Crop Circles for Beginners

The Discovery of the Music of Geometry

Contact: www.HarryEilenstein.de
Harry.Eilenstein@web.de
Harry Eilenstein at youtube

Production and publishing house: BoD - Books on Demand, Norderstedt

ISBN: 9783753473505

Table of contents

I History   **6**

II Origins   **8**
1. Natural causes   8
2. Contradictions in the "natural explanations"   9
3. Collective telekinesis   10
4. Motivation   14
5. Astrology   16

III Forms   **18**
1. Simple concentric forms   18
2. Simple elongated forms   21
3. Variations of the simple elongated form   35
4. Very long forms   36
5. Butterflies   40
6. Insects   45
7. Birds   49
8. Other animals   58
9. Eyes   66
10. Fractals   69
11. The Cabbalistic Tree of Life   78
12. Mandalas   82
   - *a) one-polar*   *82*
   - *b) two-polar*   *82*
   - *c) three-polar*   *83*
   - *d) four-polar*   *90*
   - *e) five-polar*   *100*
   - *f) six-polar*   *109*
   - *g) seven-polar*   *127*
   - *h) eight-polar*   *132*
   - *i) nine-polar*   *137*
   - *j) ten-polar*   *140*
   - *k) twelve-polar*   *141*
   - *l) thirteen-polar*   *146*
   - *m) sixteen-polar*   *148*
   - *n) eighteen-polar*   *153*
   - *o) twenty-polar*   *154*
   - *p) twenty-two-polar*   *156*

13.	Cubic forms	157
14.	Sun-like forms	159
15.	Organic forms	172
16.	Structured areas	174
17.	Complex forms	180
18.	Details	212
19.	Man-made forms	214
20.	The crop circle alphabet	224
	a) Polarity elements	*224*
	b) Structure elements	*227*
	c) Dynamics elements	*237*
	d) Complex Elements	*240*

IV Contemplation **247**

1.	The language of crop circles	247
	a) Music	*247*
	b) Astrology	*249*
	c) Physics	*250*
	d) Three-step	*251*
	e) Chakras	*252*
	f) Polarity	*252*
	g) Polarization	*252*
	h) Cabbalistic Tree of Life	*253*
	i) Dynamics of Development	*255*
	j) Self-Similarity and Fractals	*256*
	k) Golden Section	*256*
	l) Feng-Shui	*258*
	m) Ba-Gua	*258*
	n) Tribal Tattoos	*260*
	o) Power Places and Leylines	*260*
	p) Summary	*261*
2.	Life force and crop circles	262
3.	Dream journeys to the crop circles	266

V Usage **339**

	List of books	341

I History

Crop circles are areas in mostly ripe grain that are laid flat. However, in contrast to wind breakage, which are areas of grain that have been flattened by wind, the areas of crop circles have very sharp edges.

The earliest report originate from 1590 in Lorraine, France, from an indictment against some men and women who are said to have caused a crop circle by dancing in a field of grain. Eyewitnesses of this supposed dance are not known.

Around 1678 crop circles were reported in England, which were supposed to have been caused by a mowing devil.

Around 1686 in southern England circular areas in the grass were called "fairy rings".

It is possible that the fairy rings and the elf rings from legends and fairy tales are also such crop circles, but they could also be witch rings, i.e. mushrooms forming a circle.

In the 19th century such circles were called "Devils Twist" in England. The crop circles must have occurred so often that a name was established for them. German immigrants in England called them "Hexentanz" and "Teufelskreis". From this century originate several reports about crop circles from England as well as from Germany.

The first crop circle photographs are from 1932 and 1937, and are of a single circle and an arrangement of four circles, of which the inner circle was 36m in diameter.

Since about 1960, crop circles were often jokingly called "UFO nests" and associated with UFOs.

Around 1965 there were several crop circles in Canada and in Australia in reed fields and in sugar cane fields.

In 1978, Doug Bower and Dave Chorley created several simple, round crop circles by hand in southern England. These were the first crop circles that were certainly man-made.

From 1980 onwards, 150-300 crop circles appeared annually in southern England in the county of Wiltshire. This was and is the main area of crop circles distribution.

Since 1990 the shapes of crop circles have become much larger, more diverse and more detailed. They represent partly complex mathematical formations like the Mandelbrot set or structures over 100m long. Since this time the crop circles appear increasingly also in other fields – e.g. as "rape circles".

Since 1990 Rod Dickinson and John Lundberg as well as some other co-workers also produce crop circles on behalf of companies.

In 1992 a competition was organized by different persons and organizations, in which different groups had to make a given pattern as a crop circle, which these groups also succeeded quite well.

In 2003, half of the English crop circles were within a 15km radius of the Avebury stone circles.

From 2004 on, crop circles in Germany increased significantly – especially in Schleswig-Holstein, Hessen, Nordvorpommern and on Rügen. They accounted for about a quarter of the annual crop circles.

Meanwhile, about 10,000 crop circles from 60 countries are known. The longest crop circle so far was 756m long. The most complex crop circle had a diameter of 240m and consisted of 409 individual circles.

A large part of the crop circles in England originated near stone circles, burial mounds, the White Horse and similar places with prehistoric significance.

II Origins

The explanation of the origin of such a striking phenomenon as the crop circles is naturally very controversial.

II 1. Natural causes

The oldest crop circles, which appeared 350 years ago, were interpreted according to the world view of that time as the work of the devil or his followers. 50 years ago the crop circles were considered as landing places of UFOs. One often explains the incomprehensible with the unknown, thus with that, which lies outside of the known and accessible area – with the devil and/or with the extraterrestrials and their UFOs.

The attempts to explain the crop circles by weather phenomena like whirlwinds, downdrafts, tornadoes, lightnings or ball lightnings have remained so far only a very vague theory, which lacks on the one hand a conclusive explanation of the process and on the other hand the observation of such a phenomenon.

Also the attempt to explain the crop circles by the rutting dances of roebucks or by the wandering of kangaroos that have eaten opium-containing poppies is not very convincing, because this cannot explain the complex patterns and the sharp boundaries of crop circles.

Finally, since 1978 at the latest, there are also crop circles that have been made by humans. Partly crop circles in the form of cars of certain brands, company logos etc. were produced, which are obviously commissioned works to crop circle makers, who were paid by the corresponding companies.

In one case a crop circle was also created in the course of two nights. Since the crop circle did not look finished after the first night and was completed by further elements in the second night, but looked like a building site after the first night, in this case quite certainly humans were at work.

It is also striking that in Muslim countries there are almost no crop circles, but mainly in the Western civilization and in Japan. This speaks at least for a coupling of the crop circles to the "western" world view.

As a rule, the crop circles appear over night – for whatever reason …

II 2.   Contradictions in the "natural explanations"

In view of this situation, one could now conclude that all crop circles were created by humans.

But for the early crop circles this will hardly be true, because at that time it was life-threatening to be associated with such phenomena and consequently also with the devil – the pyres have not been extinguished so very long.

Then there are still five phenomena which speak against a creation by humans:

1. No non-human creation of a crop circle has been directly observed yet either. However, there are some cases in which the crop circles must have originated within one hour – which excludes their creation by humans.

2. Some crop circles are so large and so complex that the production by humans within one night seems at least questionable. Among these are areas which do not simply consist of stalks laid flat, but where the stalks have been woven or braided. Also rows of single standing stalks are not impossible to make by hand, but very complex. Finally, there are patterns that represent very complicated symmetries or shapes.

However, it is unclear what humans are ultimately capable of in terms of craftsmanship.

3. In some crop circles, the stalks have not been bent over together with the roots, nor have they been broken off, but have been bent over at a node of the stalk – as if the stalks had softened there and then become firm again.

For this phenomenon there is still no "normal" explanation – this phenomenon cannot be produced intentionally.

4. A very large part of the crop circles has a common quality, which is difficult to create by humans. One could call it a "transpersonal beauty and harmony". This quality is much more likely to be found in flowers, in a rainbow, in the course of a river, in the waves that the wind has blown in sand, and the like. In individual works of art of a person this quality is usually not present.

This form of rightness and beauty is perceived by many people, but it is not present in all crop circles. Of course, one cannot say with certainty that this quality cannot also be produced by humans. However, it is striking that so many crop circles have this quality.

5. Then there is another phenomenon which can only be determined subjectively: In fresh crop circles there is a great tension which resembles the "charge" of some old statues of gods and similar things, which one can experience e.g. also in an intensive ritual. This life force is also felt by people who have hardly any magical or spiritual experiences. This "crop circle charge", that is like a kind of airy heat and a electric tingling, disappears after a few days.

However, as mentioned, this phenomenon can only be experienced by visiting a fresh crop circle yourself. It is also unknown whether this phenomenon occurs in all crop circles.

All in all, one can say that due to the many man-made crop circles, it is hardly possible to conclude from the crop circles themselves which of them are "natural", i.e. "non man-made", and which of them are man-made.

II 3. Collective telekinesis

In order to be able to talk about crop circles at all, not only as human works of art, but also as a possibly magical-spiritual phenomenon, one must therefore take another path.

First of all one has to prove that telekinesis exists – which fortunately can be done quite easily with the "paper-wheel" experiment. This "paper-wheel" is also called "PSI-wheel". Experiments of this kind can be found under these search terms on youtube. A detailed study of telekinesis can also be found in my book "Telekinesis for Beginners".

Besides these basic telekinesis experiments which are easy to perform, there are also phenomena where larger things move, materialize or de-materialize. However, these phenomena cannot be brought about so easily.

When one has done so many experiments on this subject oneself that one is sure that telekinesis exists, one can turn to crop circles again from another starting point.

The question now is no longer "Can crop circles be telekinetically originated?" but "Is there any sense to consider a part of the crop circles as telekinetically originated?"

To be able to answer this question, one would have to find a plausible answer to two further questions: "Who practices this crop circle telekinesis?" and "Why does he practice it?"

First of all, there are several possible originators of the crop circles:

- a single person for all crop circles,
- different people for different crop circles,
- a group of people,
- mankind as a whole,
- the respective plant species as a group consciousness,
- the earth as a whole (Gaia), and
- extraterrestrials.

It can be excluded quite certainly that a certain single human being has telekinetically created all non-human-made crop circles. Who should have such a power and why should this human do this without ever showing himself?

The same argumentation exists concerning several people who created the crop circles independently of each other. Here it would be even more improbable that none of them shows his telekinetic abilities publicly. Furthermore ther should been seen diffferent styles in the crop circles.

Also a small group of humans is quite improbable as originators, because one should assume that also this group would have shown themselves sometime – and what should be their motivation?

Also extraterrestrials are very improbable as originators, because if they already make the effort to create crop circles on earth, one can ask oneself, what they intend with it and why they don't show themselves and choose a more pragmatic form of communication - after all it should be quite laborious to find us humans in the vastness of the universe at all and to seek us out ...

Thus, first of all, only three of the seven possible causers of the crop circles, which have just been enumerated, remain:

- mankind as a whole,
- the respective plant species as group consciousness, and
- the earth as a whole (Gaia).

These three possibilities have a common feature, which is not immediately obvious at first sight, but is of importance: It concerns each time a collective – all humans, all plants of a kind or the whole earth. These are three forms of the collective subconsciousness:

- the collective subconsciousness of the people,
- the collective subconsciousness of a plant species ("Elf"), and
- the collective subconsciousness of the whole earth ("Gaia").

These three possible originators have all one big "substance", so all human beings, all cereal plants and the whole earth, respectively.

The experiments with telepathy and telekinesis show that telepathy is the "eyes" of the subconsciousness of a human being and that telekinesis is the "hands" of the human subconsciousness. Since the collective subconsciousness consists of the telepathic union of the subconsciousnesses of all living people and also of all deceased people, there should be such a union also with regard to the telekinesis of all people: the collective telekinesis of the collective subconsciousness of the people.

That would be then a sufficiently strong telekinesis, which should be able to cause also such phenomena like the crop circles. This thesis would have also the advantage that there is nobody in it who could come forward and show that he has caused all these crop circles.

In the same way, one could argue for the collective subconsciousness of the grain and for the collective subconsciousness of the entire Earth. First of all, the collective subconscious of mankind seems to be the most plausible, since it would not be particularly clear at first why the "cereal elf", the "rape elf"; the "reed elf" etc. or the earth as a whole should fabricate crop circles that represent complex mathematical patterns.

But on the one hand one does not know of course what the "grain elf" is thinking, and also not what Gaia thinks about everything – or if they both simply telepathically "listen in" what the humans are thinking all day long on earth.

And there is also the constant problem that it is known that at least a part of the crop circles have been made by humans. That is not exactly the starting situation, which one wishes as a researcher – but it is now once in such a way, as it is.

The crop circle researcher must therefore also be a detective …

There is also another question: What did the collective subconsciousness of the people, the grain or the earth do with its telekinesis abilities before it created crop circles? Did this collective consciousness discover that it had telekinetic abilities only 350 years ago? That seems to be very improbable …

If a part of the crop circles has really been created by a form of collective telekinesis, then these crop circles should be actually only one example of a larger group of collective telekinetic phenomena, which should be traceable clearly further back than only 350 years.

How could one recognize such a phenomenon? It should 1. be telekinetic, 2. relate to a collective, and 3. fascinate people. This third point is probably present, but it is not a mandatory property of the phenomena we are looking for.

In the search for such phenomena one comes across above all miracles such as apparitions of the Virgin Mary, moving statues, etc., but also phenomena that occur in shamanism, such as sticks stuck in the ground that move independently and give the shaman clues as to which spirit he can use to help the person seeking advice who has come to him. Also the materializations, which appear now and then e.g. in the Spiritism, count to this topic.

These cases of telekinesis are collective magic, since it is not a single person who performs a miracle, but something happens that comes from Mary, from the being represented by the statue, or from the spirits.

It is therefore conceivable that these earlier forms of collective telekinesis have occasionally given rise to simple round crop circles, but that it was their association with UFOs that gave collective telekinesis an impetus to spread further. The extraterrestrials have taken the place of the saints – both are the "powerful ones that affect our lives from outside the accessible realm". This parallel is so exact that it is quite probable that the crop circles are a continuation of the earlier "religious miracles" in a "contemporary form".

Once this form of collective telekinesis got going, it then differentiated into more and more complex forms, i.e. the forms of the crop circles nowadays.

13

II 4. The motivation

Can it be narrowed down more precisely who or what this collective is that exercises this telekinesis? Up to now the collective subconsciousness of the people, of the grain (Elf) and of the earth (Gaia) came into question.

A common approach in the search for the answer to such a question in criminology is to examine the possible motivation. The motivation for an action, in turn, can be gauged from the consequences of that action – the result achieved is what the motivation intended. First of all, it can be said that the only recognizable concrete effect of the crop circles is their fascination for many people.

That would be a very meager motive for the cereal elf as the collective subconsciousness that makes the crop circles. Why would the grain do that? What advantage would it have from doing so? Or what could motivate the grain to do so? To begin with, no motive is discernible here.

With the collective subconsciousness of the earth, called "Gaia", the case is a little more difficult, because Gaia also includes the collective subconsciousness of the grain and the people. Everything that happens on Earth is also a part of what happens in Gaia, that is, in the collective subconsciousness of the Earth as a whole. With this statement one does not come closer to an understanding of the crop circles at first.

Also the question, what could move the earth then to the creation of the crop circles, cannot be answered first of all. Since only humans perceive the phenomenon of the crop circles consciously (but not the seagulls or the beeches), it should be a message of the earth to humans. However, this message would have been written by her rather incomprehensibly – that would not be exactly an effective form of communication …

Also the possible motivation of the earth for such a message would be very unclear. It should refer to something that the people on Earth are doing and that Earth wants to be different – always assuming that Earth actually has a preference for what should happen on it. However, considering that there have already been several ice ages, that the dinosaurs have become extinct, and that new species in general are always emerging, one may wonder what could motivate Gaia to send messages to humans. The only thing that can be found would be the complete annihilation of all life on Earth by the atomic bombs – but nowhere a reference to this possibility can be found in the crop circles …

Thus the collective subconsciousness of the people remains as the causer. Also here the question arises, what this collective subconsciousness actually wants to achieve with the crop circles. Or does it want to achieve with them possibly nothing at all?

There is finally also the possibility that there are pictures in the collective subconsciousness, which are "charged" by the large attention of humans on these pictures, whereupon the collective subconsciousness then "dreams collectively" of these pictures. Since the collective subconsciousness has not only telepathy as perception, but also telekinesis as a possibility of action, it would be conceivable that images in the collective subconsciousness, which have been very strongly charged, also express themselves in telekinetic phenomena – so to speak "telekinetically effective dreams of the collective subconsciousness".

In this interpretation the crop circles have no message, but would be simply an expression of that, what occupies the people in emotional respect just collectively most – they would be just collective dreams, which look for a telekinetic expression.

II 5. Astrology

One can ask oneself, why just from approximatly 1940 the crop circles appeared increasingly. One possibility is to see if there are astrological aspects since that time which fit to such a phenomenon.

Since about 1942 Pluto has a sextile to Neptune, which continues until today and will end only in 2039. Pluto is the intense, the collective, the extreme, the transformation, the maximum motivation, the single-mindedness, etc. Neptune is the artistic, the social, the magical, the religion, the ecology, the boundary dissolution, etc. When these two planets have a sextile to each other, that is, when they interact, artistic, social, ecological, magical impulses arise that have an existential intensity.

This can also be seen very clearly in history from about 1960, when the first people born with this Pluto/Neptune sextile in their horoscope had turned 18. From this time on, such Pluto/Neptun phenomena as the hippies, the Greens, the exploration of drugs, the interest in other cultures, an increased social engagement, globalization, etc. emerged.

So the significantly increased emergence of crop circles would fit well into the astrological phase of this Pluto/Neptune sextile, which lasts from 1942 to 2039. Of course, this does not explain anything at first, but it shows that one can and should consider the phenomenon of crop circles sensibly within a larger context.

The widespread view that the crop circles are a message of the earth to the people fits precisely to this Pluto/Neptune aspect, which refers to a large extent to collective processes. This message is generally taken as a warning about the destruction of the earth – which is also a Pluto/Neptun theme.

The collective subconsciousness is also a concept that fits well with this astrological aspect, as well as ecological and global thinking.

In art, this aspect promotes the pursuit of expression that goes beyond the individual and makes collective content visible – which is exactly the quality that makes the crop circles so fascinating to many people.

The crop circles themselves do not contain any recognizable ecological, social, artistical or magical-spiritual message, but the crop circles are associated in many ways with these very themes. This clearly shows that the crop circles are closely related to the current Pluto/Neptune sextile.

The crop circles are therefore very likely not a telekinetic message from the earth to us humans, but rather a collective self-expression of humans, which is influenced by the Pluto/Neptune sextile lasting from 1942 to 2039. So we can assume that the appearance of crop circles will last until about 2039 – probably it will end with some delay, i.e. when most of the people who are born with this Pluto/Neptun-sextile in their horoscopes have died.

Such a sextile also makes collective telekinesis much more probable and powerful: Pluto is the unity that is necessary for any effective (magical) power, and Neptune dissolves the boundaries and makes this unity work also in the material world and not only in the consciousness.

III   Forms

After these introductory considerations, it is promotive to take a closer look at the forms of the crop circles and to see if anything can be deduced from them about their origin and meaning.

III 1.   Simple concentric forms

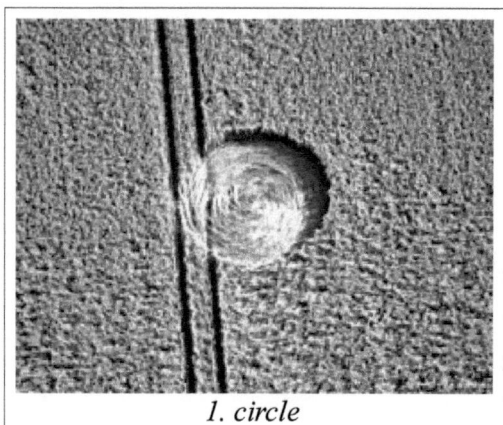

1. circle
(Wiltshire, England, 2000)

The original, simplest and for a long time also most frequent form of the crop circles was the circular form, which has been called half-jokingly also "UFO nest". This shape also gave the name "crop circle" to this phenomenon – a circular area of mostly spiral-shaped flattened grain in a crop field.

The size of the crop circles on the photos can be estimated quite easily by the tractor tracks in the grain – they are about 2.5m wide. The crop circle on the left therefore has a diameter of about 10m.

- * ❀ * -

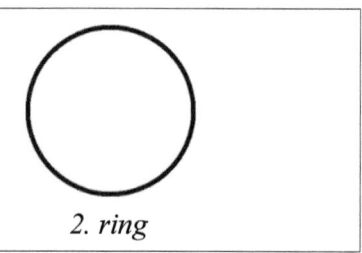

2. ring

The ring as an isolated shape is very rare, although it is the second simplest shape after the circle.

Triangles, squares, pentagons, lines and the like have not existed for a long time, but only round shapes.

- * ❀ * -

18

3. circle with ring
(place and year unknown)

The circular area with a ring was one of the first shapes that were more than just a simple circular area. It was quite common in the beginning.

- * ❀ * -

4. circle with several rings
(Wiltshire, England, 2005)

The next level of variety was the circular area surrounded by several concentric rings.

The pictured crop circle is fully concentric – it only looks so "crooked" because of the perspective when photographing it.

- * ❀ * -

19

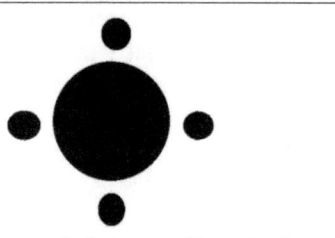

5. circle woth four smaller circles

The circular area surrounded by four "satel-lites" has been a sensation in the beginning, because this shape had a structure that went beyond concentricity.

This is the basic shape of most mandalas: the sun and the four directions or the quintessence and the four elements.

- * ❀ * -

6. circle with ring and four smaller circles
(Wiltshire, England, 2008)

This was the most complex form that could be built from the elements that had appeared so far.

20

III 2. Simple elongated forms

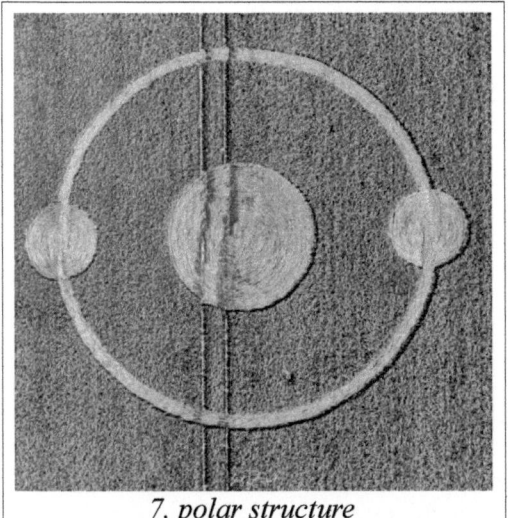

This is the simplest elongated shape: The two outer circles on the ring emphasize two opposite directions, giving a longitudinal axis that passes through the three circle of this crop circle.

7. polar structure
(Wiltshire, England, 2019)

- *  * -

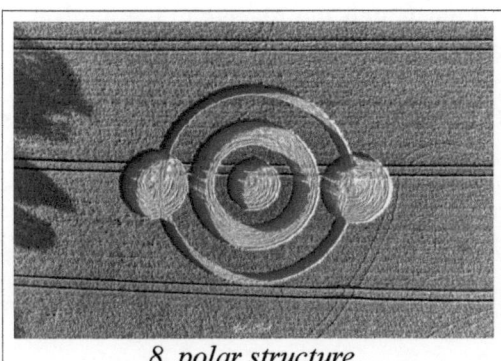

Here the basic shape of the elongated crop circle has been combined with a second, inner ring. The crop circles gradually began to evolve into more complex shapes …

8. polar structure
(Wiltshire, England, 2019)

- * ❁ * -

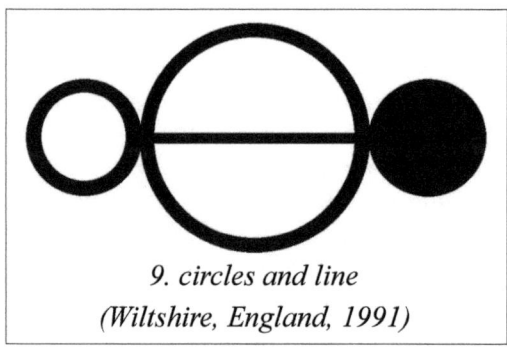

9. circles and line
(Wiltshire, England, 1991)

This crop circle, which I saw in Wiltshire in southern England, clearly shows the polar structure of this crop circle: an open circle, a closed circle, and a connecting line and a central circle.

This corresponds to the astrological sign for the opposition aspect, thus for the complementary opposition: o^o

When I entered this crop circle, I noticed that the ring on the left side feels like a mountain and the circle area on the right side feels like a cave – radiating and sucking, outward and inward, light and dark, etc. This confirms the interpretation of this structure as a complementary opposition.

On the line between these two poles there was a great, constant tension – just what one should expect between two poles.

The large ring in the middle, however, was a mystery to me at first: it felt different at every point, and the same point was not the same even after three minutes. Finally, I realized that something was flowing, circling, pulsating, rotating in this ring.

This reminded me of Rudolf Steiner's threefold system: a pole that solidifies ("Ahriman"), a pole that dissolves ("Lucifer"), and in between a pulsating system ("Christ").

The ring in the center is also the zodiac along which the planets move, with two places opposite each other on the zodiac also having opposite but complementary qualities.

So this structure was also a variation of the Yin/Yang sign: this symbol represents the two poles Yin and Yang and the eternal change that originates from them and that is described in the I Ching ("Book of Changes"). The central ring is the the ever-changing flow of life.

This crop circle therefore has a logically comprehensible structure, which can be found in various other systems.

- * ❀ * -

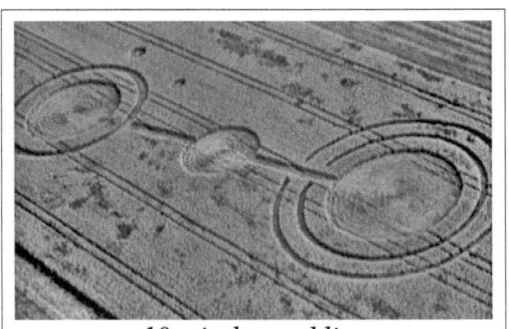

10. circles and line
(place and year unknown)

This arrangement has existed in many variations.

This crop circle consists of four elements: 1. a circular area at one end, 2. a slightly differently shaped circular area at the other end, 3. a connecting line, and 4. a circle in the center.

At the top left, there are two more small circular areas.

- * ❀ * -

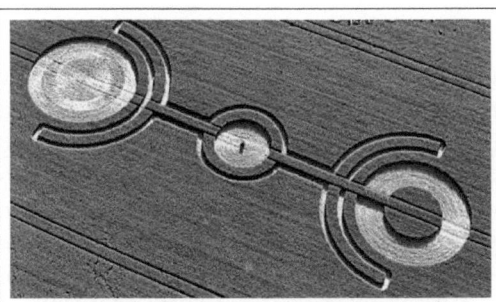

11. polar structure with "holder"
(Wiltshire, England, 2017)

This crop circle is a variation of the structure just described. Again, the two outer circles are polar – one is empty, the other is filled.

The semicircular "holders" of the two outer circles appear here as an additional element.

The whole thing just seems like a technical element.

- * ❀ * -

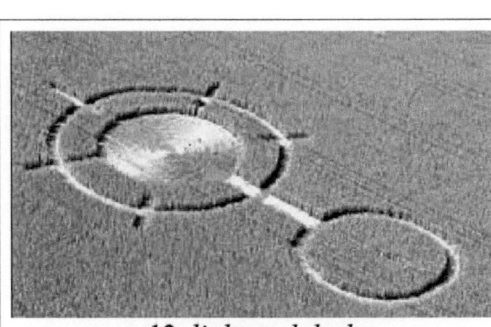

12. light and dark
(Wiltshire, England, year unknown)

Here the polar structure is very clear – one circle radiates, the other does not.

The center circle is missing.

One could also compare this structure to a magnet with its north pole and its south pole, or to a battery with its "+/–" poles. These polarities are both based on the electro-magnetic force.

- * ✿ * -

13. polar structure
(USA, 2013)

Here the polarity is only indicated by the position of the opening of the two outer circles. The center circle is missing.

- * ✿ * -

14. polar structure
(Wiltshire, England, 2010)

Here the two poles are no longer distinguished. The center circle represents the tension between the two poles in a graphically elegant way.

The two small circles are a newish element. Together with the centers of the two pole circles, they form four circles on the outer line of the central circle – are these the four elements or also the four directions?

- * ✿ * -

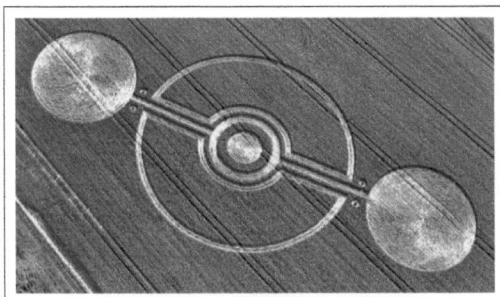

*15. complex polar structure
(Wiltshire, England, 2011)*

In this crop circle, too, the two sides are exactly identical. As in crop circle 11, the connecting line between the three circles is enveloped by another line, which here has been connected to the large ring around the center circle. This creates a new geometric shape: the "bordered half ring".

To the left and right of the straight line, in front of the outer circles, a pair of "points" can be seen, consisting of a very small circular area with a point in the center (a bundle of grain). They act like two points of attachment.

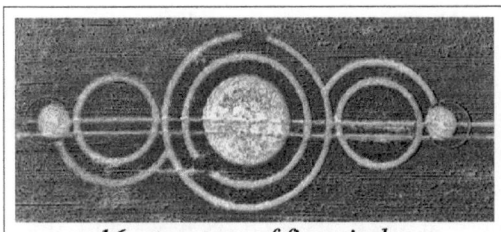

*16. structure of five circles
(Wiltshire, England, 2020)*

Here the two rings around the center circle have been interrupted – the reason for this is not apparent.

The two outer circles are distinguished by the direction in which the half rings point with them. These rings end in an additional circle, around which there is a very narrow, discreet ring. The two half circles together form an "S".

This crop circle contains quite a few "modern" elements in contrast to the "classic" crop circles.

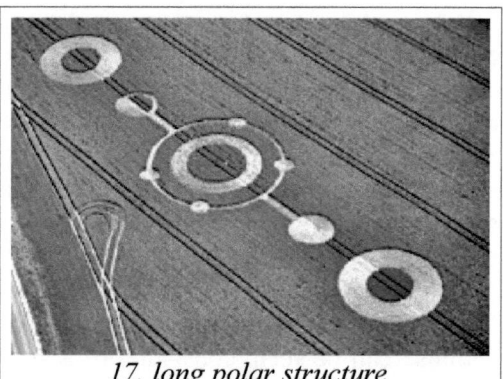

17. long polar structure
(Wiltshire, England, 1999)

Here the sovereignty of the centre is emphasized by two small rings and four small circular areas on them.

From the outer ring, two polarity lines go to two medium-sized circles, one of which is light and the other half light and half dark, representing their opposite polarity.

On the very outside is a second pair of circular rings.

- * ❀ * -

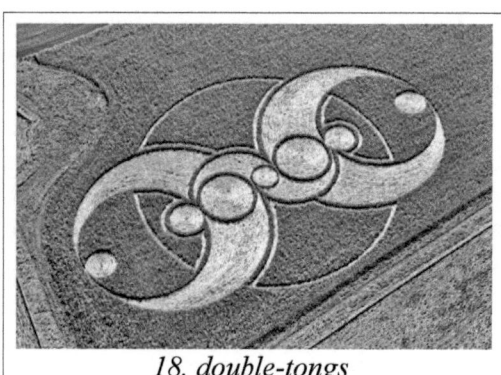

18. double-tongs
(Wiltshire, England, 2012)

Here again are found the two poles (which are represented the same) and the center circle, plus an additional S-shaped area in the center, possibly representing the connectedness of the two poles.

There are six additional small circles here at once, as well as a seventh small circle marking the center.

- * ❀ * -

19. bow-triangles
(Wiltshire, England, 1996)

Here the two pole circles have been pushed together and the center circle almost envelops them. The polarity of the two circles has been graphically represented similar to the yin/yang sign.

The two dark areas between the two pole circles ("bow triangles") may represent the tension between the two poles.

The two crescents together make two "S" shapes – once the two connected outer sides of the crescents and once the two connected inner sides of the crescents.

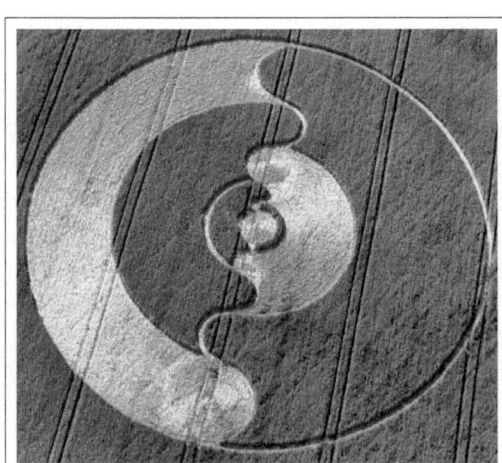

20. Chakras
(Wiltshire, England, 2001)

The two poles are clearly visible: a circle of flattened grain at the bottom of the right large face and a circle of standing grain at the top of the right large face.

The remaining surfaces are also shown polar. From the outside in, the circles are: top filled – bottom empty; top filled to the right – bottom filled to the left; top empty – bottom filled; top filled to the right – bottom empty to the left; in the center, a circle with a ring.

You have to look at this arrangement for a while to see its symmetry. It is a central circle with a narrow ring around which there are four rings.

27

This structure can be seen better if you draw some auxiliary lines:

The outer ring rotates counterclockwise;
the second outer ring rotates clockwise;
the third-outer ring rotates counterclock-wise;
the fourth outer ring rotates clockwise;
the centre is a ring.
=> This is a regular alternation.

On the left, the outer ring is alone.
On the right, the outer ring and the second-outer ring are together.
On the left, the second-outer ring and the third-outer ring are together.
On the right, the third-outer ring and the fourth-outer ring are together.
On the left, the fourth-outer ring is connected to the narrow ring of the center circle.
=> This is also a regular alternation.

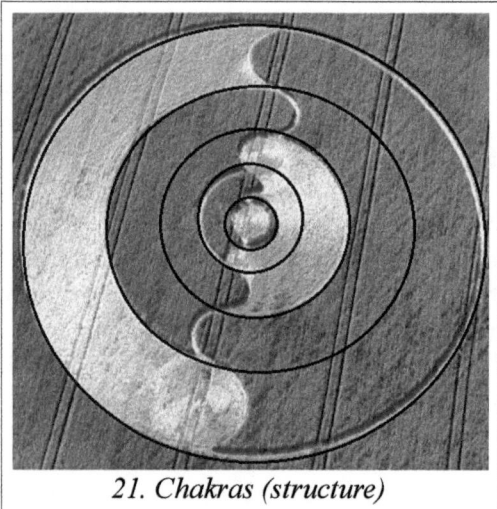

21. Chakras (structure)
(Wiltshire, England, 2001)

Altogether, the picture here is of circular rings moving like waves from the inside to the outside.

On the imaginary vertical line from the bottom to the top there are 9 circles. They could have a correspondence in yoga. Then they would be from bottom to top: Kundalini fire – root chakra – hara – solar plexus – heart chakra – throat chakra – third eye – crown chakra – bindhu light. However, it is quite uncertain whether this analogy is intended here.

- * ❀ * -

28

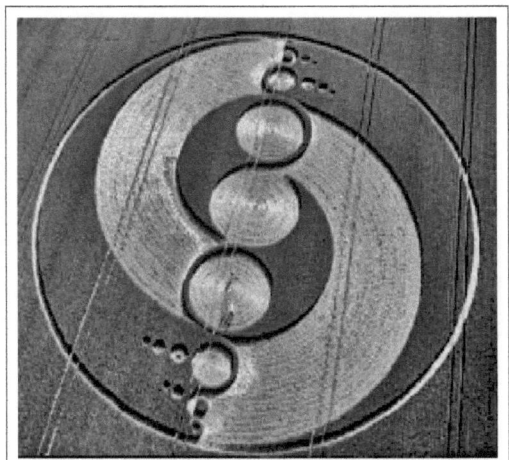

22. Chakras (strukture)
(Wiltshire, England, 2001)

This crop circle is from the same county and the same year as the previous crop circle (21).

Its central axis has exactly the same structure as the axis of the previous crop circle. By the changed distribution of the bright and the dark surfaces, however, the impression of rotating arises. Also the two dark "bow-drops" in the center as well as the two pairs of 2 and 3 points contribute to this impression.

The seven chakras plus kundalini and bindhu are in constant flux and change …

- *  * -

23. polar structure
(Wiltshire, England, 2008)

Here the two poles consist of two circles, which in turn consist of 24 small circles each, (the middle three circles belong to both circles). Does the number "2·12=24" have a deeper meaning here?

Their polarity is illustrated by the small "flames" which point outward with the left circle and inward with the right circle. If one understands the two circles as a lying "8", thus as the infinity-sign (∞), then the "flames" always point to the same side of the circle row.

In the center there is a ring with four big and four small circles – possibly they represent the two poles, the border between these poles and the four intermediate directions. It could also be a reference to resting in one's own heart chakra, in one's own center, in one's own soul. Compared to the big "∞" made of circles this center has been represented quite small. So this crop circle shows more the "Yin and Yang" than the "Tao".

- *  * -

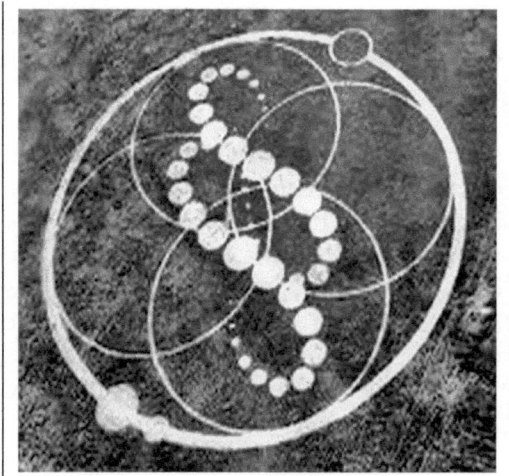

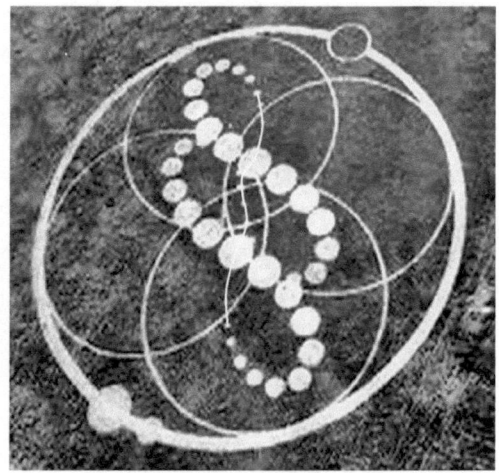

| *24. komplex polar structure* | *25. komplex polar structure* |
| *(Südkorea, 2008)* | *(the little, hardly discernable dots have been connected by a line)* |

Here the two poles have shrunk to form a large ring as well as a small ring (top) and a small circle (bottom) on this large ring.

The two ends of the double S-shape in the center are connected by small circles running through the center of the crop circle. If you count the four small circles in the center with both rows of circles, they again have a length of $2 \cdot 12 = 24$ circles, which is probably not a coincidence. Is this a reference to the 12 signs of the zodiac?

The four thin rings form a square in the middle, so a four shape – as in the previous crop circle.

- *  * -

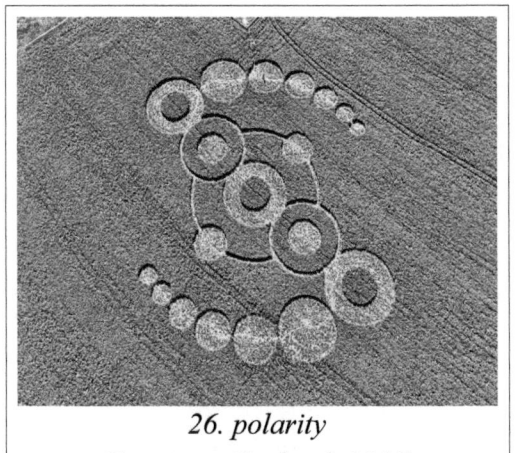

26. polarity
(Somerset, England, 2010)

Here again we can see the series of 5 circles with a central circle, which has already appeared several times. Here the rotation of the whole system is represented very vividly by 2 times 6 circles, which – if extended – would form a ring.

- * ❀ * -

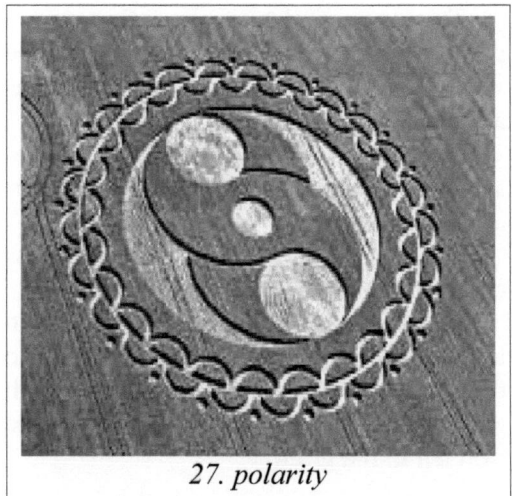

27. polarity
(Wiltshire, England, 2008)

The two poles and the two "S"s are shown here, probably symbolizing the togetherness of the two poles – a curved line similar to the Yin/Yang sign. The large circle represents the rhythm created by the polarity.

The two pole points can also be thought of as the root chakra and the crown chakra, and the point in the center as the heart chakra. The "S" would then be the life force flow of Kundalini. This structure of a center and two points also corresponds to the Buddhist Vajra symbol.

On the outside of the ring there are 25 semicircles inside and 25 semicircles outside as well as 25 points. A special symbolism of the numbers "25", "50" and "75" is not known. Overall, however, this ornamental-looking border will represent the rhythm created by the two poles.

- * ❀ * -

31

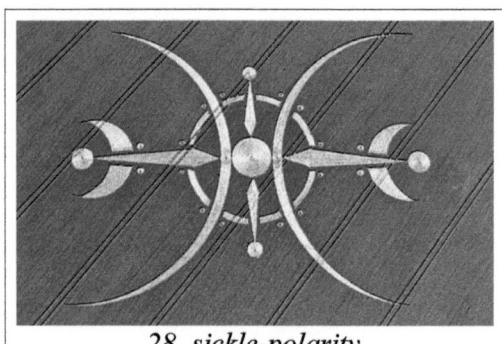

28. sickle-polarity
(Wiltshire, England, 2015)

Here, a four-part circle is found in the center – the sun and the four cardinal points or the quintessence and the four elements. The central circle is also the heart chakra.

The two circular areas on the far left and right are two poles.

The crescents correspond to the "holding" of the crop circle 9 and the crescents of the crop circles 13 and 14. On both sides two crescents each are used for holding, as separation and as connection.

There are eight of dots, which seem to act like screws holding the whole thing in place.

29. sickle-polarity
(Wiltshire, England, 2015)

This crop circle is a variation of the previous crop circle 28. It is from the same county and the same year – has anyone practiced here?

The circle area and the ring in the center are missing here, as well as the 8 pairs of dots.

Thus this crop circle looks much less centered and stable than the previous one.

Unfortunately, it is no longer possible to tell whether the straight line belongs to the crop circle, or whether it is just a path that the visiters of this crop circle have trodden in the grain.

30. double spiral
(Wiltshire, England, 2011)

Here the central circle/ring, which is quite large in most crop circles, has shrunk to a tiny circle between the two spirals.

The two spirals are double spirals, i.e. they change their direction of rotation in their centers – but in different ways. If you follow the path through these two spirals from bottom to top, you start counterclockwise at the bottom but end clockwise at the top. Here, polarity has been represented in a very creative way.

The spirals end at the top and bottom in four circles each, which, if you connect all eight of them, also run through the centers of the two spirals and through the center circle. This line, only hinted at here, corresponds to the longitudinal axis shown more clearly in other crop circles. This axis is exactly parallel to the tractor tracks.

- *  * -

31. pointed polarity
(Wiltshire, England, 2008)

In this crop circle, the center circle and the two pole circles have been depicted.

From the bottom and from the top, twelve long, narrow triangles each run to the common axis of the three circles. The "12" is the number of the sun or the radiation of the sun: the sun and the twelve-part zodiac around it.

The center circle lies completely within the triangle rays; the two pole circles lie to a small part outside of these rays.

This ray area can probably be best understood as the "magnetic field" created by the polarity of the two outer circles.

- *  * -

32. Yin and Yang
(Somerset, England, 2007)

The classic Yin/Yang polarity can be seen here. Was this sign made by humans or did the collective subconscious in this case use a commonly known symbol?

One would actually expect the eight trigrams of the I Ching around the Yin/Yang sign, into which Yin and Yang are differentiated. However, there are 12 identical signs, which is why the whole thing can be understood as the pulsating sun chakra (heart chakra) in the center with the zodiac ("sun aura") around it.

The 12 signs consist of four parallel lines, a triangle and a point in the center of this triangle. Are these supposed to be the 4 elements (fire, water, air, earth) and the 3 dynamics (cardinal = creating; fixed = shaping; mutible = using), from which the 3·4=12 signs of the zodiac result? The dots in the symbol would then indicate the identity ("heart") of each zodiac sign.

Is there even intended to show the astrological aspects? They would be:

1 (dots)	= conjunction	(0°);
2 (Yin and Yang)	= opposition	(180°);
3 (triangle)	= trine	(120°); and
4 (four lines)	= square	(90°).

III 3. Variations of the simple elongated form

Here the polarity is very clear: One "holder" contains a ring, the other holder is empty.

The two smaller circular areas, which are also found in the crop circle 7, are symmetrically arranged here. They act like "stabilizers" or something similar. They are also found on crop circles 12 and 13.

33. polar structure
(place and year unknown)

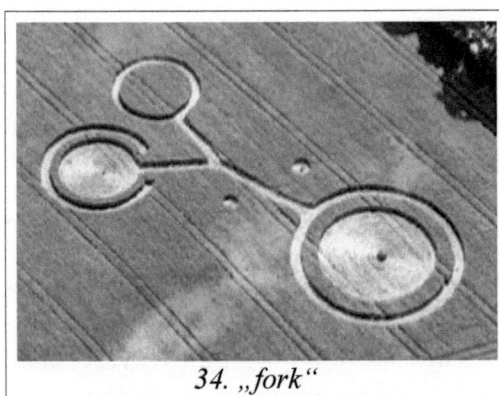

Here the two polar circles are on the left and the large "pulsating ring" is on the right, so no longer between them. In the middle, two small circular areas can be seen.

This asymmetrical form does not seem very convincing – such "forks of the way" as here do not occur otherwise with the crop circles.

Probably this crop circle is man-made – but of course this can't be said for sure …

34. „fork"
(place and year unknown)

III 4. Very long forms

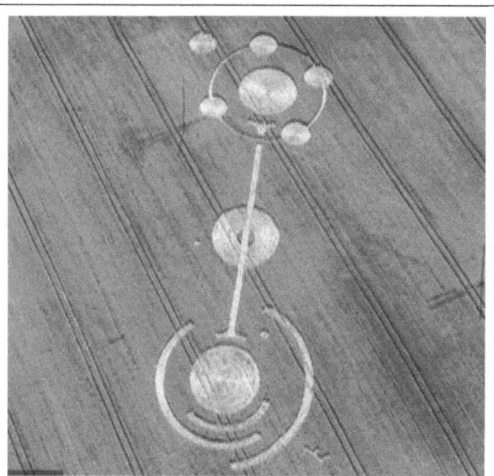

35. polar structure with additions
(place and year unknown)

For some years long crop circles were formed, some of them were more than 700m long.

At first they consisted of the already known polar structure, one pole of which has been marked here in a new way (three arcs). The four-pole structure has been moved from the center to the upper pole (four circles on a ring).

There are several new elements: the asymmetrical placement of the four smaller circles, the medium-sized circle at the upper left, the very small circle to the left of the central circle, the "T" in the upper circular ring, and the "F" at the lower left.

This crop circle is about 130m long.

- * ✺ * -

36. polar structure with additions
(Hampshire, England, 1999)

The center is the circle with the light ring and the dark ring.

From it two straight lines go out in opposite directions - it can be recognized only by the fact that in it the tractor track is missing the bright middle strip of standing grain.

The two poles are a small circular area and a large ring.

They are followed by two very small circles and a small circle, respectively.

There are several "additions". These are from top to bottom: a point, a vague shape, an "F" at the big ring, an "L" at the central circle, a semicircle and at the very bottom another "L". The meaning of these "additions" is unclear.

This crop circle is about 130m long.

37. polar structure with additions
(Wiltshire, England, 1990)

Here, too, the derivation from the polar shape is still easily recognizable: a circle with a ring in the center, a circular area to the left and right of each, and then a large circular area with ring on the very right side and a small ring as the opposite pole on the left side.

The central axis, however, goes beyond the small circle.

There are three "F" shapes, two short straight lines parallel to the axis (to the left of the central circle), and to the lower right another small circular area with two circular rings and two mini-circles.

This crop circle is about 220m long.

- * ❀ * -

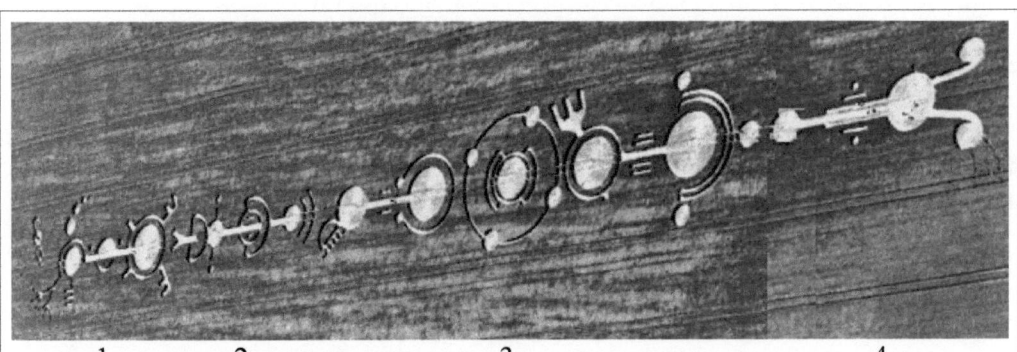

----1---- -------2------ -------------------3------------------------ -----------4-----------

38. polar structure with additions
(Wiltshire, England, 1999)

This crop circle has a length of about 350m. Such long crop circles are also mostly built up from the elements already discussed.

The three parts 1, 2, and 3 are polar structures, which here seem to have been connected in series like batteries or like magnets to achieve a higher voltage. Part 4 has a different structure and seems to be what is driven by the voltage generated by the other three parts.

The central part of the crop circle is marked "--3--" under the photo. It consists of a central circle with an inner and an outer ring and four "moons".

At the inner ring there are still two quarter arcs, which point in the direction of the axis. This is very reminiscent of the two magnets in an electric motor – which is fitting, since the energy rotates in the central ring between the two pole rings.

To the left and right of the central circle there is a double circle – directly at the central circle a circle with a ring and further away from the central circle a circle without a ring. At the straight lines between them there are a pair of straight lines as "stabilizers" between the two pole circles on each side of the central circle. On the left side there are 2·1 straight lines, on the right side 2·2 straight lines.

In the part of the crop circle marked "--2--" a second polar structure can be seen. In it, the four semicircles stand out. The two semicircles on the right seem to send the energy of part 2 to part 3 – also the three small circles on it give this impression. The semicircle in the middle seems to direct the central circle of part 2 to part 3. The semicircle on the left seems to receive the energy from part 1.

In the part marked "--1--", what stands out most are the two symmetrically arranged "F "s that seem to pass on the voltage from part 1 to part 2.

Part 4 is not a polar unit, but only a pair of circles connected to part 3 by another small circle. The two most noticeable structures on it are the two "6 "s.

On the far left, across the main axis of the crop circle, another small polar system can be seen.

This crop circle looks like a living being: Part 4 looks like neck and head. Part 3 with the central circle acts like the chest with the heart chakra. Part 2 would then be the abdomen and part 1 the tail of this living being. The two "6"s act like two antennae in this structure.

The many "appendages" are difficult to interpret. Partly they seem to be "stabilisators", partly something like "antennae" or "sense organs".

- * ❀ * -

39. polar structure with additions
(Wiltshire, England, 2008)

In this crop circle, the "poles and center circle" structure is present, but has been supplemented by quite a few "squiggles" and an eccentric ring that is only partially shown.

These "squiggles" are quite atypical in crop circles. Is this crop circle man-made?

This crop circle is about 75m long.

III 5. Butterflies

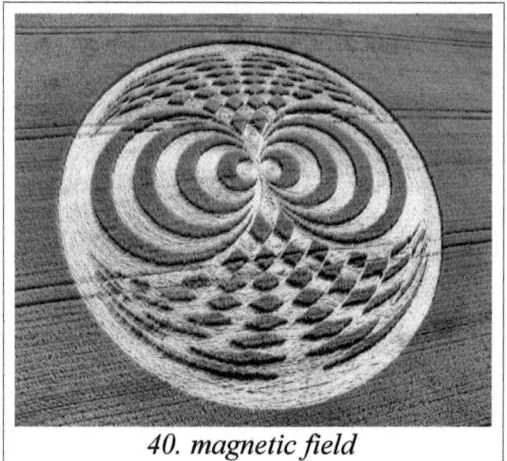

40. magnetic field
(Berkshire, England, 2006)

This crop circle is a polar system, only it has been represented differently. From the two poles arises the tension of the complementary opposition, which is represented by the 2·4 crescents. The other field of this tension is symbolized by the 2·40 rhombuses. The central circle appears here as the (unmarked) center and the outer ring.

- * ✿ * -

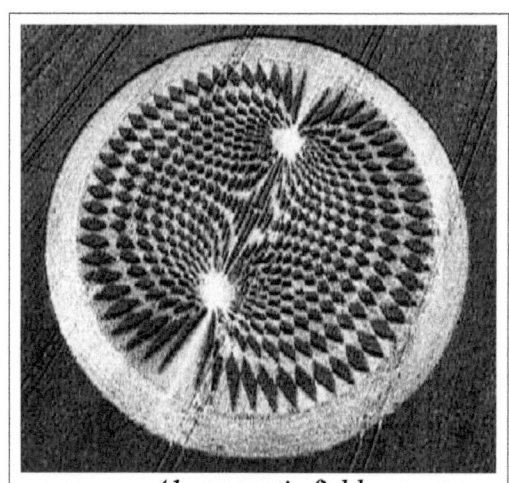

41. magnetic field
(Wiltshire, England, 2000)

Here the "polar structure with center circle" has been depicted very naturalistically – it also resembles a magnetic field.

- * ✿ * -

42. abstract butterflies
(Berlin, BRD, 2016)

Whether one should take this crop circle as the stilised representation of a magnetic field or as a schematically depicted butterfly is not quite clear at first. Since the two upper moon crescent pairs differ in the circle surfaces from the two lower pairs, it is probably rather a butterfly – if this difference is not to point to the polarity ...

The line in the center is either the bar magnet, whose field has been depicted here, or the body of the butterfly.

For the interpretation as a butterfly also speaks that a bar magnet has no 4 poles, but only 2 poles - the inspiration of this butterfly by the magnetic field grain circles, however, cannot be overlooked.

43. butterfly
(Oxfordshire, England, 2009)

This crop circle has 18 rays on the outside, each ending in a small circle with two stabilization rings and a "transmitting ring" at the top. Also in the angles between two peaks there is a small ring inside and a point in front of it.

In the center, you can see the 3D representation of 18 triangles that meet exactly in the center of the circle. The vertices of these 18 triangles are shifted upwards because of the 3D representation.

However, one can also see the two lower triangles as the body, the two upper triangles as the antennae and the 7 triangles on the left and right as the two wings of a butterfly.

It is still noticeable that the triangles of the rays are longer at the very outside above and below than at the two sides – this is not a perspective distortion.

Here, in a clever way, a perfectly point-symmetrical shape has become the image of an animal through the 3D representation.

- * ❀ * -

44. butterfly
(Oxfordshire, England, 2007)

This crop circle is clearly recognizable as a compound of a magnetic field and a butterfly. The two circular areas in the wings could correspond to the two additional circular areas also found in some of the polar constructed crop circles.

- * ❀ * -

45. butterfly
(Dorset, England, 2017)

Is this the body of a butterfly? Then it would be a luminous butterfly – it has 12 rays on each of its two sides. Since the "12" is the number of the sun (twelve signs of the zodiac in a circle around the sun), this would then be a "sun butterfly": the sunrise or a butterfly that has just hatched.

But why are there so often 2·12 rays, dots and so on?

Among Native Americans, the butterfly is also a symbol of the soul, which is often compared to the sun as well.

- * ❀ * -

42

*46. butterfly goddess
(Wiltshire, England, 2008)*

Is this again a butterfly holding the sun between its antennae? However, then the crescent would have to start at the upper "head-circle" and not at the "breast-circle".

Therefore, this is probably rather the world-wide known motive of the earth goddess who raises the sun to the sky in the morning.

She seems to be compared here to a butterfly – if the sun or the soul is a butterfly, also the mother of the sun or the souls, thus the beyond goddess, must have the shape of a butterfly. In this way, the otherworld goddess has also become a bird goddess or winged goddess – she is, after all, the mother of the soul birds.

- *  * -

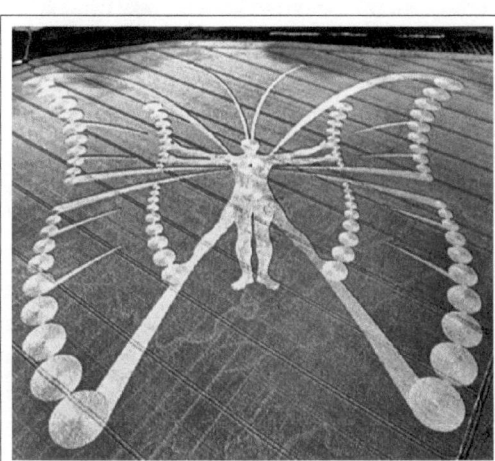

*47. butterfly man
(Netherlands, 2009)*

This form is clearly recognizable as a human with butterfly wings. If it was to be a woman, this would be the butterfly goddess, if it was to be a man, it would be the sun or a soul in the form of a butterfly.

On the inside of the wings there are four rows of 9 circles each. On the outside of the wings there are four rows of 10 circles: 9 circles plus one circle on the line that is near the other wing.

The arms are doubled and are in the posture of Leonardo da Vinci's famous study of the proportions of man. Also the legs are double in the Leonardo-way. Since Leonardo depicted a man and not a woman in his study, it is likely that a butterfly man is depicted here – but this is not certain, as it also could simply be a butterfly human.

Because of the way the grain has been flattened, the head, the heart chakra and the hara have been marked on the body of the butterfly-man: cognition, identity and inner

43

support.

48. butterfly man: detail

left botton: head;
centre: heart chakra (two people standing in the centre)
right at the top: hara

III 6. Insects

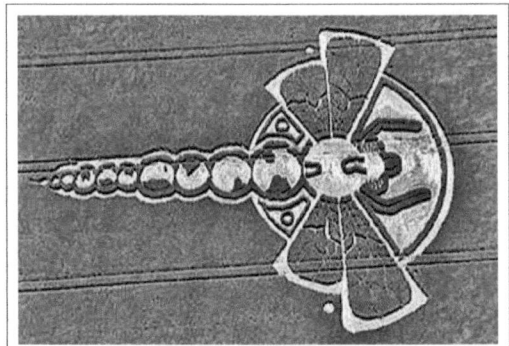

49. dragonfly
(Wiltshire, England, 2009)

This dragonfly has been depicted in a well recognizable way. However, it has been somewhat stylized: The wings are too short. The abdomen consists here of 10 circles, which have been marked in an irregular way – in nature the dragonfly abdomen consists of 7-9 segments.

The most striking element is the large circular area – is this the rest of the original crop circle or is this an emphasis of the heart chakra as in the butterfly man (crop circle 28)?

Also the central circle at the polar structures can be interpreted as heart chakra – then the two poles would be the root chakra and the crown chakra. This interpretation is also supported by the representation of two further chakras on the butterfly-man (head and hara) – whereby the interpretations as magnet, battery and chakra system do not exclude each other at all, but complement each other: They are the same form of polarity in different areas.

Between the two pairs of wings are found the now well known two small "companion circular areas".

- *  * -

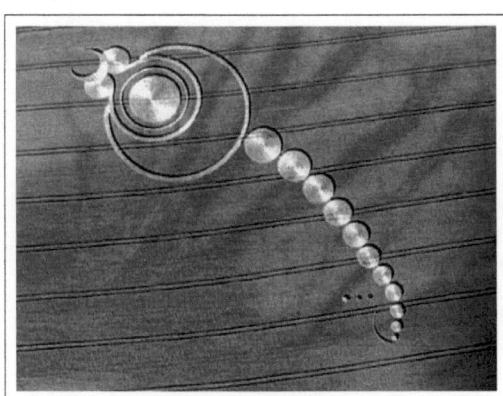

50. dragonfly
(Wiltshire, England, 1994)

Here the dragonfly's wings are missing and the abdomen has 11 segments, but since the dragonfly's large eyes and grasping pincers have been very clearly depicted, it can be clearly seen. The "pincers" at the end of the dragonfly's abdomen have also been indicated.

The circular area seems to indicate the heart chakra here as well.

At the bottom left of the abdomen, three small circular areas can be seen next to each other. Similar small shapes standing next to the main image, almost like a signature, have been seen on some other crop circles already viewed.

51. dragonfly
(Wiltshire, England, 2004)

Here is another dragonfly with a head, large antennae, a 4-piece thoracic area and a 3-piece tail area.

This dragonfly is looking at the White Horse in the background, which is a representation that probably dates back to the Neolithic period. It is created by the regular removal of the grass and humus, revealing the white limestone soil underneath.

Such references of the crop circles to mounds, stone circles and the like, of which Wiltshire is decidedly rich, are found very frequently.

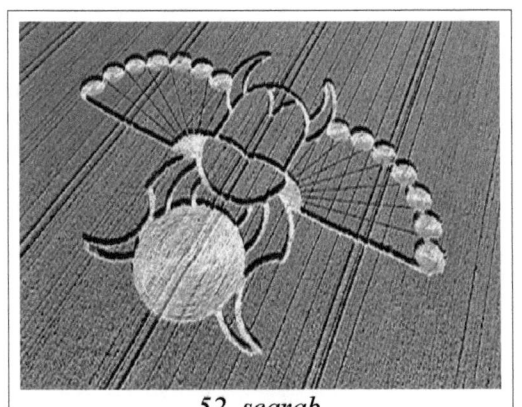

52. scarab
(Wiltshire, England, 2005)

Here is a scarab rolling the sun across the sky as in Egyptian mythology.

The connection of the butterfly, dragonfly and scarab to the sun in crop circles has now become very clear.

The sun has also been associated with the heart chakra among the Egyptians, being the "sun chakra" so to speak, as it is located in the center of the chakra system. For this reason, a scarab amulet has always been placed over the heart chakra of the deceased and wrapped with on the heart during mummification.

- * ❀ * -

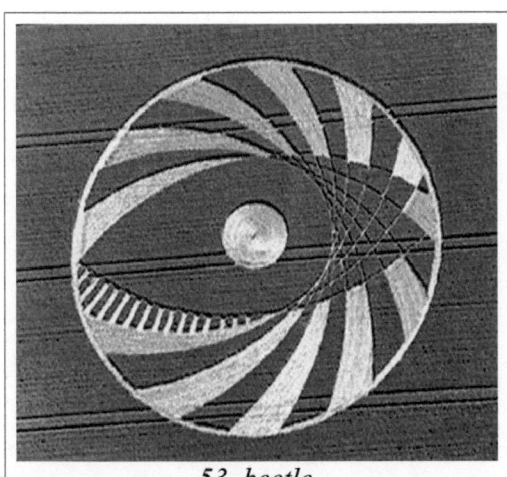

53. beetle
(Wiltshire, England, 2005)

This highly stylized form is possibly a beetle. The front part and the back part are clearly visible. It has too many legs – but maybe they are supposed to represent rays. If that should be true, the central circle would be the sun again and the beetle therefore probably a scarab.

The dashed area at the abdomen of the beetle results from graphical reasons. One could have also left two small dark triangles at the head end of the crop circle – then the bright and the dark areas at the underside would have been exchanged. However, then the body of the beetle would have become narrower.

Well … that is probably quite simply artistic freedom …

- * ❀ * -

47

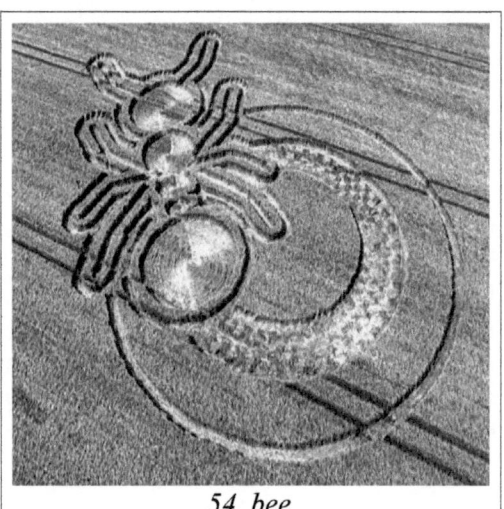

54. bee
(Surrey, England, 2019)

Here you can probably see a bee crawling over a circle with a ring.

The grain in the ring laid flat has been artfully laid down in a pattern.

III 7. Birds

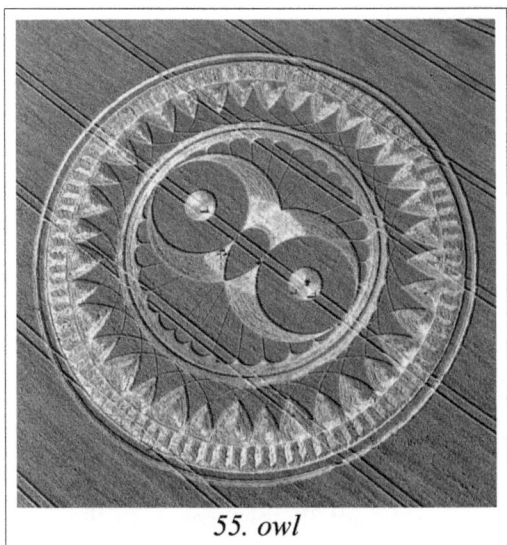

55. owl

(Wiltshire, England, 2009)

This owl has been depicted in a simple and effective manner.

There are probably 36 feathers around the head, which will correspond to the 36 rays around the head. The number "36" is derived from "3·12". However, the "12" is the sun number – and the owl is clearly an animal of the night. Should it represent the sun in the nocturnal underworld? In mythology there are some references to such an owl motif.

However, the rays are not regularly arranged, but always two rays form a pair, which are somewhat closer to each other than their distance to the next pair is. So it may not be "3·12" rays, but "2·18" rays – although the "18" has no widespread symbolism.

The grain has been artfully flattened again at the outer edge, so that it results in a pattern consisting of about 90 peaks. To each of the 18 pairs of rays belong 2 peaks and between each of the 18 pairs of rays there are 3 peaks – so there are "18·(2+3)=90" peaks in total.

The largest common number contained in 18, 36 and 90 is "9", which at least among the Nostratic peoples (Indo-Europeans, Egyptians, Semites, Hamites, Cretans, Sumerians, etc.) had the meaning "death, afterlife, afterlife journey, night, winter" and thus precisely fits the general symbolism of the owl.

It should be noted that this symbolism of the "9" is actually no longer part of the general knowledge today – if this crop circle should have been made by people, these people must have had unusually good mythological knowledge.

- * ✲ * -

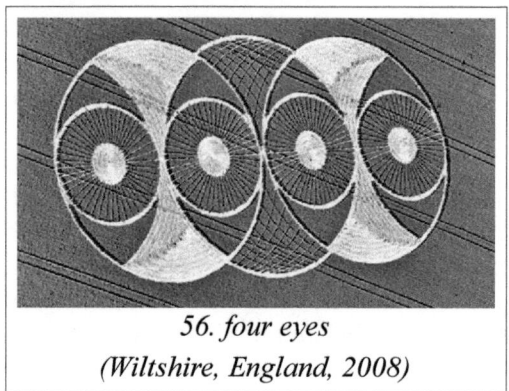

56. four eyes
(Wiltshire, England, 2008)

This shape is apparently the link between the polar crop circles and the owl motif.

The large dark central circle with the two eyes in it (the two poles) is the origin – the two large light outer circles are the complement. Are they simply to represent polarity a second time? This second pair of circles beside the polar circles has already appeared on several crop circles.

The dark arched diamonds above and below between the two middle eyes are each 8 diamonds high – there are 64 diamonds each: "1+2+3+4+5+6+7+8+7+6+5+4+3+2+1". However, these diamonds are so small on the very outside that they have hardly been represented.

"64" is a number from the binary series "1, 2, 4, 8, 16, 32, 64". The "4" of the eyes and the "8" of the arc triangles above the eyes also come from this series.

However, the eyes have 50 rays each, which does not fit this series. In the crop circle 75, 50 semicircles form an outer ring – also here the 50 rays form an outer ring.

In the white areas above and below the two outer pairs of eyes, the grain has been placed in 12 waves each – probably a reference to the zodiac.

- *  * -

50

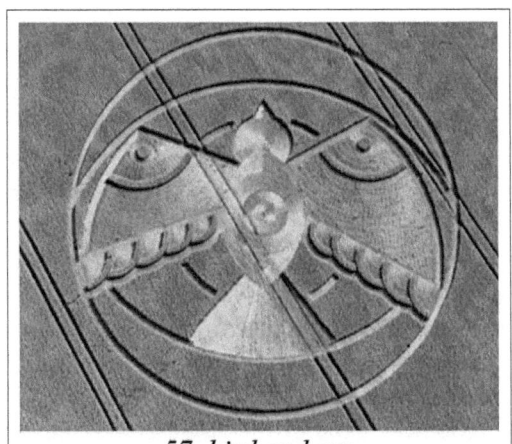

57. bird and eye
(Warwickshire, England, 2015)

The exact species of this bird is not apparent. However, it also appears to be a sun bird – it is in a circle and there is a circle in its center.

In addition, he is in an eye – the two arcs above and below him make the eye, the central circle is the iris, and the circle in the center of the bird, resulting from the way the grain is laid down, is the pupil. The sun, in turn, has been considered the "eye of God" in many religions.

The body of the bird is an eye too.

Possibly, the two dots on the wing tips are the two companion dots which are now well known.

- *  * -

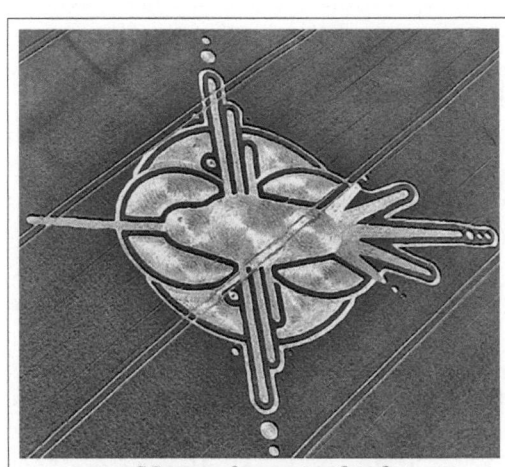

58. sun-hummingbird
(Wiltshire, England, 2009)

Here very probably a hummingbird is to be seen. It, too, is inside a sun and is therefore probably a sunbird. This connection of bird/insect and sun, so common in crop circles, is known from mythology mainly as the Winged Sun. It plays a big role especially with the Egyptians, the Persians and partly also with the Greeks (at the top at the staff of Hermes).

At the corners between the wings and the sun you can find again the two companion points; at the tips of the wings and at the tips of two tail feathers you can see two points each. At the end of the middle tail feather three points are found.

The polarity principle has also been depicted: a head pole circle around the crown chakra, a lower body pole circle around the root chakra, and the sun circle with the heart chakra (sun chakra) as the center. These three points have been additionally represented by the grain placed in the circle at the head, heart chakra and abdomen.

Between the wings and the head circle, the two companion points are found once again.

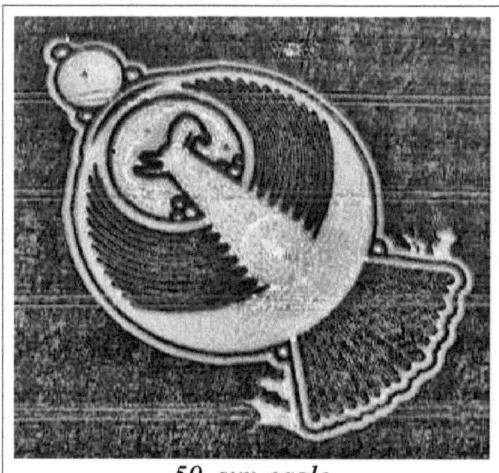

59. sun-eagle

(Wiltshire, England, 2009)

Here a sun-eagle can be seen with the center of the main circle in his heart chakra.

This type of depiction is also often found in depictions of Buddha, who sits in a circular area representing his luminous aura, the center of which is located in Buddha's heart chakra. One could also summarize Buddha's teaching as "living out of the heart chakra".

The head pole of the eagle is marked by a circle. There is also another circular area around Buddhas head – his aureole.

The lower pole has also been marked: Flames flaring up from its tail feathers. This representation corresponds exactly to the representations from Yoga and Buddhism: the Kundalini fire comes from below, the God-light comes from above and both together let the inner sun shine in the heart chakra.

The God-light coming from above, which is called "Bindhu" in Yoga, has been represented here by the circle above the eagle's head. The three small circles around this circle could represent the eternal cycle and the endless transformation and thus also the sun – at least this is the symbolism of the "3" throughout Eurasia.

The triad of small circles is repeated by the two groups of three circles between the wings and the head circle. This results in a triangle of three groups of three, with the eagle's head in the center.

The eagle has 12 wing feathers each – which is again the number of the sun. On its tail it has 16 feathers – which is, like the "8" worldwide, the number of completeness and secondarily, therefore, of perfection.

This symbolism of the "8" and derived from it also the symbolism of the "16" (8·2=16) and the "32" (16·2=32) lies in the fact that in the late Old Stone Age and in the early New Stone Age there was a binary number system: One used only the numbers "1", "2", "4", and "8". From them one put together all needed concrete numbers: 6=4+2, 13=8+4+1, 15=8+4+2+1. Larger concrete numbers were not needed at that time. The "8" as the largest number got therefore also the meanings "all" and finally also "right".

It is impressive, how uniform the symbolism of the crop circles is at a closer look. This speaks against the assumption that the crop circles were all created by humans, because these symbolisms are hardly known to anyone.

60. „phoenix"
(Wiltshire, England, 2009)

This bird has been strongly abstracted. The central circle as the sun, four concentric circles, four wing feathers each, five tail feathers.

Due to the simplicity of the draft, however, no further statements can be derived from the structure – except perhaps that the bird obviously sings ...

Is he the reborn phoenix? The phoenix symbolism comes from Egypt - at that time it was called "bennu bird", i.e. the "rising bird". The fire was the red sky in the morning and the bird itself was the reborn sun. Although it is not reported in the Egytian texts that the phoenix sang in the form of the winged sun as it rose in the morning, since birds sing in the morning, the phoenix will probably have sung along with the other birds in the morning – as it has been pictured here.

61. sun-bird
(England, 2015)

This bird has been formed in a very ornamental way. The style of this ornamentation is a mixture of the Mayan, Chinese, Greek and Perserian styles. However, it has a greater rigor than the style of these four cultures.

In the head there is the Chinese symbol for "luck, blessing".

The beak of the bird has been strongly stylized. Behind the head is a single companion point.

The border circle consists of two partial circular rings: The upper semicircle has its center in the upper breast – the 10 rays on the bird's breast also point to this

53

center. The lower semicircle has its center approximately in the root chakra.

The upper semicircle emphasizes the center of the heart chakra, the lower semicircle emphasizes the lower pole of the root chakra and the circular area above the head emphasizes the upper pole of the crown chakra.

If you look closely at the ornaments in the head, wings and tail of the bird, you can see that they are all made of spirals – they are the symbol of inward-facing self-knowledge and outward-facing unfoldment – sunset and sunrise.

62. sun-heron

(Wiltshire, England, 2012)

This rather abstract crop circle looks like a heron flying towards the sun.

The central circle with the ring is the head, the 7 circles in front of it the long beak, the straight line the neck, the big circle the body, the 11 circles on the left and the 10 circles on the right are the wings, the four circles behind the body are the tail and the 33 circles around the top right are the sun.

At first sight these numbers are quite strange, but they have a system: $3 \cdot 11 = 33$ sun circles; 10 wing circles + 11 wing circles + 1 body circle = 22 circles; 7 beak circles + 4 tail circles = 11 circles. However, the question arises, what can be meant here with the emphasis of the "11", since the "11" has no general symbolism – only a very vague symbolism as "dissolution of the 10" which has taken over the role of the "perfect number" in the decimal system. The "11" would be then like the "9" (which dissolves the perfect "8") and later the "13" (which dissolves the perfect "12"), a number of death and transformation. This would at least fit the symbolism of the phoenix and the winged sun.

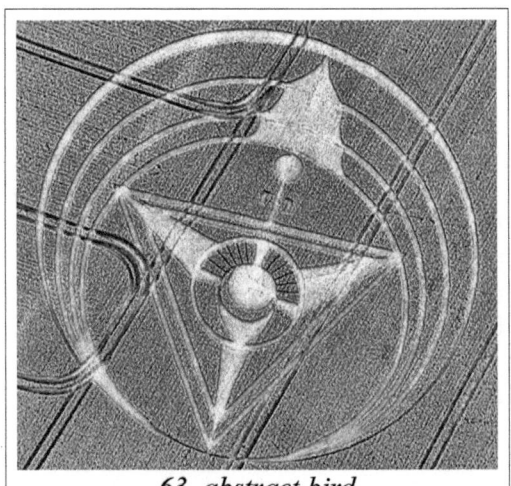

63. abstract bird
(Wiltshire, England, 2013)

This shape must first be broken down into its component parts in order to understand it.

There is an outer circle that encloses everything.

There is an axis from bottom to top that is broken in some places.

There are two triangles with three bright triangle spaces in it and in the center a circle with an incomplete cross, a crescent at the missing cross line and 12 (sun) rays.

Then there is a kind of head from which three more rings start, all meeting at the lower tip of the triangle.

At the "neck" behind the head there is a circular area and two small straight lines parallel to the axis.

The axis forms a cross with the horizontal line of the triangle, the intersection point of which is exactly in the center of the large circle.

The circular area in the ring in the triangle looks like a rising sun over which a cross has been placed, the center of which is in the center of the sun. This arrangement will again be the center of the quintessence or the sun surrounded by the four elements or the four directions. The crescent under the sun could be the sea from which the sun rises in the morning or the earth goddess who gives re-birth to the sun in the morning.

If this central circle represents the heart chakra, which is very probable because of the sun symbol, the whole triangle symbol should be the body. The three pointed triangles in the triangle would be the wings and tail of a bird.

The two short straight lines to the left and right of the bird's neck will correspond to the two lines next to the main axis of crop circles 37 and 38. Presumably they are also identical to the double holder, the double crescent, and the pairs of dots. They all seem to be something like stabilizers.

Is the circle at the base of the bird's neck the throat chakra? Then it should be where the two short straight lines are. From its position, the circle corresponds more to the atlas vertebra at the base of the skull.

The three circles starting from the head could have the general Eurasian symbolism of the "3": "cycle" and secondarily therefore also "sun".

This crop circle apparently represents a sunbird.

- * ❧ * -

64. swallows

(Wiltshire, England, 2003)

Here are three birds that have wings and V-shaped tails like swallows and swifts. The tail of the bird in front is against a circle in each case, the center of which is at the tip of the beak of the bird behind it.

So these three birds follow each other. Is the cycle symbolism of the "3" meant here? If yes, this would be again a reference to the sun, which is the archetype of the cycle. The three birds would correspond then to the circles at the head of the bird with the previous crop circle.

If one counts the circles which are behind the swallows from one side to the other, one finds the number sequence "6 – 4 – 2 – 6 – 2 – 4 – 6". These seven rows of circular spaces are each connected by a thin line. In total there are 30 circular areas.

The usual symbolism of the three numbers, however, does not lead much further: 2 = counter-set complement; 4 = directions of the sky = everywhere; 6 = group.

- * ❀ * -

65. flock of birds

(Wiltshire, England, 2008)

The same swallows or swifts are seen here as on the previous crop circle. This time there are 12 – the number of the zodiac and therefore indirectly also of the sun.

Behind the tails of the birds a total of $6 \cdot 2 = 12$ pairs of feathers of 4 long feathers each can be seen – a total of 48 feathers.

In the center, behind the tails of the birds, there are a total of $6 \cdot 2 = 12$ pairs of feathers, each with 4 short feathers – again a total of 48 feathers.

At the horizontal center line there are $6 \cdot 2 = 12$ crescents.

At the top and bottom, there are $2 \cdot 6 = 12$ almost symmetrical arched triangles.

In the center there are $6 \cdot 2 = 12$ asymmetrical arch triangles.

In the center are 6 dark almond shapes and 3 light almond shapes.

The "12" has been emphasized in an extreme way in this crop circle. In total, there are $12 \cdot 12 = 144$ shapes in the outer area: 12 birds, 48 long feathers, 48 short feathers,

12 crescents, 12 symmetrical arch triangles and 12 asymmetrical arch triangles. In addition, there are the 9 almond shapes on the center line.

It can be assumed that these swallows are also sunbirds.

III 8.   Other animals

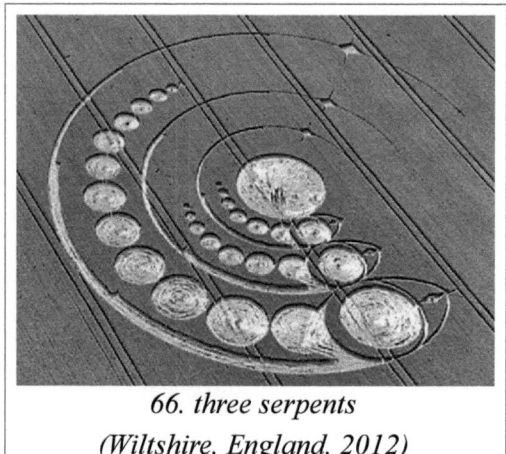

66. three serpents
(Wiltshire, England, 2012)

In this crop circle three snakes seem to crawl around a central circle. However, these snakes are also very reminiscent of the representation of the swallows in the previous crop circles.

The outer snake has the largest head-circle; the middle snake has the middle head-circle; the inner snake has the smallest head-circle. All three have a crescent-shaped, almost complete ring around their head-circle.

In front of the heads of the snakes, the tongues of the snakes could be represented.

The outer snake has 12 circles behind it; the middle 7 and the innermost 6.

The outer line at the arc behind the outer snake becomes 4 times gradually narrower; the arc of the middle snake 3 times and the arc of the inner snake 2 times.

If you draw a line through the central circle and through the three head circles, you can see the different angles from here:

- The tips of the heads extend forward about 22.5°, or about 1/16 circle.
- The first step on the arc of the innermost snake is at about 90°, that is, at 1/4 circle behind the head.
- The three "stars" at the end of the three circular arcs are at about 225° behind the heads, i.e. at 5/8 circle behind the heads.
- The ends of the circular arcs are at about 247.5°, that is, at 11/16 circle.
- Also, the various arc stages are all at a multiple of a 1/16 circle.

The crop circle appears to be based on a 16-rayed star. If you start with the head tip, you get the following positions:

- 0/16 circle: tip of the head
- 1/16 circle: center of the head
- 2/16 circle (1/18 circle):   -
- 3/16 circle: -
- 4/16 circle (1/4 circle):   1st step middle and outer arc

- 5/16 circle:	1st step outer arc
- 6/16 circle (3/8 circle):	2nd step outer arc
- 7/16 circle:	2nd step middle arc
- 8/16 circle (1/2 circle):	3rd step outer circular arc
- 9/16 circle:	-
- 10/16 circle (5/8 circle):	last step of all three arcs
- 11/16 circle:	three stars
- 12/16 circle (3/4 circle):	-
- 13/16 circle:	end of the three arcs
- 14/16 circle (7/8 circle):	-
- 15/16 circle:	-
- 16/16 circle (1 circle):	tip of the head

The "16", like the "8", is a symbol of completeness and perfection and is therefore used also as a sun symbol in Eurasia, Australia and in America.

The symbolism of the three "stars" is unclear. Overall, however, the same sunbird symbolism will have been depicted here again as in the previous crop circle.

- * ❁ * -

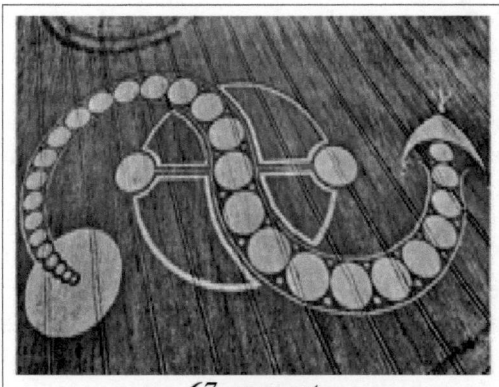

67. serpent
(Wiltshire, England, 2011)

Here a snake can be seen quite clearly. It too has the arc-triangle known from the Swallow crop circles as its head.

The background is formed by a polar system: a ring with two circles on it.

The snake itself, which has the shape of an "S", apparently represents the flow of energy caused by the polar system – the magnetic field, the flowing current, the blood circulation, the Kundalini, etc.

If one would draw the shape of the snake further on, one would get the ∞-symbol to which the "S" has already been expanded in crop circle 23. This could indicate the endless flow of life force.

On the snake there are 29 circles – a symbolism of this number is not known. However, humans have 29 dorsal vertebrae, which makes the interpretation of the snake as Kundalini quite likely, since it rises within the body from the root chakra between the genitals and anus, in front of the dorsal vertebrae, along to the crown chakra on top of the head.

59

Snakes have far more vertebrae – on average there are about 200 vertebrae, but there can be as many as 435 vertebrae.

Between each of these circles you can see 2 points that act like stabilizers or parts of joints. These combinations of circles can also be seen as the dorsal vertebrae of the snake.

The circle from which the snake emerges will be the root chakra from which it rises. It could also be associated with the nest or egg of the snake. In addition, "kundalini" has the meaning "that what lies in the pit (kunda)". Therefore, this circle will be the "pit" of Kundalini, i.e. the root chakra.

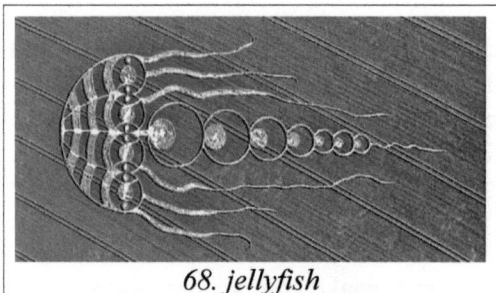

68. jellyfish
(Oxfordshire, England, 2008)

At first glance, this is simply a jellyfish – but at second glance, there is more to it.

The most interesting thing is found at the baseline of the hemisphere on the left, which is the "head" of the jellyfish. It consists of four circles next to each other, which all have the same inner structure: a large central circle and next to it on the left and on the right two smaller polar circles, which are separated from the central circle by a sickle each.

This arrangement is already well known from the polar crop circles. Here apparently four such polar crop circles have been connected in a series. This is reminiscent of four magnets or batteries placed one behind the other to increase their power.

Can one imagine this jellyfish head as a hemisphere with a total of eight such polar grain circles connected in series in a circle? What then would be the effect of eight such batteries or magnets arranged in a circle?

If the analogy to the magnet should be correct, in the center of the magnets in a right angle to the surface on which they are located, a radiating magnetic field would have to develop. Such a radial magnetic field, which emerges at the rotation poles, every sun and every planet possesses – they are called "jets".

These jets have an interesting analogy in yoga: the vertical line in the body through which the life force flows and at which the seven chakras are located. This "life force jet" is called the "sushumna" in yoga.

In the case of the jellyfish, there are seven spheres where you should expect to find this jet. These spheres all contain a small sphere, which is not in the center, but on the edge towards the "jellyfish head". Is this shift of the circular area in the ring towards the "jellyfish head" an indication of the "magnetic" attraction by the polar circles connected in the series? It would at least fit well.

There are interestingly exactly 12 dark areas on the jellyfish head – they are the already so often appeared number of the "sun aura", thus of the zodiac.

There are not only 7 spheres in the "jellyfish tail", but also 7 threads on the jellyfish and its tail. Since the 7 spheres are in a row and the threads are also arranged as a "3+1+3" group, this number could refer to the chakras, which are also a "3+1+3" group – and which are located on the jet (sushumna).

The chakras are structured as follows:

The structure of the chakra system			
Chakra	*Location*	*Quality*	*Symmetry*
Crown Chakra	on the head	spiritual contact	
Third Eye	between the eyebrows	outer structure: orientation	
Throat chakra	larynx	social self-expression	
Heart Chakra	chest center	identity, "temple of the soul	
Solar Plexus	under the costal arch	physical self-expression	
Hara	just below the navel	inner structure: inner support	
Root Chakra	between genitals and anus	physical contact	

A center acts outward in three steps: (center) – impulse – form – contact.

These three steps are also found in the solar system: (sun) – solar wind – shock front – bow wave.

They are also represented by the Indian Vajra symbol: (sphere) – lotus – elephant head – elephant trunk.

(A more detailed description of these systems and connections can be found in my book "Chakra Magic for Beginners").

Therefore, the arrangement of the 7 tentacles of the jellyfish as a "3+1+3" group will hardly be a coincidence, but with the help of the aesthetically beautiful picture of the jellyfish will represent the chakra system and its dynamics.

It is impressive on the one hand, how uniform and conclusive the symbolism of the crop circles is at a closer look, and on the other hand also, with which elegance these structures and connections are represented. One could call them a little poetically "pictures of the inner dynamics of life".

- *  * -

69. sun-cat
(Wiltshire, England, 2016)

Here is the largely naturalistic head of a cat. Above him is a circular area – probably the sun again.

In Egypt, the panther goddess Mafdet, the lion goddess Sachmet, and to some extent the cat goddess Bastet, were considered to be the power of the sun. Sachmet is also almost always depicted with the sun disk as a crown. The big predator (big cats and bears) has the symbolism of strength in almost all peoples and is often associated with the sun.

This cat head has two wings – a common motif for Egyptian goddesses. These two wings have 17 feathers each. A general symbolism of the "17" is not known.

Only the strength of the sun seems to have been represented here.

- *  * -

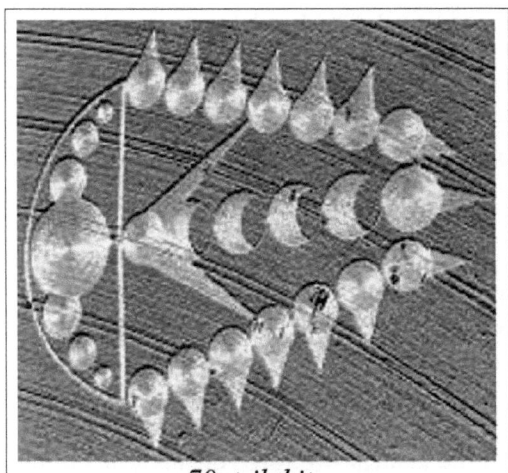

70. trilobite
(Wiltshire, England, 2009)

Trilobites are marine animals with an exoskeleton like that of crabs. They once populated the oceans but have long been extinct. They look very much like this crop circle.

On the head plate of the trilobite there is a large central circle and three smaller circles to the left and right of it. This will be taken as a reference to the seven chakras with the heart chakra in the center.

This seven number is also represented on the left and right side of the body of the trilobite by the seven "circles with prongs". This corresponds to the hook-shaped legs of the trilobite – however, it had 10 and not 7 legs on both sides. The "7" was chosen here probably for symbolic reasons.

On the central axis of the trilobite there are again 7 circles – if one counts the central head circle and the circle in the arc triangle too.

The arc triangle interestingly points with its three tips from the middle circle (third eye) below the crown chakra on the head to the two middle circles (heart chakra) on the sides.

Of the 7 circles in the center, 4 circles each contain a crescent – do they represent the cohesion of these circles ("dorsal vertebrae") or are they, like the circles on the jellyfish, supposed to indicate the "magnetic attraction" on the central axis? Possibly both …

- *  * -

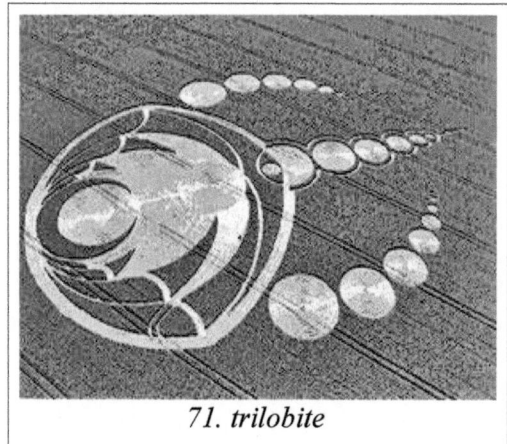

71. trilobite
(Wiltshire, England, 2004)

This trilobite has been somewhat more stylized than the previous one, but its three body segments are also represented by seven circles each. The middle circles are each surrounded by a ring, fused together to form a kind of shell of the circles.

Here again the 7 chakras are represented. The seventh circle of the middle row is already in the "head" and can only be seen as a pattern in the flat-laid grain.

Possibly one can understand the three rows of circles also as a correspondence to the central life force channel Sushumna and the two life force side channels Ida and Pingala in Yoga.

The representation of the trilobite's head is somewhat confusing at first glance. The structure is reminiscent of a flower with three petals on each side, in the center of which is a sphere. This motif is known from Egypt, India and Central America: a lotus or a water lily that rises from the water underworld and brings the soul or the sun back to this world – the rebirth of the soul or the sun.

The head circle, on closer inspection, is an almond shape and not a circle.

One will be able to understand this central circle and the twice 3 petals again as a representation of the 7 chakras with the "sun chakra" in the center.

In the central circle row, the second uppermost circle contains a smaller circle located where the base of the skull rests on the atlas vertebra. This arrangement was also found in crop circle 63, which represents a bird, and in crop circle 68, which has the shape of a jellyfish (there is a short line between the tail and the head).

What is this point all about? It is known from yoga as a place where one often gets into trouble when the Kundalini rises, because of one's parents' ideas about how one should behave in social contexts. This is the backside of the third eye. However, the reason for the emphasis on this point in three different crop circles is unclear for now.

- * ❀ * -

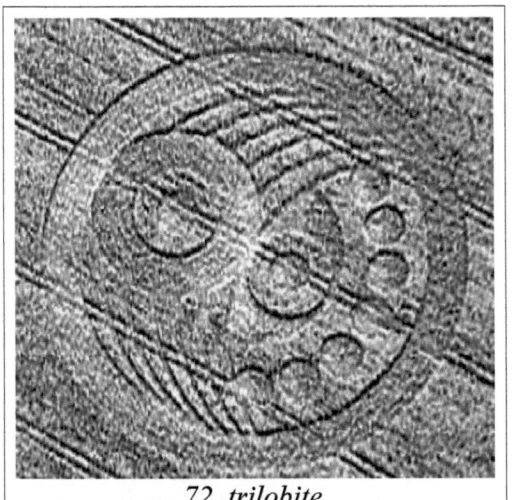

72. trilobite
(Wiltshire, England, 2010)

This is a very simple trilobite. There are again the 7 head circles (right), the heart chakra circle and additionally a large circle (left) instead of the differentiated representation of the body. The twice 7 legs have been depicted here more naturalistically than on the other two trilobites.

III 9. Eyes

The motif of the eye was already found on crop circle 53, where it could also be a beetle with its heart chakra, as well as on crop circle 57, where it appears on the body of a bird and also rather represents the heart chakra.

- - -

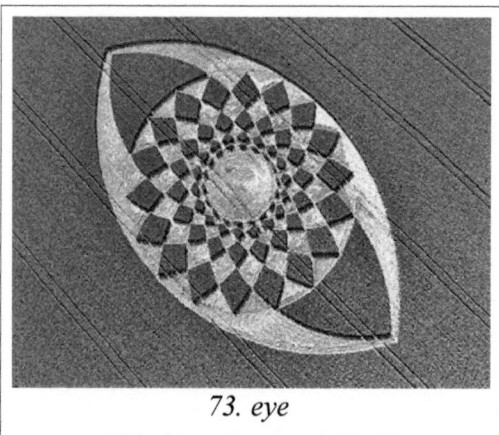

73. eye
(Wiltshire, England, 2005)

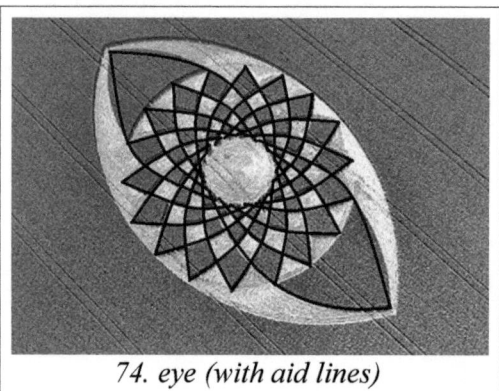

74. eye (with aid lines)

This crop circle unmistakably represents an eye. However, there are some peculiarities, which are worth looking at more closely.

Left and right of the iris of the eye one should actually expect the white of the eye. Instead, there are two arched triangles – as in crop circles 64 and 65, where they represent both bird bodies and gaps, in crop circle 66 bird or snake heads, and in crop circle 67 a snake head.

The motif of the "snake in the eye" is known from the Teutons, the Indians and the Chinese: the Kundalini snake risen into the Third Eye. However, this interpretation is still very uncertain for the time being, since it is based only on the shape of the arch-triangle.

The iris of the eye consists of four rings of 18 arched diamonds each. These rhomboids are obtained by drawing 18 arcs from the pupil of the eye that give clockwise to the outside and 18 arcs that go counterclockwise to the outside. These 36 arcs overlap at regular intervals and form the total of 72 diamonds.

This pattern becomes clearer when these guide lines are drawn into the crop circle (see Figure 74).

Why are there 4·18=72 diamonds? Does this actually mean 9·8=72 diamonds? Then it would be the transformation or the death (9) of the perfection (8). This could also be a paraphrase for the solar cycle – and the sun is often understood as the eye of heaven. However, this interpretation is only a vague conjecture for the time being.

66

75. eye
(Warwickshire, England, 2010)

This eye has been depicted differently. Its iris is a uniform surface, but the whites of the eye here have been divided by arcs into arc diamonds.

Counting from the inside to the outside, there are "9+7+5+3+1" rhomboids, so 25 rhomboids in total. If one takes both sides together, it is 50 diamonds. In the crop circle 27 there were $2 \cdot 25 = 50$ semicircles. Whether this number in both circles is based on the same symbolism, is unclear at first – after all both "$2 \cdot 25 = 50$" forms surround a center, which can also be understood as the sun.

The arched rhombuses of this eye are created by $2 \cdot 10 = 20$ instead of $2 \cdot 18 = 36$ arcs. Also here it is unclear at first whether the numbers have a meaning.

The eye is surrounded by 12 dark arc-stripes and by 12 light arc-stripes. These stripes as a whole result in a vortex – if one imagines the eye away and adds the background according to the stripes, this vortex becomes visible. The interpretation of the eye as the sun's eye is thus quite certain – the "12" is the zodiac surrounding the sun.

The "12" is the basic structure not only in astrology, but also in physics: the basic unit in today's physics is the superstring ("superstring theory"), which is a circle consisting of 12 equal sections forming a standing wave. So the importance and symbolism of the "12" is well established.

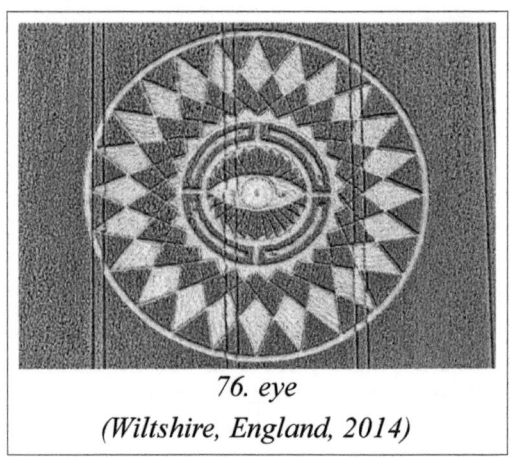

76. eye

(Wiltshire, England, 2014)

This eye is the most naturalistic of the three crop circle eyes.

Above the eye are 12 rays (as you would expect). However, below the eye, unexpectedly, there are 14 rays. Why? $2 \cdot 7$ chakras? Or do crop circle creators also make mistakes? Or is there another reason for this?

Around the eye are two rings with four "gates" which will correspond to the four directions or the four elements.

Outside around these two rings, which are broken four times, there are 2 rows of 24 arc-rhombs each – so 48 arc-rhombs in total. This number also existed in the flock of birds in crop circle 65, in which 48 long and 48 short feathers were represented, which could also be sunbeams.

Given the quadripartition of the circular ring around the sun, as well as the twelve-partition ($2 \cdot 12 = 24$) of this ring, the "48" would be the combination of these two symbolisms.

If one counts the bright diamonds on the very outside, one comes to 72 diamonds – also the eye in the crop circle 73 is surrounded by 72 diamonds. This seems to be no coincidence.

III 10. Fractals

A fractal is a certain mathematical-geometrical form, which can be very complex. However, its basic principle is quite simple: a certain process is repeated endlessly. For example, at the sides of a triangle one can place again and again a small triangle whose side is only one third as long – again and again. Then the following series is formed:

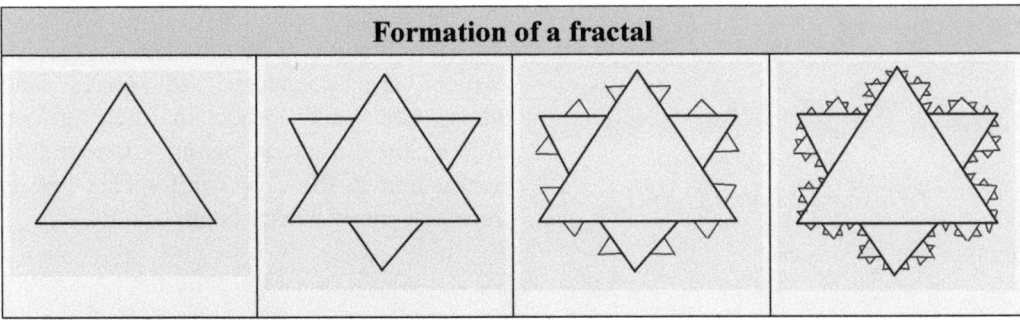

Formation of a fractal

In nature, fractals are very common – e.g. snowflakes are formed in a fractal shape and also the leaves of a flower are often arranged as a fractal. Of course, depending on which replication-rule is applied each time, completely different shapes can be created.

The fractal is a simple growth principle, which extends a thing according to the same rule always one step further.

- - -

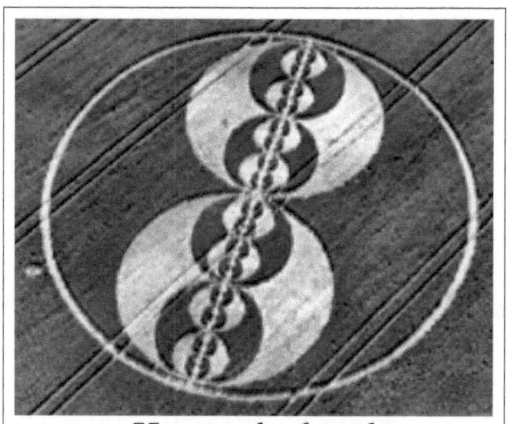

77. two-polar fractal
(Wiltshire, England, 2001)

In a ring there are two circles: the polar system – the "magnet" or the "battery".

Each of the 2 circles is again a ring in which there are two circles – a sequence of two "magnets" or "batteries".

Each of the 4 circles is again a ring in which there are two circles – a sequence of 8 "magnets" or "batteries".

Thus a sequence of ever more and ever smaller "magnets" or "batteries" results, which are connected in series and strengthen each other in their effect. Finally they create a "beam" – the straight white line in the crop circle. This line is reminiscent of a laser beam.

- * ✿ * -

78. two-polar fractal
(Hampshire, England, 2000)

The initial form of this fractal is the well known structure of two pole circles and a central circle.

The fractal formula with this grain circle is very simple: Add to each circle two more circles, just under half the size, in such a way that all circles have the same distance from each other.

This is true for the central circle – the two pole circles are opposite each other.

Then, like the central circle, the pole circles form a center, which can be seen as a semicircle, and let two more circles sprout out of it.

This process is repeated several times:

- 1 central circle
- 2 pole circles
- 4 pole circles
- 8 pole circles
- 16 pole circles
- 32 pole circles

70

On the very outside there are $2 \cdot 13=26$ rows of 3 points each with decreasing size. This odd number results from the fact that some of the outer circles overlap. One could understand this as three three-steps, thus as "impulse – form – contact". However, it is not sure if that is what is meant here.

- *  * -

79. four-polar fractal
(Mammendorf, FRG, 2016)

This fractal is 4-polar, but not as regular as the previous one. Several steps occur:

- 1 sphere-"bud" (extension).
- 2 sphere "bud" (branch)
- 3 sphere "bud" (addition to hexagon)
- 4 sphere-"buds".

Therefore, this shape looks like a fractal, but is ultimately no fractal ...

- *  * -

71

80. tree-fraktal
(Hampshire, England, 2002)

The rule in this fractal is "division at the end of a line into two lines half as long, pointing left and right at a 60° angle". This gives the shape of a tree.

The hexagons (honeycombs) at the ends of these lines look like leaves or apples.

Since the angle of 60°, in which the new lines branch off from the old line, creates 3 120° angles between these 3 lines, the hexagon, which is also based on the 120° angle, fits best to this kind of "tree".

The angles have not been kept quite precisely – otherwise this crop circle would look even more symmetrical.

Here another principle is shown, which is closely related to the fractal: the self-similarity. This principle means that in a system the same structures can be found in the most different places.

- *  * -

81. two-polar fractal
(Wiltshire, England, 2009)

Here the "S" is the formative shape. The two rows of 6 circles are connected by seven thin lines running across the center circle.

The two pole circles also each contain an "S".

In total, there is a large central circle on the central axis, and three small circles above and below it – the seven main chakras with the heart chakra in the center.

The big "S" as well as the two small "S"s seem to represent the flow of life force in the chakras: the Kundalini.

But why the big "S" consists of two times 6 circles and once 7 lines is not really clear: Has the heart chakra not been counted with the six circles? Or are the increasingly larger circles supposed to represent the flow velocity, which would then be greatest in the heart chakra? That would fit to the fact that the heart chakra is presumably the pump in the life force cycle.

Whether one can understand the structure of this crop circle as a fractal is unclear. The structure "central circle + 2 polar circles" is repeated purely graphically in the two polar circles, giving rise to the twice 3 outer circles, but in terms of content the two outer triads of circles are the extension and self-expression of the central circle, i.e. the heart chakra.

- *  * -

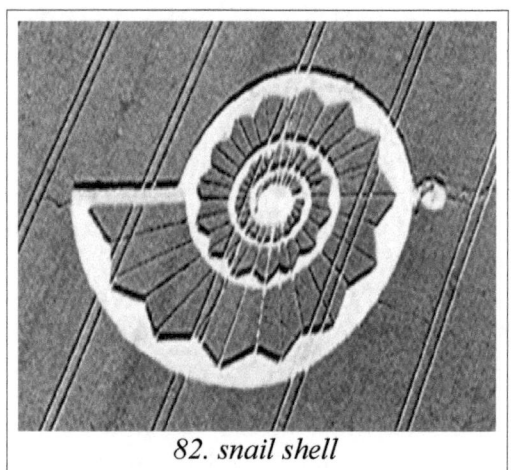

82. snail shell
(Wiltshire, England, 2002)

This snail shell unfolds as a spiral – one of the simplest fractal forms. Each limb of the spiral consists of two irregular rectangles that together form a ray. There seem to be 50 such rays – but the exact number cannot be seen clearly.

Strictly speaking, one sees "rays", but if one looks at the "open end" of the snail shell, it becomes clear that the units are actually "recesses".

On the right, there is a small circular area on the snail. Its significance is unknown.

The snail has pretty much 3 turns. The "3" has the symbolism of development – which fits extremely well with the coils of a snail shell.

- * ✿ * -

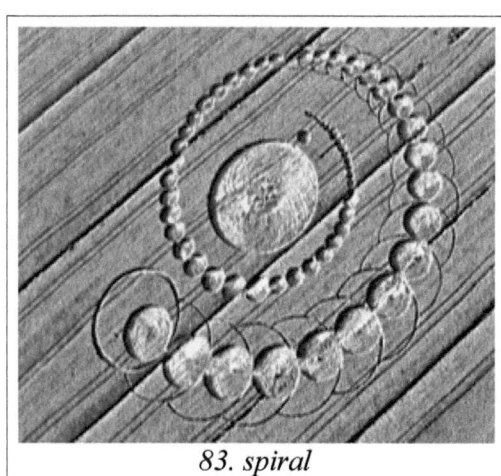

83. spiral
(Italy, 2012)

This spiral consists of about 69 circles.

The 20 first, larger circles are surrounded by a ring. However, the circles are located in these circular rings at the back end and not in the middle. This arrangement, which can also be found on the trilobite (crop circle 70), obviously represents something like a dorsal vertebrae, an anatomical coherence.

In the center a large circle is to be seen, beside which lies a smaller circle. Is the big circle the center from which this spiral movement starts? And what is the meaning of the small circle that is also next to the snail shell (crop circle 82)?

- * ✿ * -

74

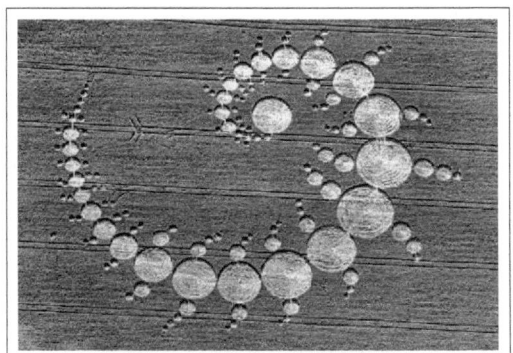

84. one-polar Julia-set
(Wiltshire, England, 1996)

A Julia set is a particular mathematical shape that is also a fractal in most cases. It is a variant of the spiral. The mathematician who discovered this set was named Gaston Maurice Julia.

The Julia set shown here consists of a single line, which consists of a central circle and 35 smaller circles. To the left and right of these circles are short rows of small circles.

Seen from the central circle these are:

- 1 central circle without companion
- 2 circles without companion
- 4 circles with 2 times 1 companion
- 6 circles with 2 times 2 companions
- 8 circles with 2 times 3 companions
- 6 circles with 2 times 2 companions
- 4 circles with 2 times 1 companion
- 5 circles without circles

The symmetry is obvious – if we ignore the fact that the simple circles without companions become smaller and smaller at the end and therefore have a larger number than the expected "2".

- * ✿ * -

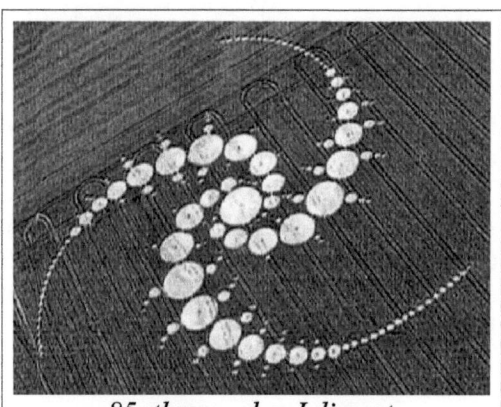

*85. three-polar Julia-set
(Wiltshire, England, 1996)*

Here, the Julia set has three arms. The arms also have a different structure:

- 1 central sphere surrounded by 3 large circles and 9 small circles.
- 2 circles without companion
- 1 circle with 1 companion
- 1 circle with 2 companions
- 3 circles with 3 companions
- 3 circles with 2 companions
- 2 circles with 1 companion
- 18 circles without companion

These are the numbers for the lower arm. The other two arms differ slightly. In brackets is the length of the companion rows.

- lower arm: 2 (0) - 1 (1) - 1 (2) - 3 (3) - 3 (2) - 2(1) - 18 (0)
- right arm: 2 (0) - 1 (1) - 1 (2) - 4 (3) - 1 (2) - 1(1) - 18 (0)
- left arm: 2 (0) - 1 (1) - 1 (2) - 3 (3) - 2 (2) - 1(1) - 18 (0)

One could take this form as "triple expansion", that is, the emergence of the 3 chakra pairs from the heart chakra.

- * ❀ * -

76

86. six-polar Julia-set

(Wiltshire, England, 2001)

This sixfold Julia set could be seen, according to the previous interpretation, as the emergence of the six outer chakras out of the heart chakra.

The single Julia set would then be the expansion itself, the triple Juliet set the three steps outward, and the sixfold Juliet set the emergence of the six outer chakras. Since no double, quadruple, fivefold or sevenfold Julia sets are known as crop circles, one can take this interpretation for the time being.

All six arms are built up uniformly. The numbers in the brackets indicate the length of the companions: 1 (1) – 3 (2) – 5 (3) – 4 (2).

- *  * -

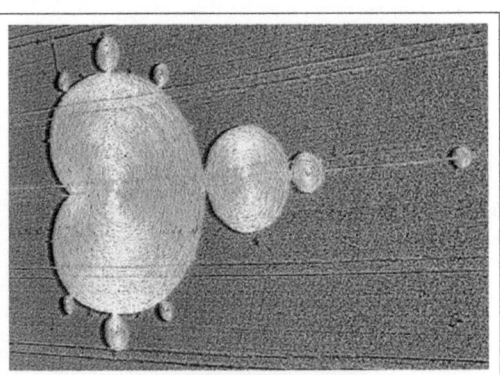

87. Mandelbrot-set

(Oxfordshire, England, 1991)

This fractal has been named after the mathematician Benoit Mandelbrot, who lives in Oxford, where this crop circle also appeared.

The Mandelbrot set is a fractal and closely related to both the Julia set and chaos theory.

It is a picture of the very complex and varied forms that arise when a simple principle is constantly repeated – so it is a fractal picture … probably the most memorable fractal form.

Also living beings are created according to the fractal principle: few rules result in complex living forms by their ordered interaction – thus living beings.

III 11. The Kabbalistic Tree of Life

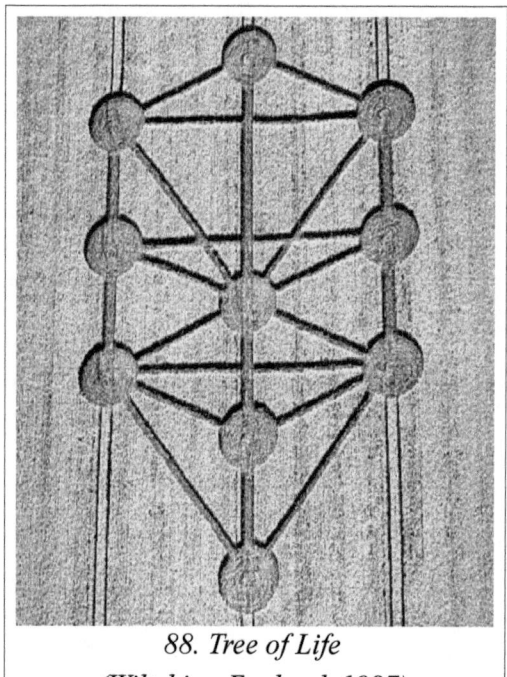

88. Tree of Life
(Wiltshire, England, 1997)

The cabbalistic tree of life is related to the fractals in a certain way. It is a structure which can be found in all systems, since it is based on the simplest of all fractal principles: on the three-step "impulse – form – contact" already mentioned several times. The two poles of this structure are unity (upper sphere) and multiplicity (lower sphere), between which the organical system, i.e. the heart chakra stands (middle sphere).

However, the system is too complex to explain here.

It is noticeable that the three "pillars" of the tree of life lie exactly on three tractor tracks.

- * ❀ * -

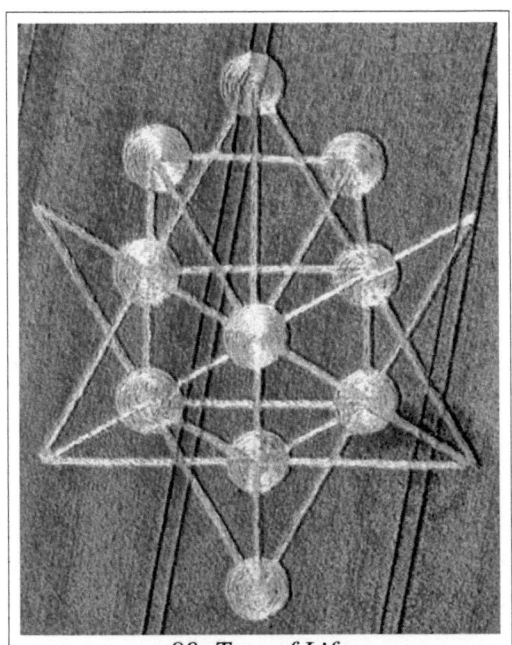

89. Tree of Life
(Wiltshire, England, 2017)

Here again the tree of life can be seen, which has been supplemented by some auxiliary lines, one forming a penta-gram with a point pointing downward, and the other a triangle pointing upward. These two forms do not belong to the classical figure of the Kabbalistic Tree of Life.

The Tree of Life, like the formation of the chakras and like many forms in the crop circles, is based on the "three-step", but it is a form developed by human beings. Therefore, it should be considered that it may have been created by humans.

90. three step
(Wiltshire, England, 1991)

Here a part of the three-step has been represented, on which among other things also the tree of life is based. The starting point (central point) can be seen on the top right, the expansion (six flames) below and the structure (six angles) on the left.

The starting point on the upper right corresponds to the heart chakra, the expansion below to the solar plexus and the throat chakra, and the structure on the upper left to the hara and the third eye. The correspondence to the two contact chakras (root and crown chakra) are not shown in this diagram.

This shape also fits the spheres in the

Tree of Life graphic: the circle at the top right corresponds to the sphere at the top of the Tree of Life (Hebrew name: "Kether"), the circle at the bottom corresponds to the sphere at the top right of the Tree of Life (Hebrew name: "Chokmah"), and the circle at the top left corresponds to the sphere at the top left of the Tree of Life (Hebrew name: "Binah").

The three-step principle is represented fourfold in the crop circle:

     - by the three circles,
     - by the triangle,
     - by the circle and the two rings, as well as
     - by the three lines emanating from the three circles and meeting in the centre.

- * ✸ * -

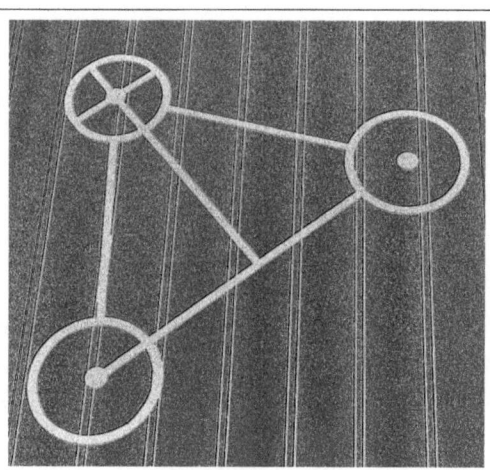

91. three step
(place and year unknown)

Here the upper triangle of the Tree of Life has been represented in a slightly different form:

Point = origin ("Kether");
Line = extension ("Chokmah")
Cross = shape ("Binah")

The vertical line fits graphically into the picture, but if it was to be a section of the Tree of Life, it would have to run from the right circle (top of the Tree of Life) to the center of the opposite line (see Tree of Life graphic).

- * ✸ * -

80

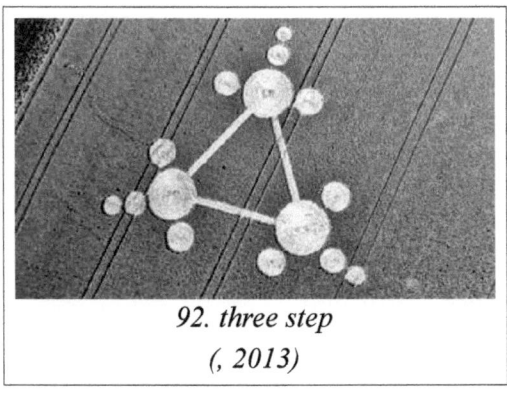

92. three step
(, 2013)

Here the three-step or three-polarity has been represented by the triangle, by three lines, by three circles as well as by three small circles at each circle.

The expansion dynamics of the "3" has been expressed here by the additional small circle at the three tips, through which the crop circle gets something radiant.

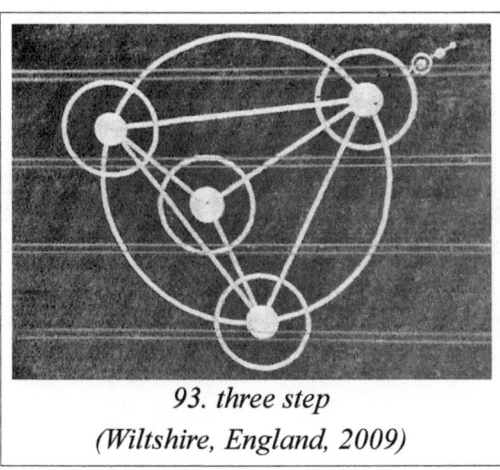

93. three step
(Wiltshire, England, 2009)

Here again the same principle has been illustrated, but this time without markings of the qualities of the three circles.

In the large circle that connects the centers of the three outer circles, there is a triangular pyramid whose apex is decentralized and located above another circle. The meaning of this point is unclear and differs both from the structures of the Kabbalistic Tree of Life and from the crop circle structures found so far. The top of the three circles on the upper right, however, is typical for a crop circle.

One can understand this crop circle also as a 3D representation of a tetrahedron (equilateral triangle pyramid). Then the representation would be conclusive.

81

III 12.   Mandalas

A mandala is a concentric and symmetrical magical-spiritual land-map used in meditations and rituals. However, most concentric symmetrical structures are now called "mandala".

III 12. a)   Mandalas – unipolar

Single-polar crop circles consist of only one circular area and one or more circular rings. This is the simplest form of mandala. It corresponds in astrology to conjunction and in physics to gravitation – both pull everything together into one unit.

III 12. b)   Mandalas – bipolar

The bipolar mandalas have already been discussed – these are the polar built crop circles, which consist of two poles, which set in motion a cycle, pulsation, rotation or the like. They correspond to the opposition in astrology and to the electromagnetic force in physics.

III 12. c)   Mandalas – three-polar

There are several three-polar structures in the world. Fortunately, they all have the quality of solid cohesion, which can therefore be assumed in three-polar mandalas. The two most important of these structures are the astrological trine (120° = third circle) and the strong interaction, also called "color force", which has three polarities that together give the neutral state. This force is called "color force" because its three poles have been called "red", "yellow" and "blue" which together give the neutral "white".

This quality of solid cohesion is also found in stone healing with the trigonal crystallization form.

The crop circles, which consist of three circles and have already been described in the chapter about the tree of life (crop circle 90, 91, 92 and 93), also belong to the three-polar mandalas.

- - -

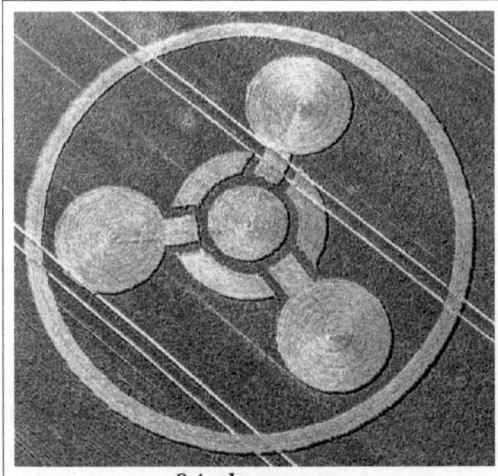

94. three axes
(Wiltshire, England, 2018)

This simple crop circle represents presumably only the firm cohesion which exists in three-polar systems.

In a proton e.g. the "red" quark, the "yellow" quark and the "blue" quark are held together by the color force and form together the outwardly neutral, "white" state. If you want to take a quark out of this connection, you have to spend so much energy that three new quarks are created from it, i.e. a new proton is created – and the proton, from which you wanted to snatch a quark, remains un-harmed. More cohesion is not possible …

So, this crop circle can be understood as a proton or neutron with the three quarks in it, which are held together by the color force.

- * ☸ * -

95. three poles
(Wiltshire, England, 2000)

Here the cohesion has been shown even more impressively:

In each of the three directions, the centers of the three poles can be seen. They are each surrounded by two bright lines, which together with the center form a trinity.

The two inner lines run around the entire shape and, together with the center of the entire shape, form another trinity.

Finally, the large ring that runs through the three pole centers and has its own center in the middle of the overall shape further emphasizes the unity of the three poles.

- * ❀ * -

96. three centres
(Ammersee, FRG, 2014)

Once again, the three pole circles and the center circle can be seen. The three poles here consist of a center and three circular rings. Is this an allusion to the center and the three steps of unfolding (impulse – structure – contact)?

Around them something is depicted which looks like the force field of this arrangement and apparently holds the whole thing together. This force field consists of the meanwhile already well known arched rhombuses. There are in each case 1+3+5+7=16 arc rhombs. Was the perfection symbolism of the "16" intentionally aimed at here?

Together the three force fields have 48 rhombs – this number was already found at the rhombs around the eye (crop circle 76) and at the short and long feathers of the bird flock (crop circle 65). Since the number "48" in these three crop circles comes about in different ways, thus is not based on the same geometry, it could be intended. Therefore, the "4·12=48"

84

symbolism could be meant, which combines the 4-division of the circle around the center with the 12-division of the zodiac, which is also a circle around a center.

- *  * -

97. three rays
(Hampshire, England, 2016)

This crop circle is not so easy to interpret.

In its center are three leaves that look like tobacco leaves. Between them sprout three small leaves – so the transition to the six-polar form is indicated. The central circle is followed by three more leaves, which are only outlined.

The leaf area is backed by a pattern of arc triangles, the tips of which point to the center of the crop circle.

Around this leaf area are 20 symbols that look a bit like Tibetan or Indian letters. There seem to be 10·2 signs – several times the same signs are exactly opposite to each other. Their meaning is completely unclear.

The outer border of the crop circle consists of two circular rings, the outer of which has 33 connections to the outside. Thus, 11 such connections correspond to each of the three thirds of the circle.

This crop circle has three unusual elements: the tobacco leaves, the non-concentric background of arc triangles, and the letters. It could therefore be a candidate for the man-made crop circle group.

- *  * -

98. three sickles
(Wiltshire, England, 1999)

Not much can be said about this simple crop circle. In it, a rotating movement has been represented by three crescents, which is given stability by a narrow ring.

The center is an arc triangle.

- * ❀ * -

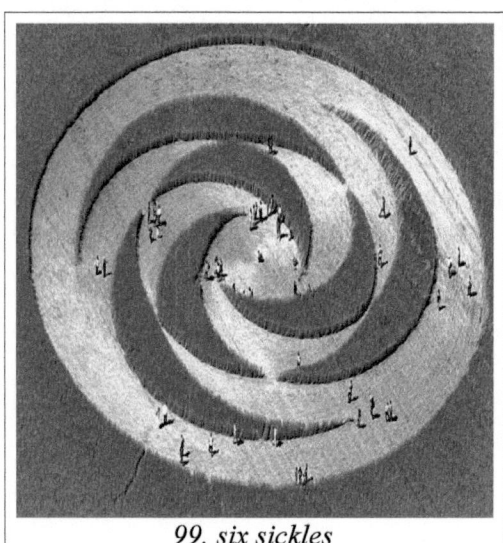

99. six sickles
(Swiss, 2007)

This crop circle is a variation of the previous crop circle: three pairs of crescents form a three-polar mandala that appears to rotate because of the arrangement of the crescents.

Here the ring has been omitted. The center is a circle.

- * ❀ * -

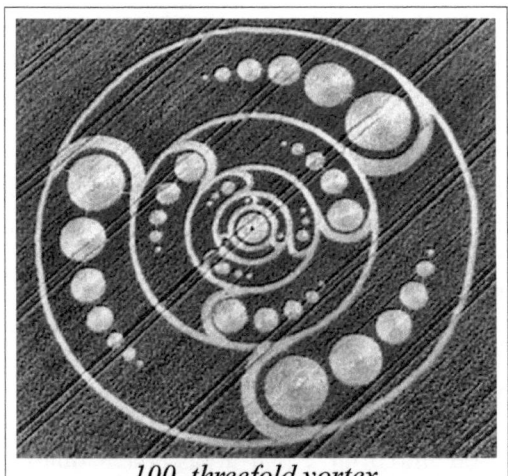

*100. threefold vortex
(Wiltshire, England, 2001)*

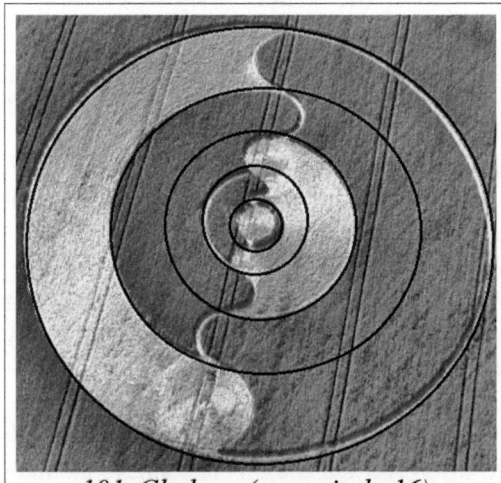

101. Chakras (crop circle 16)

Here is a central circle and around it four rings, which in turn consist of three thirds. Each third consists of a circle as well as a crescent in front of it and some circles behind it: In the outer ring there are once 7 circles and two times 6 circles, in the second outermost ring 5 circles each, in the second innermost ring 3 circles, and in the innermost ring 1 circle. This gives the series "7 – 5 – 3 – 1".

Here the three-polarity is represented fourfold. All rings rotate in the same direction.

The principle "center and 4 rings" was already found once in a very similar way, but without the tripolarity at the crop circle 21 shown on the left again. There this structure has been interpreted as the 7 chakras plus Kundalini fire (below) and Bindhu light (above).

This can be transferred also to the crop circle 100, whereby then not the single chakras, but only the areas would have been represented:

- center: heart chakra
  - inner ring: solar plexus and throat chakra
  - second inner ring: hara and third eye
  - second outer ring: root chakra and crown chakra
  - outer ring: Kundalini fire and Bindhu light

This interpretation, however, does not explain why the four rings are divided into three parts and why different numbers of circles have been depicted in them. Is something completely different meant here? Or does the tripartition stand for the development out of the heart chakra?

- * ❀ * -

87

102. threefold vortex
(Wiltshire 2016)

Aesthetically pleasing and intellectually confusing … In the center a three-polar structure and outside two four-part rings with symbols.

The symbols in the two circular rings occur in groups of 4 and 12. This will be a hint to the usual 4-division (directions, elements) and 12-division (zodiac, super-string) of the rings.

The outer circle is completely identical with the outer circle of crop circle 229, in which there are two wings.

The ring is divided by two thick areas each into four equal areas. Each quarter contains $2 \cdot 12 = 24$ strokes, $2 \cdot 2 = 4$ squares and 4 double spirals – the complex symbols are in the center.

What us the meaning of these double spirals? When the water of a stream flows into a lake, double spirals are formed – the same is true wherever an impulse enters a still medium. The penis and the ovaries also have this form.

So we can assume that this double spiral indicates that an impulse is going from the inside to the outside, creating this double vortex. The position of the double spirals on the outer circle shows that the impulse comes from the inside and goes to the outside.

If the 4 double spirals are the double vortices caused by the penetrating impulse, then the 12 strokes on the left and on the right of it would be waves, which go out from it and the 2 squares in the two corners would be surfaces, which remain largely calm. So the ornaments on the outer circle are a flow pattern.

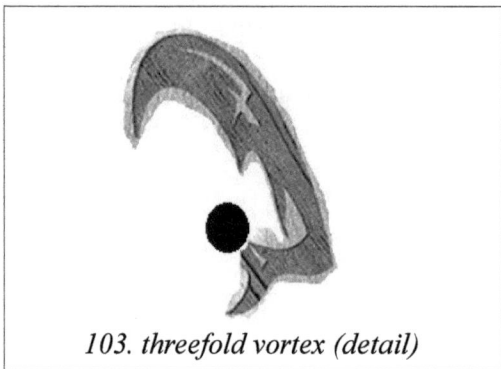

103. threefold vortex (detail)

The triple shape in the center is difficult to interpret. On the left is a single element of this triple shape. The black circle represents the center. The shape is most reminiscent of a fish – the head at the top left and the tail fin at the bottom.

The interpretation of this very unusual motif must remain open for now.

- * ✹ * -

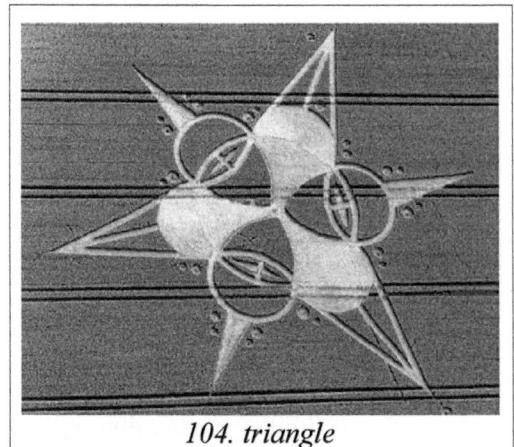

104. triangle

(Wiltshire, England, 2011)

The centerpiece of this crop circle consists of the three polar circles and the central circle, which has been represented only as a ring passing through the centers of the three polar circles.

The three light polar circles have been supplemented by three further dark circles to form a hexagon.

From each of these six circles a pointed triangle projects outward, the triangles belonging to the light and to the dark circles having two different shapes. The three lines of the triangles belonging to the light circles once again emphasize the "3".

The three dark drop-like shapes almost give the impression of three faces looking towards the center. This shape has evolved into the "alien face" that will be discussed later.

At the corners between the circles and the triangles are 2 dots each – a total of 24 dots. Again, they give the impression of fastening screws.

89

III 12. d)   Mandalas – four-polar

In astrology the square, i.e. the 90° aspect, represents the separation and thus the spanning of a space and the stability of a form. The same is found in physics: the electric wave of a photon is always at right angle (90°) to the magnetic wave of a photon – when one wave is at its maximum, the other is always at "0". In stone healing the cubic crystallization form has the property of separating, space-creating and ordering.

- - -

105. mandala
(Wiltshire, England, 2002)

This is the basic 4-polar mandala: a center and a 4-divided surrounding space. This can be the sun and the 4 cardinal directions, the 4 elements and the quintessence, the 5 Dhyani Buddhas, Osiris and the four sons of Horus, etc.

- * ❀ * -

106. „game board"
(Oxfordshire, England, 2008)

This 4-polar mandala has a very harmonic structure:

- From the central circle, 5 circles emanate in each of the 4 directions, increasing in size in a regular manner.

- From the circles of these 4 "arms" 0, 1, 2 and 3 circles go off to the left and right respectively, which become smaller in a regular way.

- In the corners there is an even smaller point. Except for these 4 corner points and the center, the diagonals are "circle-free".

There is a stabilization point at each of the angles between two circles and at the tips of the rows of circles.

- * ❀ * -

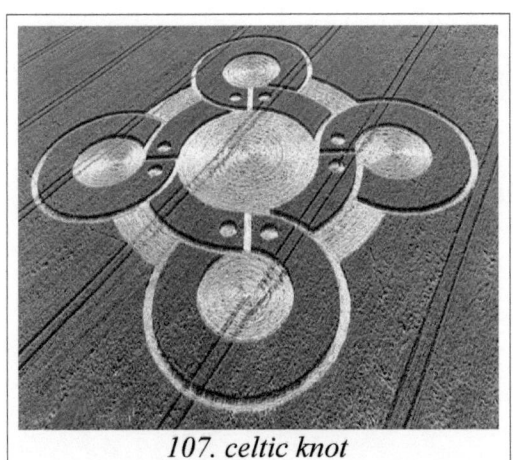

107. celtic knot
(Wiltshire, England, 2017)

Here a bright central circular area and a bright ring around it can be seen. The dark band forms a second central ring and four attached circles. This band is interrupted 4 times and is apparently held together at these points by 2 points each.

- * ❀ * -

91

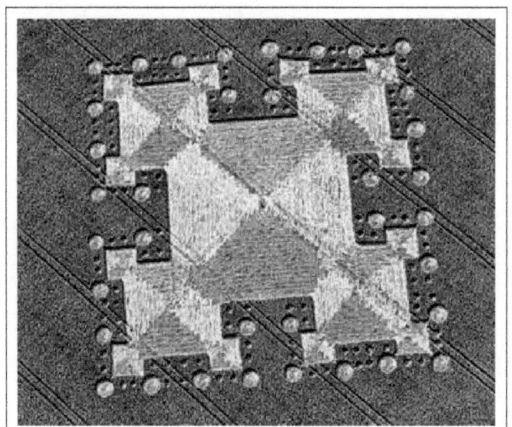

108. square-fraktal
(Wiltshire, England, 1999)

This is a plain square fractal. Its construction formula is: "To each corner, add a square whose side length is 1/3 as large." This process has created three sizes of squares.

In all squares, the grain has been laid down in square patterns. In the large square, the grain seems to be laid down in 16 rows, in the medium sized squares in 8 rows, and in the small squares in 4 rows. This is obviously intentional.

Around the square, small circles and very small circles have been arranged in a square pattern. Just as the squares are each only 1/3 as large as their reference square, the space is also divided into thirds by two small circles and two very small circles (together they take up an area just as large as a small circle).

There are 17 squares and 156 points in total, which does not reveal any other symbolism.

- * ❁ * -

92

109. step-fractal
(Wiltshire, England, 1999)

This mandala is a fractal – this is seen clearer when adding some construction-lines:

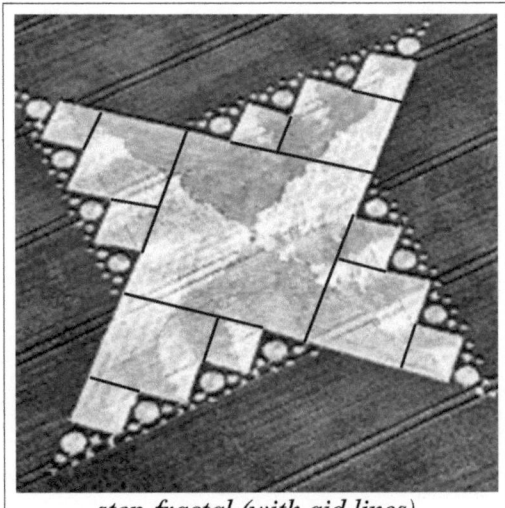

step-fractal (with aid lines)

This fractal is constructed in six steps:

    1. a square ($2^0 = 1$ square)

    2. a half as large square at the right side of the each side of the central square that is looking away from the centre, i.e. all four sides ($2^2 = 4$ squares)

    3. a half as large square at the right side of the each side of a square that is looking away from the centre ($2^3 = 8$ squares)

    4. a half as large circle at the right side of the each side of a square that is looking away from the centre ($2^4 = 16$ circle)

    5. a half as large circle at the right side of the each side of a circle that is looking away from the centre ($2^5 = 32$ circle)

    6. a half as large circle at the right side of the each side of a circle that is looking away from the centre ($2^3 = 64$ circle)

- * ❀ * -

93

110. luck-symbol
(Dorset, England, 2015)

In the center the well-known Chinese symbol for luck and blessing has been depicted, which is also on the head of the sun bird (crop circle 61).

The four circles on the outside have been added in a way, that the whole gives a rotating impression.

- * 🌀 * -

111. force field
(Wiltshire, England, 2006)

This crop circle has a fourfold structure, but it still looks like a polar structure with additions. The upper and lower circles consist of 3+4 crescents, while the other two circles consist of two circular rings (or a central circle with 3 circular rings). Presumably, the circles on the left and right are the 2 poles (center + 3 rings) and the two 7-part rings are the force field created by the two poles.

The chakra system consists of the heart chakra in the center and two chakras in each of the three circular rings around it – thus 1 central chakra and 3 pairs of chakras. This may be the meaning of the left and right ring-system.

The upper and lower groups of seven crescents each could also be an allusion to the seven chakras. But why are these to groups not symmetrical but point in the same direction?

- * 🌀 * -

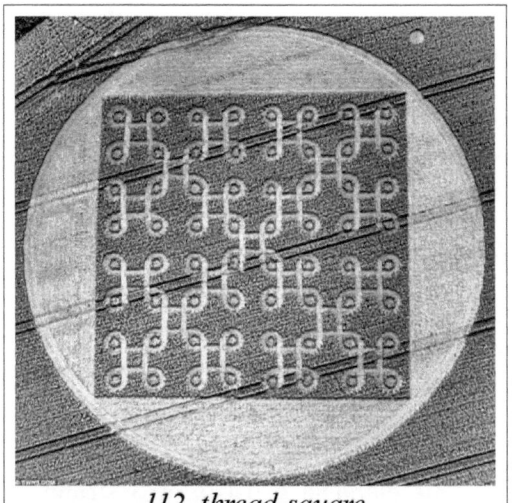

112. thread-square
(Hampshire, England, 2012)

In the center is a square of 4·4=16 squares, which in turn consist of 4 circles each, for a total of 64 circles. These 64 circles are held together by a single long thread, as in a Celtic weave pattern, and therefore form a unit – which is also expressed by the circle surrounding the square.

No further structure can be discerned here.

At the top right, a small companion circle has once again been added.

113. blossom-castle
(Wiltshire, England, 2009)

This crop circle consists of a large circle, one-eighth of which can be seen in the center of each of the four sides.

At each of the four corners is a good half of a smaller circle.

A small attachment point has been placed at each of the transitions.

The area around the square in the center has been carefully flattened in patterns.

On the very inside is a circle of four leaves. Around it are four four-petaled flowers, the inner leaf of which has been tilted 90° so that it forms the circle in the center. All these leaves consist of two quarter circles.

Around this center are 16 flowers, each again consisting of 16 leaves.

So from the center outward there is an abundance of 4s, 8s and 16s:

In the center, 1 diamond with 4 corners.
In the whole centre a total of 16 leaves.
Around it 16 flowers with 16 leaves each.
At the very outside 1 large circle with 4 medium sized circles.
At the very outside one circle at each of the 4 corners.
At the very outside 8 bows.
Attached to it 8 small holder points.

Obviously, the intention here was to show the 4 and 16 structure in as many ways as possible.

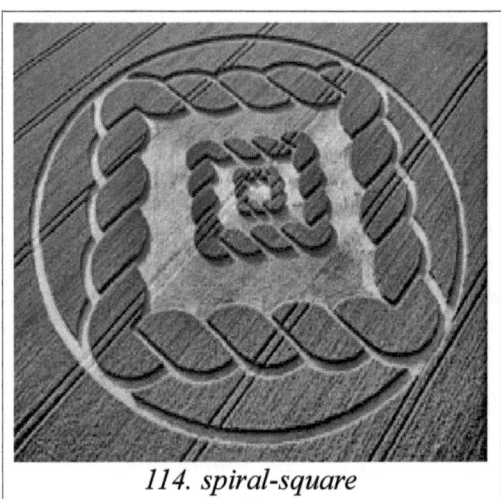

114. spiral-square
(Wiltshire, England, 2002)

This mandala consists of 3 strings of 2·4=8, 2·4=12 and 4·4=16 turns.

You can also think of these strings as 8, 12 and 16 "S "s, that is, a flow of energy.

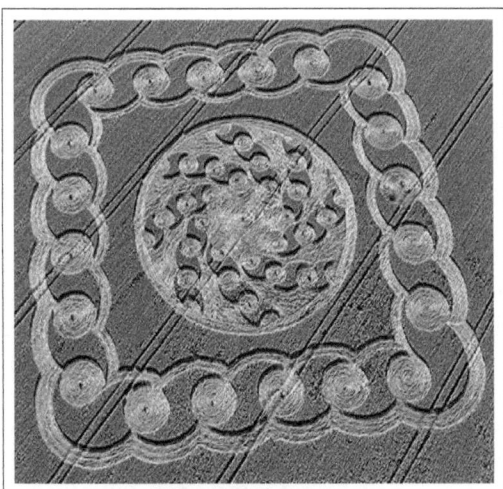

*115. spiral-square
(Oxfordshire, England, 2020)*

The outer surface is a square, the middle part is eight-polar.

Both the 8 spiral arms in the center and the 4 spiral straight lines outside are made of circles and the "S" shape: fixed points and the flow of energy or life force.

Inside there are 3 circles and 3 times an "S" – the 3 steps of development "impulse – form – contact". These are 24 circles and 24 "S"s.

Outside there are a total of 4·5=20 times a circle and 4·5=20 times an "S".

The total impression is therefore "bended and in itself resting energy in a solid form". Circles and square = form; "S" = flowing energy; square = rest, protection, stability; central circle = autonomy.

- * ❀ * -

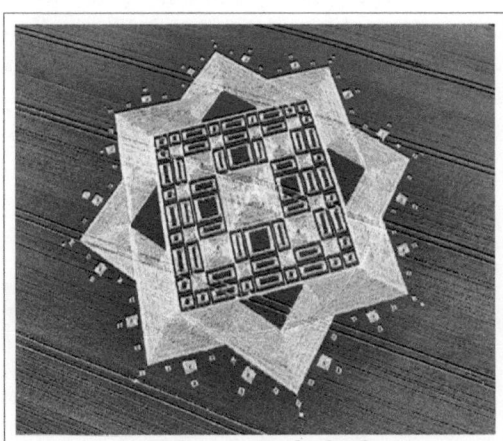

*116. square-fraktal
(Wiltshire, England, 2005)*

If it were not for the square in the center, this shape would have to be counted among the octagons - which has been shown twice as a border.

However, the square has such a prominent filling that it seems to be the main quality of this crop circle.

The numbers in the following overview are only auxiliary units – the smallest square in the middle square of this crop circle is called "1·1-square" here for the sake of simplicity and overview.

In the center is a 4·4 square, then follows a 2·2 square at each corner, which again has a 1·1 square at each corner. These are the light squares, arranged as in a fractal.

On the remaining faces you will find "filled squares". These are 20 1·1 squares, 36

97

2·1 rectangles and 4 2·2 squares.

On the very outside there is 1 small square on each of the 16 sides of the 8-corner star and around it 3 more very small squares. That makes 16 small squares plus 48 very small squares, for a total of 64 outside squares – all now well known numbers, but here they arise simply from geometry.

A ring can be seen that has been divided into regular square areas. The size of the dark squares in these areas decreases from the inside out – but the centers of the squares in a row all lie on the same straight line. There are a total of 80 squares in the circle (8·8+4·4=80).

Both upwards and downwards there is a "mountain" with six steps on the left and on the right, which again results in the well-known "12" – the number of the surrounding space (zodiac, superstring).

The whole thing looks like a heart chakra with the sushumna (life force channel) – although in this interpretation the emphasis on the "4" und the "8" is surprising.

117. heart chakra und sushumna (Hampshire, England, 2005)

118. poly-polar mandala
(Oxfordshire, England, 2005)

Is this crop circle primarily 4-polar, 6-polar, or a circle?

The "6" in the center is simply represented by 6 diamonds, which look quite lively because of the dot in their centers – the dots look like the nuclei in six cells.

Between the diamonds there are 6·10 rays or petals each on the outside. If one would count the empty areas as 2 rays each, there would be 6·12 rays – but only 6·10 rays have been depicted.

Around it there is a square, which consists of 16 squares, which again consist of 8 rectangles each, which form a spiral (8·16=128). If you look at these spirals more closely, you can see that they all turn counterclockwise and that the outer starting point of the spirals is always shifted one corner further (seen counterclockwise, the starting points change from bottom left to bottom right to top right to top left to bottom left, etc.).

On the very outside you can see 4·18 rays (the 19 rays on the top left will probably be a mistake). Does the 72 rays here again mean the "9·8" symbolism of the solar cycle?

In general, the 4-fold mandals seem to have little dynamics – they are just mainly a spatial structure like the astrological square and the right angle in the electromagnetic wave.

119. poly-polar mandala
spiral-pattern

- * ❁ * -

99

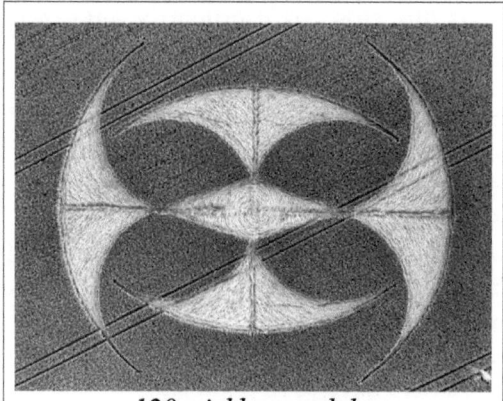

120. sickle-mandala
(Auchy-les-Mines, France, 2019)

1 rhombus and 4 arc triangles form an irregular 4-polar structure.

The outer line of the two large arc triangles (left and right) are two quarters of a large, common circle.

The outer lines of the two inner (horizontal) arc triangles meet exactly the center of the outer arc of the two outer (vertical) arc triangles and thus form the already known eye symbol.

For clarification, the crop circle is shown below once again with auxiliary lines. The basic form can be designed with three large circles; the finer points can be constructed with six more circles lying on two axes; to these are added the four straight lines of the rhombus in the center.

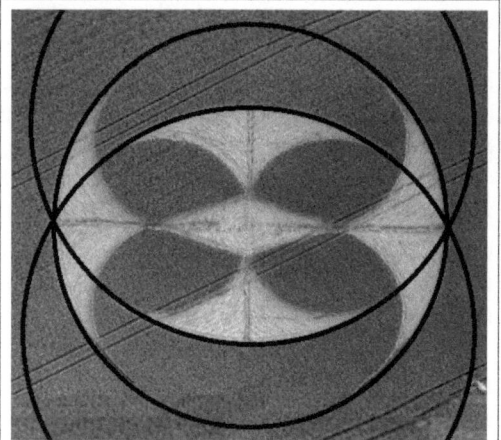

121. sickle-mandala (with aid lines)
„eye"

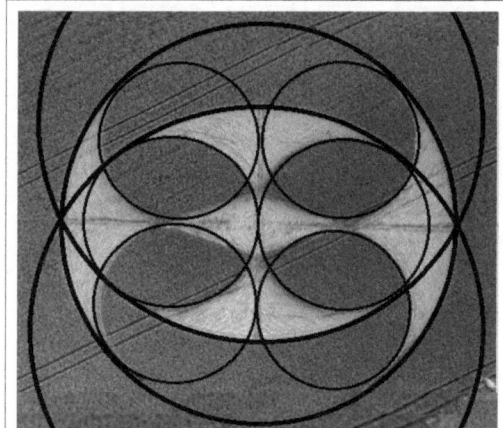

122. sickle-mandala (with aid lines)
construction-pattern

III 12. e) Mandalas – five-polar

The "5" has no traditional symbolism – but it has been used as a symbol for man at least since Leonardo da Vinci. In magic, the pentagram is an important invocation and banishment symbol. The pentagram and the pentagon are also both associated with Mars – that's why the U.S. Department of Defense has the shape of a pentagon.

- - -

123. ray-pentagram
(Wiltshire, England, 2017)

In this pentagram, there is a circle of swirled cornstalks in each corner of the pentagram.

These circles are surrounded by 2 attachment points as well as two ray points.

This is a very uniformly structured crop circle.

- * ❀ * -

101

124. ray-pentagram
(Bedfordshire, England, 2003)

A pentagram with 5 irregular numbers of rays (clockwise from the bottom): 25, 24, 23, 21, 25. 5·5=25 rays each would have been more conclusive.

- * ❀ * -

125. double pentagram
(Wiltshire, England, 2020)

In the center is a pentagram with a central point. Around it are areas that become understandable only when you draw in the auxiliary lines.

Except for the really very clever geometrical construction and its realization as a crop circle, there is unfortunately nothing to discover.

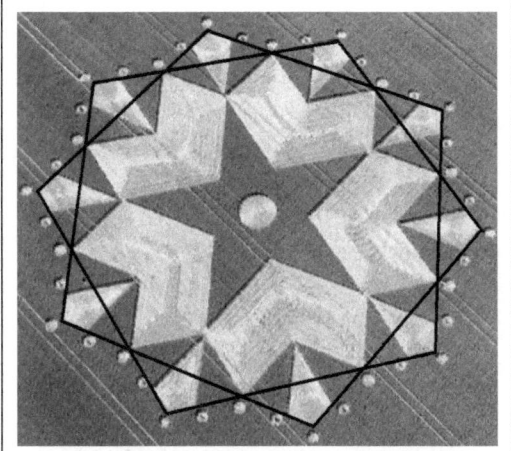

126. double pentagram (aid lines)
2 pentagons

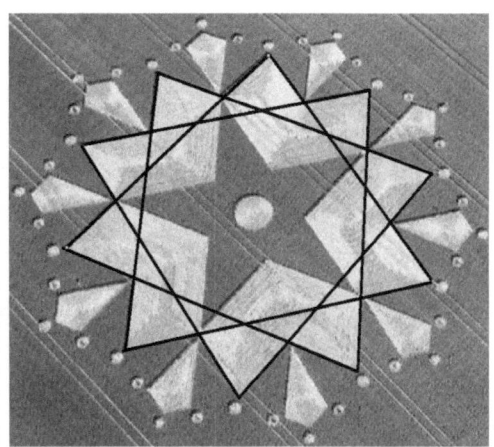

127. double pentagram (aid lines)
10-rays star

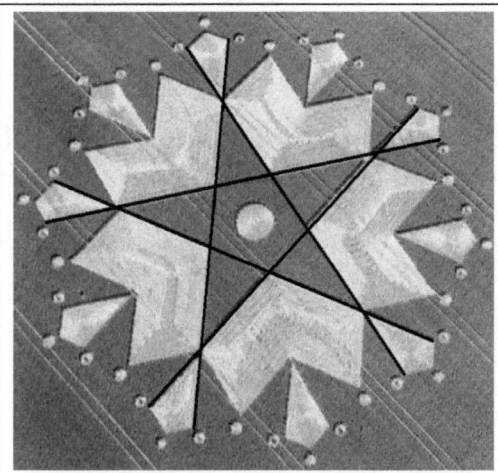

128. double pentagram (aid lines)
pentagram 1

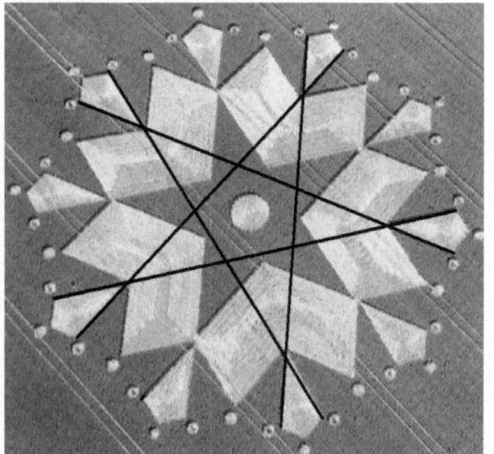

129. double pentagram (aid lines)
pentagram 2

- * ❀ * -

130. pentagon-pentagram
(East Sussex, England, 2014)

This crop circle, on the other hand, is constructed very simply: a pentagram and around it, alternately, a circle and a pentagon.

In total, that's 5 shapes of five (1 pentagram and 4 pentagons) and 5 circles.

The construction is coherent, but not particularly interesting.

- * ❃ * -

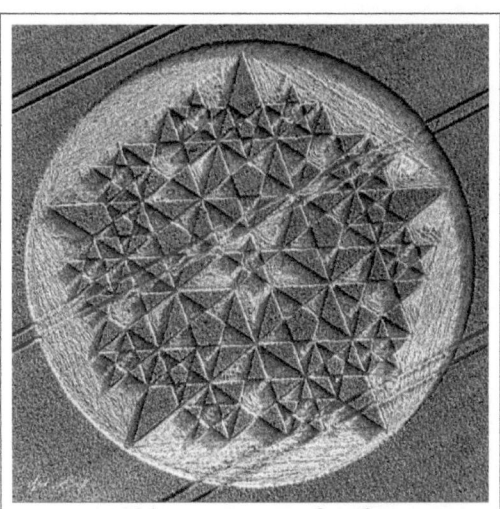

131. pentagram-family
(Wiltshire, England, 2018)

Here geometric skill is found above all else. If you look closely enough at this crop circle, you will find:

1 large pentagram,
1 half-size pentagram
5 medium pentagrams,
16 small pentagrams
1 large pentagon,
10 medium pentagons,
16 small pentagons.

The whole shape is constructed exclusively from pentagrams and pentagons. It is a near-fractal.

- * ❃ * -

104

A pentagram in the middle of penta-grams which together form a pentagram in a pentagon in a pentagon … a conclu-sive construction …

132. pentagon-pentagram
(Wiltshire, England, 2003)

- * 🌀 * -

A pentagram in a pentagon of pentagon stars in a pentagon with pentagram points – its a pentagram/pentagon-fractal.

It seems that pentagrams invite to play with geometry …

133. spiny pentagram fractal
(Wiltshire, England, 2007)

- * 🌀 * -

A central circular ring in a pentagram of 5 triangles, between each of which 5 circles form 5 rays in a ring – most 5-polar corn-circle mandalas definitely have a variety and a coherent structure, but little inner dynamics.

134. pentagram-star
(Hampshire, England, 2001)

- * ❀ * -

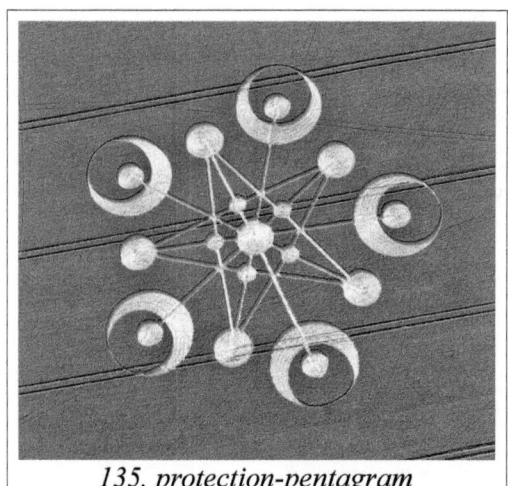

Here is a somewhat more complex pentagram with a distinct central circle.

It has a medium sized circle at each of its tips, which gives it stability and something round.

Where the 5 connecting lines between the center and the 5 points intersect the pentagram, there are 5 more smaller circles, giving it even more stability.

Between these 5 rays, another 5 rays go from the center to the outside, ending in a crescent with a central circle. These crescents have something supporting in relation to the center circle in front of them, giving the pentagram something protective.

135. protection-pentagram
(Dorset, England, 2014)

- * ❀ * -

106

136. weapon
(Wiltshire, England, 2003)

This crop circle, which was created 11 years before the previous crop circle, conveys a different feeling.

It too is centralized, but in it the crescents are found at the tips and have no center circle. The 5 points of the pentagram are not structured by further lines, but are just pointed lozenges, which gives the impression of a pointed weapon. The sickles are round, but they still give the impression of something sharp, pointed, defensive.

Only the double line around the center circle, which merges into the outer circle along the five rays, conveys something resting, round, whole, stable.

- * ❀ * -

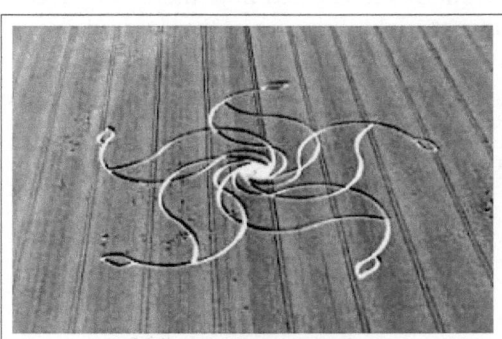

137. wind-pentagram
(Dissenhofen, Swiss, 2008)

This crop circle is 5-polar, but it conveys something very moving and airy, unlike the 5-polar crop circles considered so far.

It consists of a center circle and 5 "S" shapes ending in a "leaf". Because of this "leaf", the "S"s do not appear pointed.

The whole thing gives the impression of a flower and something rotating.

- * ❀ * -

107

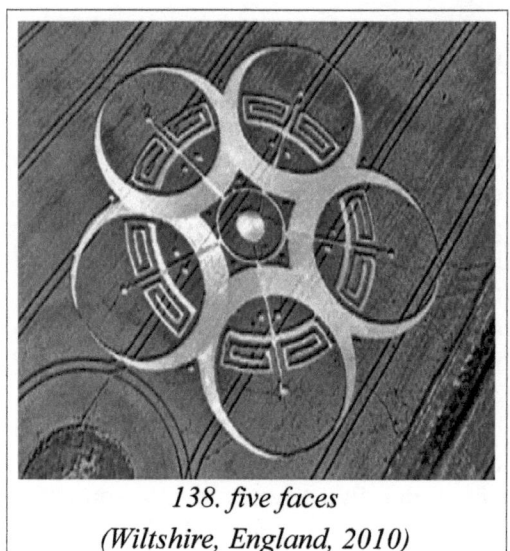

138. five faces
(Wiltshire, England, 2010)

In the center of this crop circle is the only arc pentagon I know of. It contains a central circle, a central ring, and 5 small "attachment points".

The 5 outer circles are irregularly thick, so that they almost become sickles. Thus they seem to concentrate their power in the center and radiate outward.

The five circular spaces look like faces. The eyes remind of the Chinese luck symbol. The line from the nose to the crown and further to the central ring gives the impression that the five faces execute the will of the central circle.

The direction of rotation of the double spirals shows that here an impulse rises from the bottom to the top via the third eye to the crown chakra: Five people doing a joint Kundalini-meditation?

Above the eyebrows, to the left and to the right of the vertical line, there is a "fixing point" each. These points, together with the straight line, give the impression of determination. One would not want to mess with this "gang of five" …

There is a fixing-point on the inside and on the outside end of the area, where these faces meet each other.

This is the most creative of the five-ray crop circles.

III 12. f) Mandalas – six-polar

There are a large number of 6-polar crop circles – just as there are a large number of 6-polar shapes in nature. The 6-polar shape results when balls of the same size are stored as closely as possible – e.g. marbles of the same size in a bucket or neutrons and protons in an atomic nucleus. In the plane, six circles of the same size are always adjacent to a central circle of the same size.

In astrology the sextile aspect (60°) describes the agglomeration of equals to a group. In nature, water molecules cluster together to form snowflakes. On the orbit of a planet two moons can fly if they are 60° apart – thus a maximum of 6 moons fit on the same orbit. On a smaller scale, six electrons can orbit around an atomic nucleus on a d-orbital. The hexagonal crystallisation form of minerals also has this cooperative group character in crystal healing.

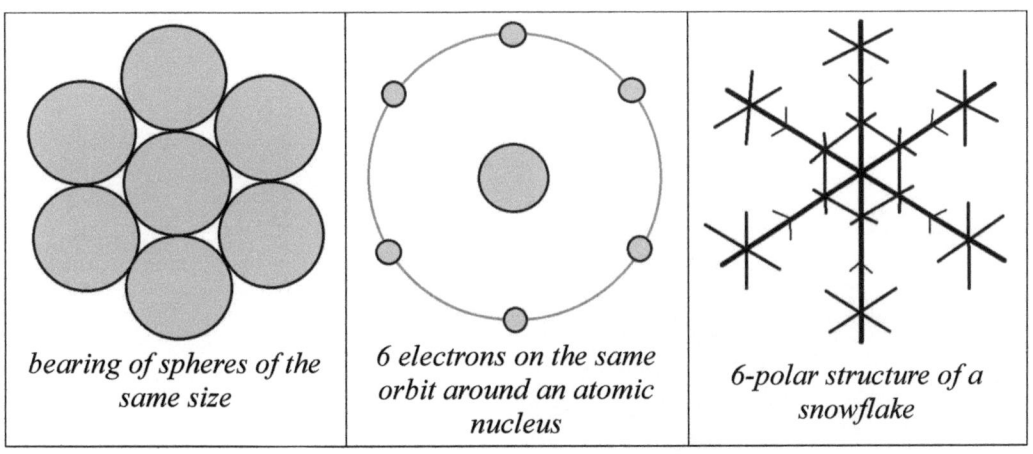

| bearing of spheres of the same size | 6 electrons on the same orbit around an atomic nucleus | 6-polar structure of a snowflake |

- - -

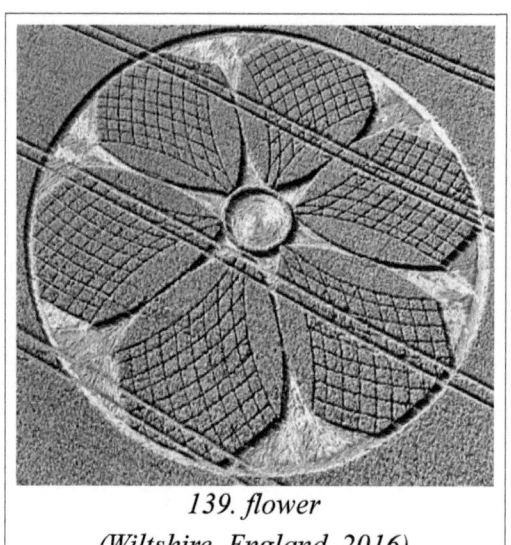

139. flower
(Wiltshire, England, 2016)

Here a central circle with six petals can be seen.

On the leaves go out from both sides 9 rows of rhombuses. On one leaf there are 72 diamonds – a well known number by now. In total there are 432 diamonds in the flower.

- * ❀ * -

140. flower
(Oxfordshire, England, 2008)

This is another flower – this time with narrow petals and a broad ring around the outside.

- * ❀ * -

110

This is a hexagram with pentagram quality: there is something very pointed about it because of the 6 diamonds and the 6·12=72 triangles. The bright, round area in the centre, bounded by the lateral corners of the diamonds as well as the bases of the inner triangles, takes away a bit of the usual resting quality of hexagrams from this crop circle.

141. circles and rays
(Warwickshire, England, 2012)

- * ❁ * -

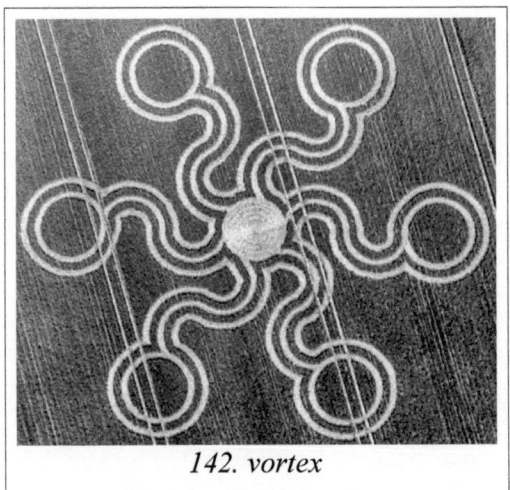

From the central circle emanate 6 "S"-forms, which in turn end in six circles.

This will probably be the outer form (6 circles) created by the protrusion ("S") of the central circle (center).

Are these "S "s perhaps sperms or snakes?

142. vortex
(Wiltshire, England, 2019)

- * ❁ * -

143. sickles
(England, 2014)

This crop circle can be constructed in 3 steps:
- one central circle:
- six circles of the same size, whose center is always on the intersection of an outer circle with the center circle;
- another 6 circles of the same size, whose center is always exactly between the intersections of the previous six circles.

The way in which the surfaces thus created are connected or separated gives the impression of a vortex.

Inside at the edge of the inner circle six of the now well known arc triangles can be seen. They are also found on the outer edge.

The cornstalks in the $3 \cdot 6 = 18$ areas of this crop circle have been artfully symmetrically flattened.

- *  * -

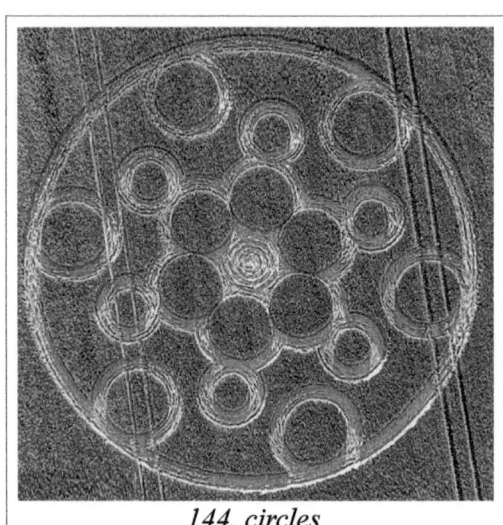

144. circles
(Wiltshire, England, 2017)

Here is a 6-polar crop circle made of 1 central circle and $3 \cdot 6 = 18$ rings. Because of their arrangement and their different sizes, this crop circle, although it consists only of circles, has something unsteady.

- * ❀ * -

145. circles
(Wiltshire, England, 2007)

The large central circle is surrounded by 6 smaller circles in a row, whose centers lie on the circumference of the central circle.

All 7 circles contain two rings each. The outer rings are designed to create a circular motion.

There is an attachment point between each of the six outer rings.

- * ❀ * -

146. circles
(Wiltshire, England, 2003)

Here, too, circles were mainly used. Only the central hexagon and its 6 rays contain other elements. An additional, rather discreet structure is created by the 12 small rings and the 6 large outer rings. The intersections of the large rings create "almands".

Overall, this crop circle appears quite organic.

- * ❀ * -

147. hexagonal fraktal
(Wiltshire, England, 1997)

This crop circle has been constructed as a fractal. The outer shape is a hexagram with attached triangles. The inner shape is a six-pointed star with attached hexagons. On the very outside, small circles have been added – 3 at the main points and 2 at the secondary points.

There are 42 hexagons and 156 points. The square fractal (crop circle 108) is also surrounded by 156 points. However, whether this has a deeper meaning is questionable.

148. hexagonal circle-fraktal
(Wiltshire, England, 2010)

This crop circle has a rudimentary fractal design: a central circle surrounded by 6 circles, which in turn are surrounded by 6 circles each.

Between each of these circles are four points. The 2 points on the axis of the two circles act as connecting elements – the two points to the left and right of them act as stabilizers.

The centers of the circles all lie on three axes each, which run through the grain circle (the three directions of the six-polar structure).

Three of the axes, running from lower left to upper right, are drawn as thin lines. Why is there this irregularity?

The sides of the 6 arc triangles are parts of the rings around the 7 main circles. There are a total of 205 circles and dots to be seen – a task requiring great diligence …

*149. six-polar magnetic field
(Wiltshire, England, 2002)*

Here the 6-polarity has been represented as a force field.

In the center is a hexagram of six diamonds. Around it a hexagon can be seen, which is divided into different diamonds by straight lines. Next to it there are 6 rounded surfaces, which are divided by straight lines into different shaped rhombuses. These lines end in the 66 rhombuses that form the outer circle.

There are 6 lines running through the entire crop circle including the hexagram in the center and the six white poles.

- * ❀ * -

*150. flowers and circles
(Wiltshire, England, 2010)*

The center circle and the 6 outer circles are connected by almond-shaped petals. They start at the edge of the inner circle and extend into the outer circles – thus the center circle is the starting point and the outer circles are the elaboration of the quality of the center point.

The outer ring is formed by 5 points each between the six large outer circles.

The inner ring consists of bisected circles, which by their arrangements become a series of "S"s and therefore suggest the flow of a force.

Next to the circle in the lower right is a companion ring.

- * ❀ * -

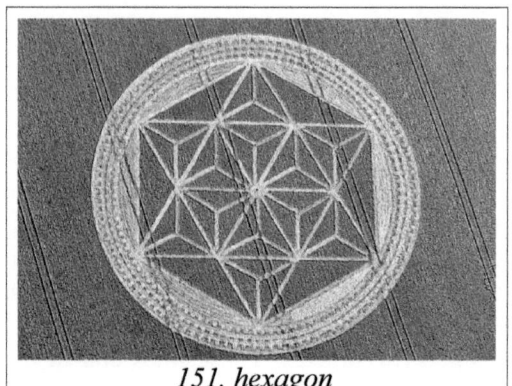

151. hexagon
(Wiltshire, England, 2011)

Here a hexagram has been filled with 12 triangular pyramids.

The flattened grain in the outer ring has been interwoven in three rows of $6 \cdot 19 = 114$ times each of a light and a dark area. So this is a total of 3 rows $\cdot$ 114 areas = 342 areas. A meaning of this number is not evident.

The 114 can be represented as $2 \cdot 3 \cdot 19$, which has however also no recognizable symbolism.

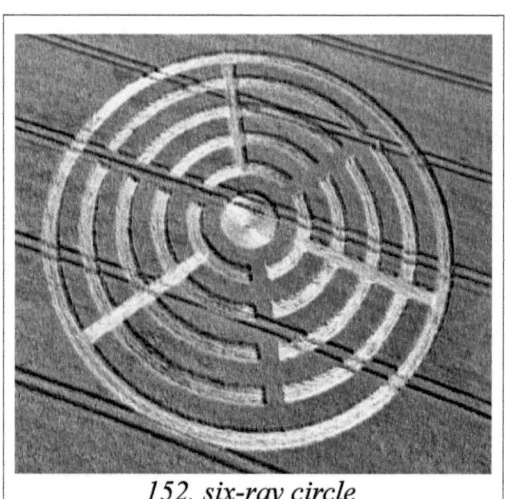

152. six-ray circle
(Wiltshire, England, 2007)

A very simple crop circle: 1 central circle + 5 rings = 6 round forms; 6 rays = 6 straight forms.

The rays are alternating flat-laid and standing grain.

116

153. two triangles
(Hampshire, England, 2019)

Here it has been emphasized that the hexagram consists of two triangles of different quality. In the zodiac, these are, for example, the triangle of the three fire signs in combination with the triangle of the three air signs. (or water and earth signs).

The hexagram is in a hexagon (honeycomb) and this in a circle.

The shapes in the triangle are interesting. They are formed by 5 circular arcs each, whose centers are in the three corners of the triangle, and 4 straight lines each, which are parallel to the sides of the triangle.

This creates the well known arc triangle in the center as well as 3·15=45 other shapes, thar are irregular hegagons. At the edge of the central arc triangle there are 3·9=27 arc squares, in the center 3·6=18 arc hexagons.

So here it is shown that both the sides of the triangle act towards the center (4 straight "waves") and the corners of the triangle act towards the center (3·5=15 curved "waves").

Thus, this is an introverted, meditative crop circle.

- *  * -

117

154. two triangles
(Borough of Swindon, England, 1999)

As in the previous crop circle, the hexagram has been divided into two triangles. The 3 points of one of these triangles have been characterized here as "pointed and radiating" – the 3 rays of the other triangle as "round and receiving".

Due to the large center circle and the emphasis on only 3 of the 6 axes, the crop circle appears very stable. One of the 3 axes ist parallel to the traktor tracks.

The stabilizer pairs on each of the 3 rays consist of a straight line as well as a large and a small point. These groups are a new element, as otherwise only single straight lines, double straight lines, and pairs of dots have appeared as stabilizers.

- *  * -

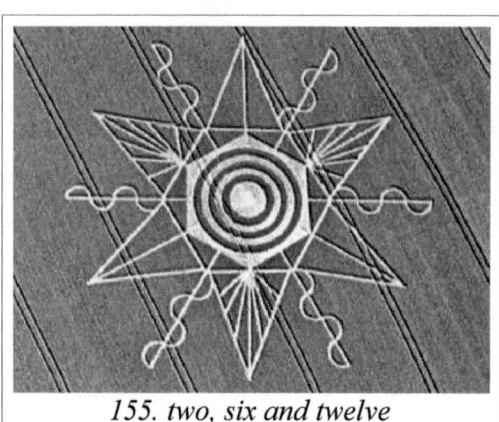

155. two, six and twelve
(Dorset, England, 2014)

The hexagon with the three circular rings in the center looks very powerful. It is surrounded by a second hexagon ring, which is rather inconspicuous at first. Adjacent to this hexagon are 6 triangles that do not form a hexagram, but are longer and narrower and therefore push outward more.

This is in contrast to the previous crop circle an extroverted, acting crop circle.

From the corners and the side centers of the inner hexagon, one line each goes outward, for a total of 12 rays (signs of the zodiac).

3 of the 6 outer triangles contain 7 rays (chakras) each; the other 3 triangles contain only a single ray. Here again the dissimilarity of the two triangles that make up the hexagram is emphasized.

The remaining 6 rays are encircled by a "double S" (serpentine line). They radiate power outward, which amplifies the extroverted character of this crop circle.

118

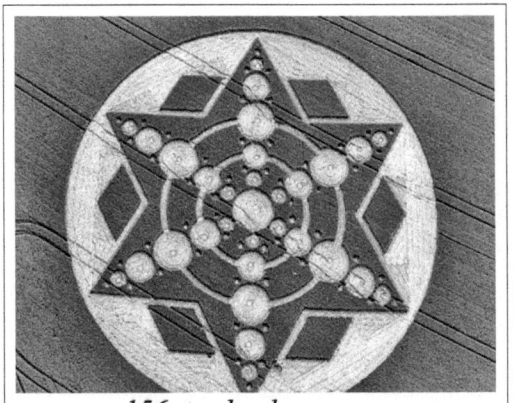

156. twelve-hexagram
(Wiltshire, England, 1999)

A combined hexagram-hexagon can be seen here. In the hexagram are a central circle and two rings. The rays consist of 6 circles and 4·2 companion points each.

The shape seems very coherent, but like most crop circle mandalas, it has little momentum.

- * ✿ * -

157. pointed mandala
(Wiltshire, England, 2013)

A ring can be seen with 6 small circles on it. Each of the 6 circles is inside an acute triangle. These triangles have an angle of 40° in the center, that is, of a ninth of a circle. The gaps between these triangles have an angle of 20° inside. So the circle has been divided first into 18 segments of 20° each.

The dark triangles have been reduced on their outside by an equilateral triangle whose apex lies in the centre of the small circle and whose baselines connects the two outer points of the triangles. These baselines are also emphasized by a different layering of the cornstalks.

The whole arrangement gives a "biting" impression, which is very untypical for 6-polar shapes. This is due, among other things, to the fact that the formative angle is not 60°, but only 40°, which corresponds to a division into 9 ninths instead of 6 sixths.

- * ✿ * -

119

Essentially, this is a small ring within a large ring that has a small circle as a companion (top right).

These 2 braod rings are complemented by 4 narrow rings – so there are 6 rings in total.

Above these 6 rings, 6 narrower rings have been drawn, whose diameter is half that of the large ring and equal to that of the central ring. The centres of these 6 rings are all on the small ring in the centre. This arrangement creates 6 petals.

Has the execution of this design not been precise? At the upper end of the crop circle, the 6 smaller rings do not fit together exactly, so that a double ring has been created. Probably the centre of the 6 "petal rings" should not have been on the outside of the central circle, but in the middle of the central circle. This looks like "work of human hands" …

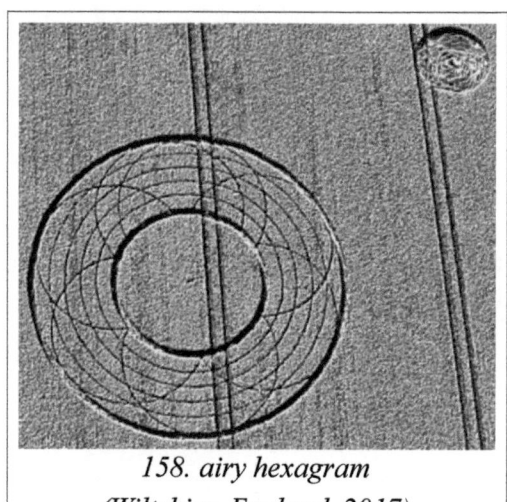

158. airy hexagram
(Wiltshire, England, 2017)

- * ❁ * -

This crop circle, on the other hand, is very harmonious in a Hexagram-typical way.

It has been constructed like the "Flower of Life" from equal circles: a circle in the center, on the edge of which are the centers of 6 other circles of the same size. Their centres always lie on the inter-section of an outer circle with the inner circle.

This shape is then completed by some arcs, which have the same length and curvature as the arcs resulting from the initial construction.

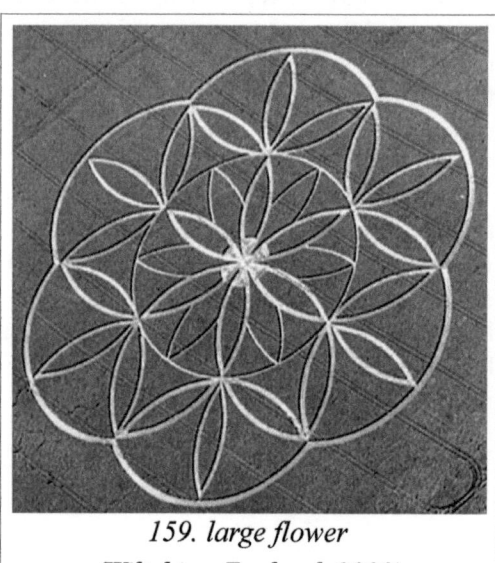

159. large flower
(Wiltshire, England, 2003)

This crop circle, consisting of 6 crescents, is reminiscent of Christ's crown of thorns.

The elaborate flower-like hexagram in the center is barely visible (3 almonds and a circle in the center).

Is this supposed to be a flower surrounded by spikes?

160. sickle-wreath
(Warwickshire, England, 2010)

- * ❀ * -

This crop circle looks soft like a flower and light like a butterfly.

Its geometric base is a thin ring that passes through the centers of the 6 small circular rings and through the innermost circles of the petal edges.

Six more rings with the same radius as the central ring form the almond-shaped petals. However, only 2/3 of these rings are visible – the rest, which would be outside the flower, has not been executed.

The central star consists of a small circle as well as 12 narrow almands, which lie on the lines of the 6 outer rings.

The edges of the petals consist of 6 large and 8 small circles each and another large circle at the tip.

161. flower
(Italy, 2010)

121

The 6 rings inside the petals are also interesting because they contain different numbers of dots in different arrangements. Clockwise from the bottom, these are: 13, 6, 15, 7, 15, 13. No system is apparent here. This irregularity clearly adds to the lightness of this crop circle.

- *  * -

This crop circle has already been discussed with the qua-dratic mandalas (crop circle 118). It is cited here again because of the beautiful hexagram in its center.

162. poly-polar mandala
(Oxfordshire, England, 2013)

- *  * -

163. eighteen cubes
(Wiltshire, England, 2007)

Around the central hexagram are 18 hexagons that have been designed into 3D cubes. Is this supposed to be more than just a visual gimmick? If so, what?

On the outside there are 4 rows of 36 triangles each. So that's a total of $4 \cdot 36 = 144 = 12 \cdot 12$ triangles, which may be an allusion to the "12" of the zodiac.

The triangles increase in size from the inside to the outside, creating a radiant impression.

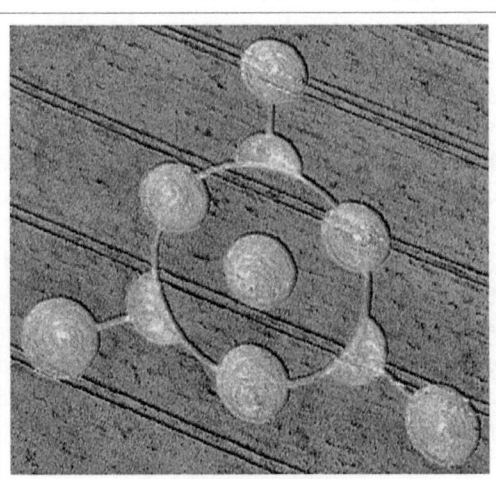

164. molecule
(Wiltshire, England, 2009)

Here again the dissimilarity of the two triangles is emphasized – 3 of the circles on the ring can be seen whole and 3 only half. The 3 circles on the very outside also emphasize this dissimilarity.

One does not know whether the "group" quality of the 6 or the "cohesion" quality of the 3 is the more formative element here.

Does this crop circle represent the (inaccurate) 3D model of a benzene ring (C_6H_6) with the hydrogen atoms attached? If so, however, 3 H would be missing. It would be a C_6H_3 - i.e. Benzenetriyl. In both cases the central circle would not be a part of the molecule.

123

165. triangle-pyramids
(Wiltshire, England, 2012)

This hexagram consists of 2 triangular paramids with their bottoms on top of each other – only the top of the upper triangle can be seen, but not the top of the lower triangle.

- * ✺ * -

166. triangle-pyramids
(Wiltshire, England, 2017)

The center of this crop circle (upper triangle) has been constructed from 4 triangular pyramids. The 3 peaks of the lower triangle don't really fit this 3D representation.

The hexagram is surrounded by a barely visible ring. At each of the 6 peaks of the hexagram there is a circle. between these circles again 2 connecting circles can be seen like e.g. also at the crop circles 87, 88, 112 and 114. They are only half filled, but do not form a dynamic "S", but are static. The rings around the 6 outer circles, which are only half visible, also reinforce the impression of a baroque fortification.

- * ✺ * -

167. stronghold
(Wiltshire, England, 2008)

This crop circle gives even more of an impression of a baroque fortress.

The hexagram in the center has been designed as a vortex, which is again surrounded by the static and "defensive" bisected circles lying on a hexagon surrounded by a second hexagon. The outer line of the crop circle is formed by a 3rd hexagon.

The 12 triangles in the outer hexagon act as defenders and the 6 triangles on the outside of the hexagon act as bastions. In front of the top of each bastion are three small circles.

The overall impression: concentrated power in a fortress.

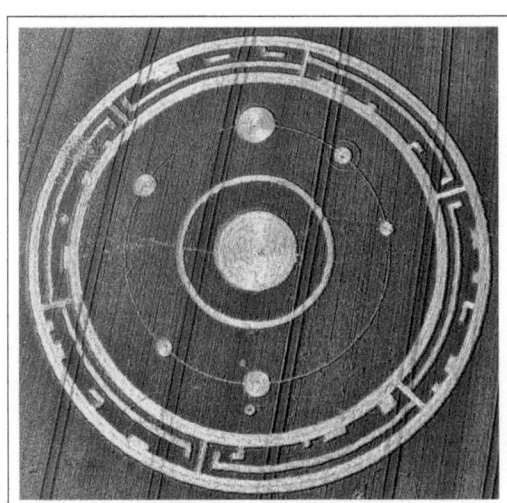

168. ring of planets
(Dorchester, England, 2015)

Here the 6-polarity is only visible at second glance: the outer circle is divided into 6 sixths. In contrast, the central circle, the inner ring, the middle ring ("sun") with the "planets" and the outer ring, which altogether give an impression of being oriented towards the center, are formative.

The sixths of the circular ring all contain the same elongated "L", but different additional small elements that look a bit like lines of writing or a code.

It is noticeable that the 6 "planets" are irregularly distributed and are not in the stable position with a distance of 60° each – this can't last long … The "planet" on the upper right has a "ring" and the "planet" on the lower left has 2 "moons".

Did someone want to give the impression that this is a message from another star system? The probability that this is a man-made crop circle is decidedly high.

169. unicursal hexagram
(Dorset, England, 2014)

This hexagram is probably also man-made – presumably by Crowleyans, since this hexagram has the shape of the "unicursal hexagram" designed by Aleister Crowley.

The striking stylized face, which does not occur elsewhere in this form, fits this assumption.

III 12. g)   Mandalas - seven polar

The "7" is commonly associated with the 7 planets, but since this is only a traditional symbolism based on the random number of planets visible to the naked eye, the "7" has no basic structure like the "2", the "3", the "4" or the "6". It is therefore comparable to the "5", which also has a traditional symbolism, but no structural one.

However, this is only true for the 7-polarity – the 7-series usually corresponds to the 7 chakras, whose structure is a fundamental structure in the world.

- - -

170. heptagram and sickle
(Wiltshire, England, 2016)

This crop circle, seen from the inside out, consists of a heptagon, 7 petals (diamonds), a heptagram, a crescent (sockle) and a circle with 2 rows of $7 \cdot 12 = 84$ squares each – the usual reference to the zodiac as the structure of the space ("aura") surrounding the center.

The "7" is associated in magic with Venus. Venus and partly also the moon (crescent) belong to the Sumerian goddess Inanna. Should this possibly be intentional?

- * 🪷 * -

127

171. star-flower

(Italy, 2011)

Here, the combination of ring and heptagram can be seen inside, with line petals around it and area petals around it. The whole makes the impression of a "star-flower".

On the outer petals are in different arrangements different numbers of dots – from below clockwise these are: 4, 4, 5, 3, 3, 4 and 4 dots – altogether 27 dots. A system is not apparent here. The effect of these dots is that they break up the strictness of the form – just as the curved forms of the petals ("arched triangles") do.

Between the outer petals are rows of 7 dots each, which are partly filled (1) and partly empty (0). Starting from the row of dots at the bottom left clockwise, there are different sequences (counting from the inside to the outside).

1st row:	0 0 1 0 1 0 0	=> 2·1
2nd row:	1 0 1 1 1 1 1	=> 2·1
3rd row:	0 1 1 1 0 1 0	=> 4·1
4th row:	0 0 1 1 1 1 0	=> 4·1
5th row:	0 1 1 1 0 1 0	=> 4·1
6th row:	0 0 1 0 0 0 1	=> 2·1
7th row:	0 0 1 0 1 0 0	=> 2·1

The 1st row corresponds to the 7th row and the 3rd row corresponds to the 5th row. If the 6th row were a little different, these sequences would be symmetrical around the 4th row (up in the middle).

The meaning of the dots on the petals and the filled dots on the dot lines is unknown.

Each side of the 7 petals is surrounded by 12 dots – the classic zodiac symbolism. Since the endpoints of these dot lines each belong to 2 petals, this makes a total of 14·11=151 dots.

- * ❀ * -

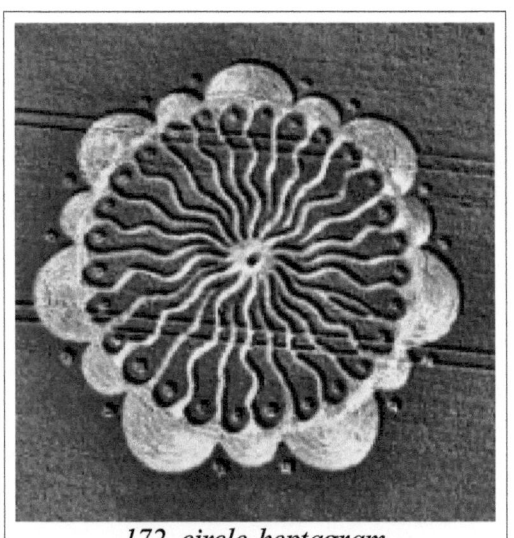

172. circle-heptagram
(Wiltshire, England, 2009)

The outer shape consists of 7 large circles connected by 7 small circles. The centers of these 14 circles are all on the same ring. At the corners between each of these circles is an attachment point.

In the center there is a point from which 7·4=28 "worms" crawl outwards. One could also take them for snakes, larvae, sperms and so on. In any case they represent an "organic expansion". They are also an organical variant of the "S", which represents the flow of a force.

This crop circle appears soft and alive – which is more of a moon symbolism than a Venus symbolism.

173. star-heptagram
(Dorset, England, 2018)

A hexagram surrounded by a ring of 14 Greek spirals, one pair of each, representing the Chinese symbol of luck.

On the outside, there are 7 more circles in front of the tips of the heptagram.

- * ❀ * -

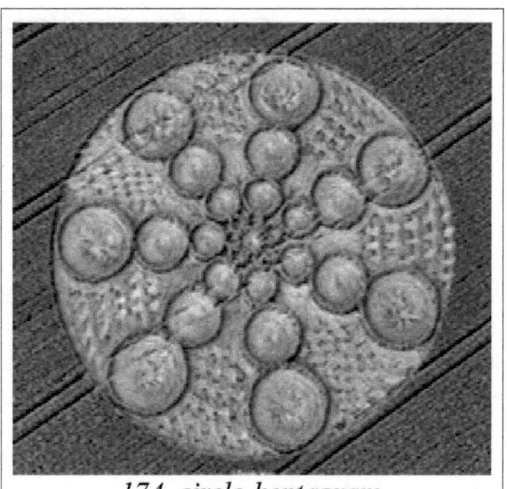

174. circle-heptagram
(Wiltshire, England, 1999)

7 rows of 4 circular rings each emanate from 1 central circle.

The striking thing about this crop circle is the woven grain in the areas between the circular rings.

- *  * -

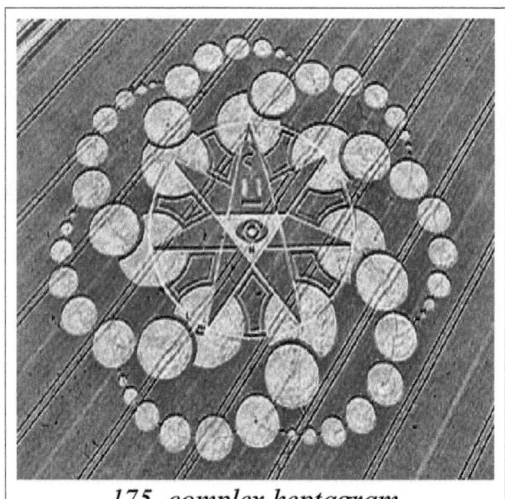

175. complex heptagram
(Wiltshire, England, 2008)

There is clearly more going on here … but it is unclear where is up and where is down in this crop circle – it is not a completely symmetric mandala. Since it is unclear from which side one should look at this crop circle, both possibilities are given here.

In version 175 there is an eye in a triangle in the center – a well-known symbol of God. However, the triangle stands on the head – is therefore the devil meant?

The heptagram stands with the point upwards, thus striving upwards.

In the upper tip of the heptagram a horizontal and two vertical lines as well as an ascending snake can be seen. Are these a fundament, two supports and the rising Kundalini? Or the root chakra, Ida, Pingala and Sushumna or Kundalini? The snake corresponds to the "worms" in the crop circle 172 – also there they move from the inside to the outside.

The tips of the heptagram end in circles whose centers all lie on a ring. This ring

130

separates the inner from the outer area of this crop circle.

From the 7 circles 8 further circles go out in a curved line – thus totally 9 circles each. The rings, of which these curved lines are a part, all run through the center of the crop circle. These arcs of 9 circles each give the crop circle the impression of rotating.

Finally, the dark areas between the tips of the heptagram are interesting. On the one hand they seem almost organic and on the other hand they look like arrowheads and are remotely reminiscent of a penis.

176. complex heptagram

If you turn this crop circle upside down (version 176), the eye stands in an upright triangle, which results in the usual God symbol.

However, the snake then crawls downwards – and the symbolism of a descending snake is not known. Should it perhaps represent the incarnation, thus the witnessing, instead of the enlightenment symbolism of the ascending snake? That would fit to the snakes or sperm from the crop circle 172.

Is the heptagram with one point downwards the shadow of venus, i.e. Lilith?

Or is the "7" here the the number of the mother goddess who makes possible the incarnation of the people? Probably this is all thought much too mythologically …

131

III 12. h)   Mandalas – eight-polar

Some eight-polar forms have already been considered – especially in connection with the square mandalas: from two squares an octagram results. The "8" has the symbolism of completeness and perfection since the Paleolithic. It is found in late formations, for example, as a division of the Germanic sun discs and as the ground plan of the Romanesque churches. For this reason Buddha also called his teachings the "eightfold path", i.e. "the perfect path".

- - -

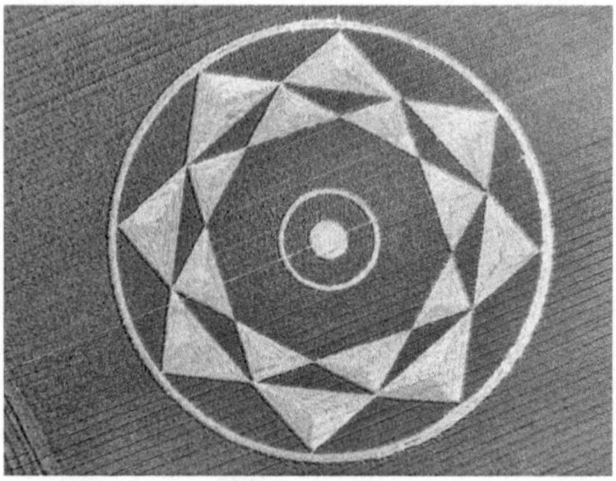

177. oktagon
(place and year unknown)

The 8-polarity seems very static – and it is. It is, so to speak, the "ordered variety of the relaxed forms of a whole". The crop circle on the left illustrates this quality very clearly. The octagon is the "soft version" of the square.

Inside is a circle, around it follows a ring, then two octagrams (two combined squares each) and on the very outside again a ring.

- * ❀ * -

In the center and on the outside there is an octagram each. Their tips are each connected by an almond-shaped petal.

The whole is given support and cohesion by a wide outer ring.

*178. oktagon-flower
(Wiltshire, England, 2000)*

- * ❀ * -

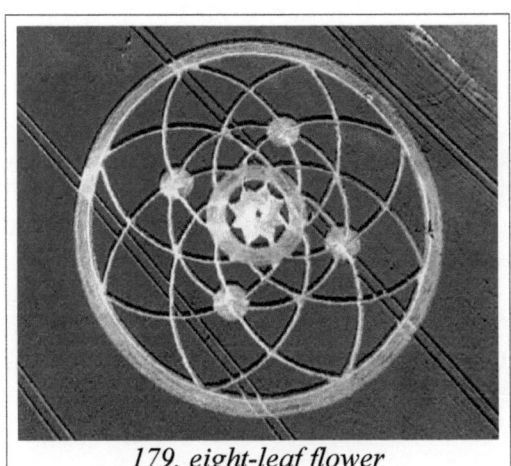

*179. eight-leaf flower
(Wiltshire, England, 2013)*

Here is a softer and more organic version of the 8-polarity.

There is an octagram in the center and a thick ring around it. These two shapes give the impression of a stable, orderly, resting and constant center.

Around this center are 8 almond-shaped leaves, whose outer tip lies on the outer ring and whose inner tip lies on the opposite side of the inner circular ring.

The inner intersections of these leaves have been connected to another ring, on which there are 4 more circles. From the geometry, there could have been 8 such circles, since there are 8 equal intersections. However, 8 such circles would not have given such a strong impression of stability as the restriction to four circles – stability is a quality of the "4".

The whole gives the image of a stable, grown form.

- * ❀ * -

180. Escher-oktagram
(Fürstenfeldbruck, FRG, 2015)

This is an octagram of a single continuous line. This line has been designed according to Escher's principle of "impossible geometric shape".

- * ❀ * -

181. wheel of fire
(Hampshire, England, 2019)

This crop circle can be seen as a rotating eight-spoked wheel surrounded by flames on the outside: the fiery sun wheel of the Indo-Europeans, who conceived the sun as such a wheel.

This crop circle is a double swastika, that is, the symbol that once represented the sun, the wheel, completeness, rightness, and perfection.

- * ❀ * -

182. eight claws
(Wiltshire, England, 2008)

This crop circle consists of a center circle with 8 rotating leaves and with 8 claws. This 8-polar shape looks amazingly aggressive – that is quite unusual for octagrams and octagons.

- * ❀ * -

183. double-four
(Italy, 2013)

This crop circle is quite simple at first glance: a white central circle, a narrow eight-pointed ring, a white ring, a wide eight-pointed ring, an octagram (eight-pointed star), and a narrow ring. The alternation of light and dark triangles on the very outside also creates a cross – an emphasis on the "4".

The inner ring, however, contains a "code". Starting at the bottom center clockwise, it reads: o•oo – •o•• – o•oo – •ooo – o•oo – o•oo – o•o• - oo••. "o•oo" occurs three times, the other combinations only once.

On one of the eighth segments of this circular ring there is a triangle, on another a double triangle.

In the bright triangle on the upper left there are also six small triangles.
The meaning of both "codes" (if they have any) is unknown.

135

- * ⊛ * -

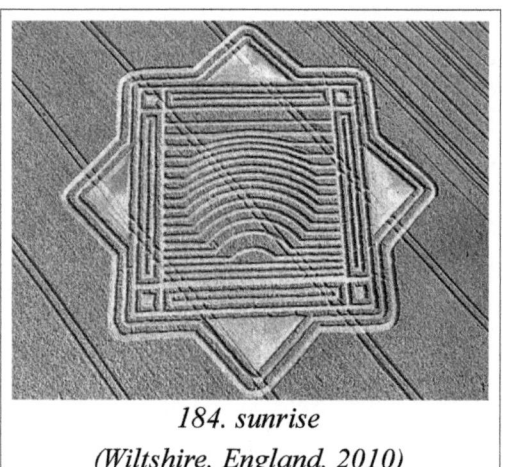

184. sunrise
(Wiltshire, England, 2010)

Here an octagram has been formed from two squares.

In the inner square, a circle has been drawn in a clever way by bending the transverse lines. Because the lines are narrow at the bottom and wide at the top, the impression of a sunrise in the fog is created.

In the square, the corners and the sides are emphasized.

- * ⊛ * -

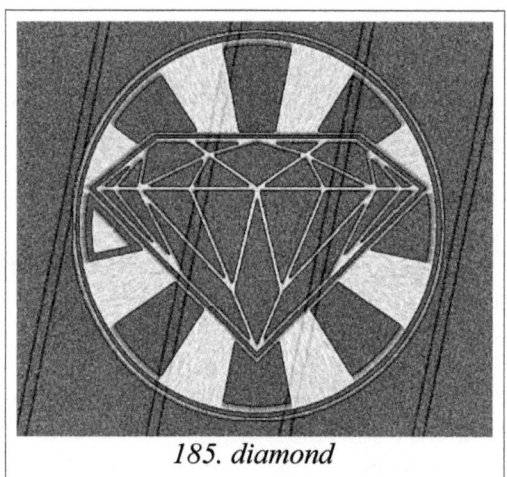

185. diamond
(Wiltshire, England, 2008)

The background is eight rays in a circle, and it is noticeable that the dark-small ray on the left is "hollow" unlike the other rays – why? Since this deviation is not repeated anywhere and no other deviation can be seen, it cannot be interpreted.

The diamond has an octagon as its base, as can be seen from the cut shown. An octagon as the central surface is common in many different diamond cuts.

III 12. i)   Mandalas – nine-polar

As the "8" is the ideal number, the "9" is the destruction of this ideal, correct state – death. After "12" displaced "8" during the middle Neolithic and became the ideal number, "13" became the "destroyer of 12" – Judas, the 13th apostle.

Whether this death symbolism of the "9" is also found in the 9-polar mandalas has yet to be examined – after all, it is not a natural symbolism, but a traditional symbolism (albeit a very old one).

- - -

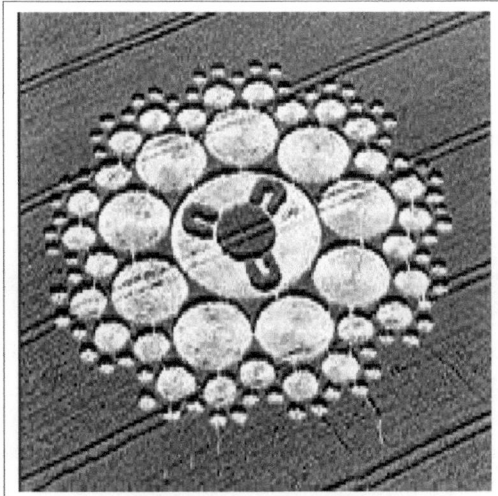

186. circle-nonagram
(Wiltshire, England, 1998)

The center is a circle surrounded by a large ring in which there are three "U"s. These "U"s act like buds or horseshoe magnets – like the power of the central circle.

Around the ring are 9 large circles. In the outer angle between each of them there is a central circle, which are connected by two more circles.

The same principle is repeated again on the very outside with most of the small circles.

This results in a sequence from the inside to the outside, which is created by multiplying by "3": 1 circle – 3 "U" – 9 circles – 27 circles (– 63 circles).

In this mandala, although the 9 circles stand out the most as a structure, it is basically a 3-polar circle.

- * 🌀 * -

187. vortex-nonagram
(Wiltshire, England, 2001)

Here, on the other hand, the 9-polarity is very clear: 1 central circle, 9 outer circles, 9 arcs, 2 rings.

- * ❁ * -

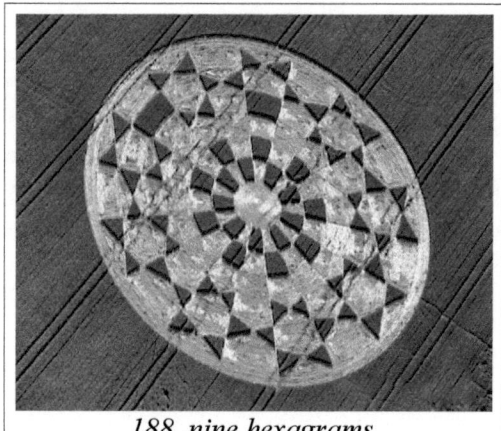

188. nine hexagrams
(Wiltshire, England, 2015)

Didn't this crop circle get quite finished? At the top and top left, 2 shapes of each of the 9 hexagrams are still hanging together.

Around the circle in the center are two circles of 9 light and 9 dark rectangles each.

What should this quite unconventional grain circle express? 9 individuals uniting to a group? But that is the symbolism of the "6". And if these are 9 groups – what are they doing together?

- * ❁ * -

189. nonagram-stronghold
(Wiltshire, England, 2007)

Here the core is a again a circle surrounded by a "3" – here a triangle. Around it is a 9-rayed star.

In the following ring there is a crescent – similar to the 7-star in crop circle 170. What does this sickle mean, which occurs quite often after all? It is not a crescent moon, but a ring of different thickness. It creates a shift, a dynamic to one side, a connection, a contact.

In the ring that surrounds the nonagram and the crescent, the three main directions defined by the triangle in the center are marked by three small triangles.

The outer ring consists of 9 arc segments, which in turn are composed of 2 "L" each – is this an "angular S", i.e. a flow of energy? Or minimal spirals with the same symbolism?

On the very outside there are 9 triangles which "protect" the 9 "gates" between the ring-segments.

139

III 12. j) Mandalas – ten-polar

The "10" is indeed the formative number in the decimal system and it also appears in the animal world as 10 fingers and 10 toes as well as the 10 limbs of the early animals with exoskeleton (precursors of the crustaceans, insects and spiders), but the 10 has no structural symbolism.

- - -

190. cobweb
(Wiltshire, England, 1994)

A 10-pole spider web ... The symmetric spider webs in nature consist of about 20 radial threads and only one spiral thread, which also has about 20 turns. Furthermore the spiral threads do not all hang towards the center like in this crop circle, but of course downwards.

However, the spider web principle is clearly visible in this crop circle.

The sun in the center then probably corresponds to the spider.

140

III 12. k)   Mandalas – twelve-polar

The "12" is the number of the zodiac and the superstrings and thus the number of the structure of the surrounding space, the structure of the aura (life force body). Among the crop circles considered so far, quite a few have already contained a 12-fold structure.

- - -

191. circle of leaves
(Wiltshire, England, 2020)

This 12-structure is quite simple: one ring inside and one ring outside, 12 triangles around the inner ring and then 12 leaf-like structures. The construction of the leaf is shown in Figure 192.

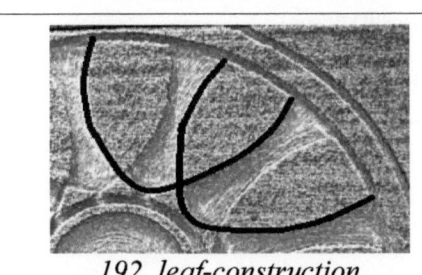

192. leaf-construction

- * ❀ * -

193. circle of points
(Andechs, Bayern, BRD, 2012)

1 center circle, 12 6-rayed triangles, a complex outer ring – apart from the shape of the triangles, which look very pointed and dynamic, there is nothing remarkable about this grain circle.

The outer rim consists of 3 rows of dark squares. There are 12·13=156 squares in a row – 468 in total. Should these squares be seen as a beam of 3 squares in front of each point plus 3 rows of 12 squares in between?

Crop circle 151 consists of a hexagon surrounded by a similar outer ring – in that case there are 3·114=342 squares.

- *  * -

194. circular saw blade
(Italy, 2014)

The structure is very simple: a circular area is surrounded by 4 circles of 12 "saw teeth" each. The combination of the "4" with the "12" is found very often.

- * * -

195. ornamental circle
(Oxfordshire, England, 2009)

This crop circle is much more complex than the previous one.

A circle in the middle, around it 12 areas that look stable and delineated because of their rectangular shape, that look sovereign and alive because of the dot in them, and that look radiant and expanding because of the location of the dot near the outer edge.

Then follow two rings of each approximatly 4·12=48 squares – there are 49 squares on the inside and 53 on the outside.

The two rings on the outside consists of approcimately 6·12=72 squares – there are 72 squares on the inside and 75 squares on the outside.

Between the two circular rings there are 12 blossoms of 4 petals each, each connected by a small ring. The petals are surrounded in each case by 4 very small fastening points, which in this case are rings.

The whole thing looks earthy-harmonic.

- * ✤ * -

196. circle of triangles
(Wiltshire, England, 2011)

At first glance, this crop circle looks very regular: Central circle, twelve multipart rays, outer ring.

In addition, there is an inner ring consisting of 12 arc squares, each containing a small circular area with a central point. This acts as a stabilizing ring. From each of these arc-squares a dark ray of equal length emanates to the outside.

These rays seem to rotate clockwise because the light-colored borders at their back (looking in clockwise direction) are broader than the borders at their front.

However, the dark rays emanating from the inside are of different lengths. If you start at the bottom left of the short ray and go clockwise, these rays extend only the following fraction into the white area: 1/4 – 1/2 – 2/3 – 1/3 – 2/3 – 1/3 – 1/2 – 1/4 – 2/3 – 1/2 – 3/4 – 2/3. The only regularity in this "code" is that there are never two rays of the same length next to each other.

- * ❀ * -

197. circle of prongs
(Wiltshire, England, 2015)

A central circle, surrounded by a wide ring, then 12 rays, another narrow ring, 12 prongs (lightning bolts? angular "S"s?), a ring with 4 thickenings each containing a circle, 4 prong lines going further on to the outside, and finally a ring.

The central ring and the outer ring combined are the astrological symbol of the sun. Is this crop circle a twelve-armed swastica? A "zodiac-swastica"?

From the central circle, 12-fold energy radiates outward, stabilized by four circles on a "pedestal" – probably the rising sun half above the horizon.

- * ❀ * -

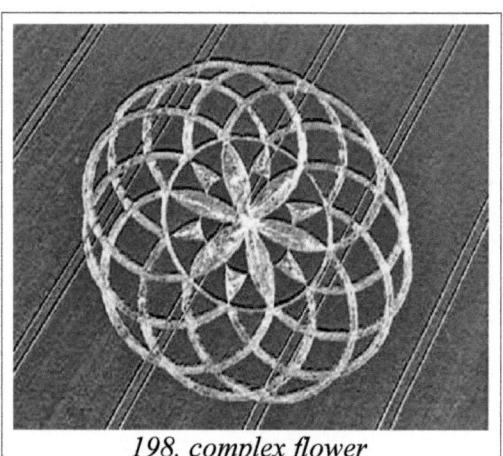

198. complex flower
(Wiltshire, England, 2009)

Here a 6-petaled flower has been extended by 6 half-petals to a 12-petaled flower – this flower motif has been seen many times before.

The arcs on the outside result when the outer arcs of the 12 leaves are expanded to form circles – a very simple concept.

144

199. 3D-Zodiac
(Wiltshire, England, 2006)

The center is a simple 12-rayed star, but the rays emanating from it are square 3D columns.

They are arranged in 3 groups of 4 columns of increasing size. This probably corresponds to the signs of the zodiac, which are created by the 3 dynamics (cardinal, fixed, mutable) of the 4 elements (fire, water, air, earth).

A drastic representation, which reminds a little of graffiti art.

The dark dots in the centre are people who are standing there.

III 12. l) Mandalas – thirteen-polar

The "13" has the symbolism of "destroying the order of the 12": death and transformation for example Judas, the 13. apostle or the 13. Tarot card „death". However, this is a traditional and not a structural symbolism, i.e. it is not found in nature, but only in mythology.

- - -

200. sunflower
(Wiltshire, England, 2003)

This crop circle reminds a little of a 13-petaled sunflower. The overall impression of this crop circle is something restlessly radiant: with the 13-polarity there are no regularities at which the view could rest, since the "13" is a prime number.

While the triangles inside still seem quite peaceful, the diamonds outside make a latent-aggressive impression, which, however, is weakened again by the 13 circles on the very outside.

Without the narrow ring around the whole, it would lack cohesion.

- * ❀ * -

146

201. four and thirteen
(Wiltshire, England, 2015)

Here a four-pointed star has been combined with a crescent. They are surrounded by a ring with 13 arc segments – for whatever reason …

The "16" shares the symbolism of the "8" and is a greater version of it: fullness and perfection. This is a traditional symbolism, not a natural structure.

- - -

202. eight and sixteen
(Warwickshire, England, 2011)

This crop circle mandala has 16 rays on the outside, but an 8-rayed star as the core.

Especially interesting is the transition between both stars: the 8 diamonds inside as well as the 8 petals in the center and the 8 triangles outside are each divided – the triangles even twice.

Does this division signify a polarity? The petals are divided at the level of the tips of the diamonds. In the rhombus and the corresponding triangle, the light/dark markings alternate regularly.

There is also an alternation in the shape of these three geometrical forms: diamonds = technical-angular; leaves organical-round; triangles = technical-angular.

The 8 long triangles on the outside are also two-colored – the 8 short triangles on the outside, on the other hand, are all one-color-dark.

In the middle, a central circle and two rings have still been marked by way of laying the grain flat.

- * ❀ * -

148

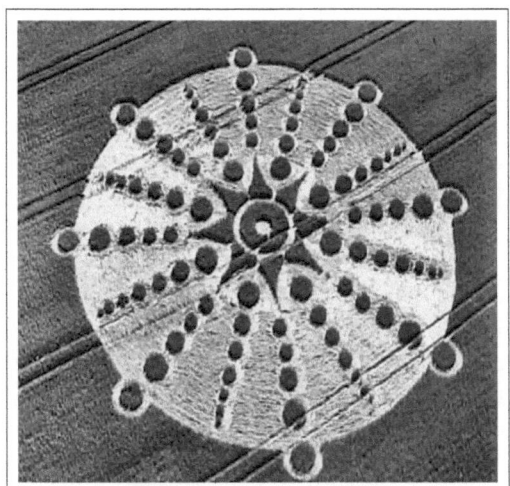

203. eight and sixteen
(Wiltshire, England, 2011)

Here we find a similar principle as in the previous crop circle mandala: inside an 8-rayed star, outside a 16-rayed star.

Because of the dark ring in the center, this mandala appears more centered, and because of the arc triangles of the 8-rayed star, it also appears a bit more aggressive.

The rows of circles starting from the tips of the 8-rayed star consist of 5 circles whose size increases and whose largest circle is on the outside of the total circular area of this mandala – this looks like the start of a conquest.

In between there are rows of 7 circles whose size decreases. The rows of 5 circles look like an expansion outwards, the rows of 7 circles look like a normal ray.

Possibly this crop circle should be considered 8-polar rather than 16-polar, since the 7-rows act like the gaps between the rays of the 5-rows.

- *  * -

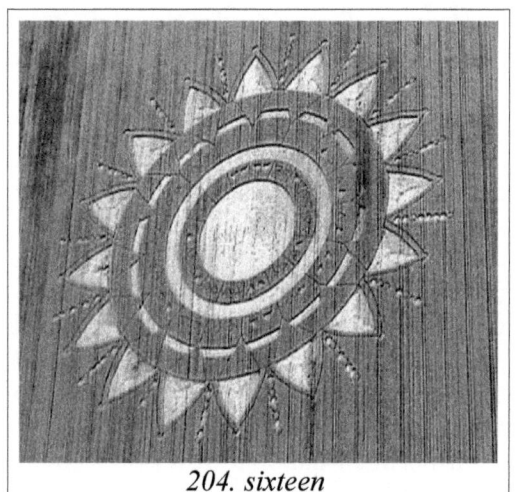

204. sixteen
(Turin, Italy, 2015)

This crop circle has 16 arc triangles on the outside and is consequently a true 16-polar mandala. Between each of these "petals" is a ray of eight small circles, so that this crop circle also has a 32-polar structure.

The circles in these rays are partly filled and partly empty. There is no regularity in the distribution of the fillings.

Also the inner ring consists of 16 elements. In each segment there are two small triangles pointing inwards – so 32 triangles in total. They appear concentrating and relating to the large circular area in the center.

Similarly, the middle ring is composed of 16 segments. However, each segment contains two small triangles and therefore also has a 32 structure. These triangles, pointing outward, give the impression of unity and alignment. They point to the small triangles in the outer ring, which are the base of the rays.

The outer ring, on the other hand, consists of 16 large triangles that form the base of the leaves and 16 small triangles whose apexes "emit" the rays.

205. sixteen (another photo)

By combining the triangles in the outer ring with the petals and the rays, the triangle/leaf combination has a passive-defensive effect and the triangle/ray combination has an active-expansive effect.

In this crop circle mandala there is a harmonious balance between concentration, protection and expansion.

The throat chakra has 16 petals in the traditional representations – should a healing of the throat chakra have been represented here? I.e. the ability to show oneself to others and also to be able to see others? That would be then the unhindered social self-expression …

On the detail picture (205) it is recognizable that the fillings in the rays, which consist of 8 small circles, are irregularly distributed. Also the two opposite rays on the

150

lower left and upper right, which are visible here, are displaced.

The distribution of the small triangles in the inner and the middle ring is also irregular.

If we take "•" for a filled triangle or circle, "o" for an empty triangle or circle, "-" for the absence of a triangle and start at the bottom and continue clockwise, we get the following three series:

The "crop circle code"																
rays	•	•	o	•	o	•	•	o	o	o	•	o	o	o	o	o
	•	o	•	•	•	o	•	•	o	•	o	•	•	•	o	•
	o	o	o	o	o	o	o	o	•	o	o	•	o	o	o	o
	•	o	o	•	•	o	o	•	•	o	•	o	o	•	o	•
	o	•	•	o	•	•	•	•	o	o	o	•	•	•	•	•
	•	o	o	o	o	o	o	o	o	o	o	o	o	o	o	•
	o	o	o	o	o	o	o	o	o	•	o	o	o	o	o	o
	•	•	•	•	•	•	•	•	•	•	•	•	•	•	•	•
middle circle	oo	oo	oo	oo	--	--	--	•o	o•	o•	••	•o	••	oo	oo	•o
inner circle	oo	•-	--	--	••	••	oo	•o	oo	oo	•o	oo	••	oo	oo	•o

Are the rays a binary code? At least there are combinations of eight "•/o" as in binary code, where there are eight combinations of "0/1".

There are a few regularities:

- The sequence "•• oo oo •o oo" is present in both circles (the last 4 pairs plus the first pair).
- Every ray starts with a "•" at its inner end.
- The following rays are identical: 2 and 6; 3 and 13; 5 and 8; 8 and 14.

Probably this is not an binary code, for every combination beginns with an "•" and there not equaly many "•" and "o" in the rays: 57 "•" and 71 "o"

Whether the different kinds of "code" in these crop circles have a meaning remains unclear until someone finds a conclusive interpretation – which is quite unlikely in view of the altogether very few code signs and the lack of clues to their possible meaning. Therefore these manifold-irregular elements in the crop circles remain for the time being merely "elements which loosen up the geometrical strictness".

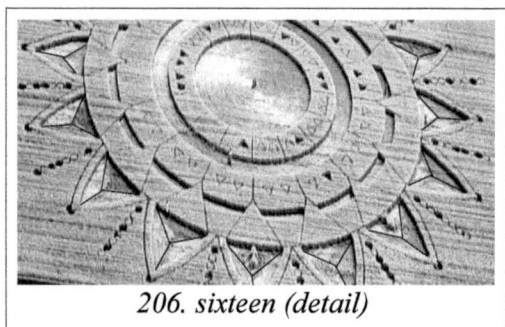

206. sixteen (detail)

In the detail picture 206 one can see in which careful way the grain has been laid flat in the petals.

152

III 12. n)   Mandalas – eighteen-polar

The "18" has no structural or traditional meaning. It is sometimes interpreted as a "double 9", but even that is extremely rare.

- - -

207. butterfly
(Oxfordshire, England, 2009)

This 18-polar crop circle, reminiscent of a butterfly, has already been discussed as crop circle 43.

- *  * -

208. flower
(Wiltshire, England, 2007)

This crop circle consists of four rows of petals: the inner row has the "almond shape" consisting of 2 arcs, while the three outer rows have the shape of triangles consisting of 3 arcs.

The "slant" of the pattern of this corn-circle is only due to the distortion caused by the photography angle.

III 12. o)   Mandalas – twenty-polar

A general symbolism of the "20" is not known.

- - -

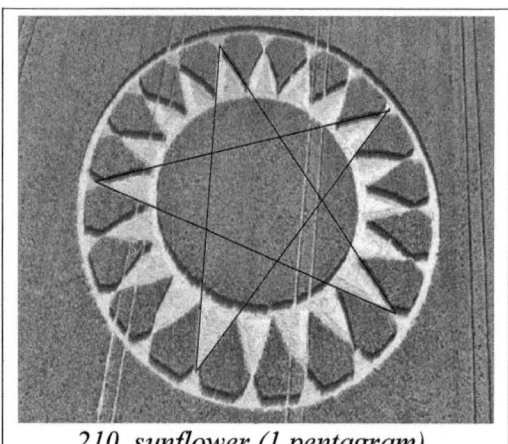

209. sunflower
(Warwickshire, England, 2016)

This crop circle has an exceptionally large inner circular area, which in combination with the 20 bright petals looks like a sunflower.

On the outside there are 20 pentagonal "diamonds".

If you extend the lines of the diamonds or the petals, you get 4 pentagrams. This is not necessarily so: It could also have been 5 squares, 2 ten-pointed stars, a continuous twenty-pointed star, or no geometric shape at all – it depends on the leaf angle chosen.

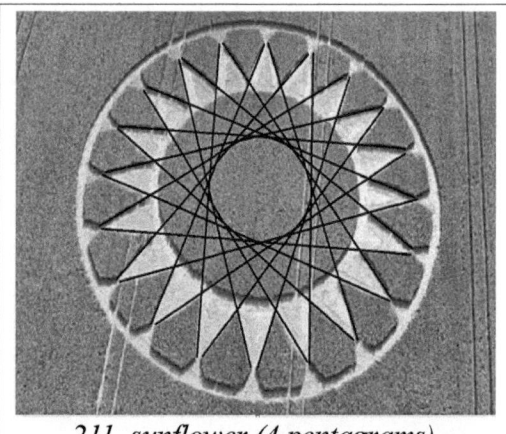

210. sunflower (1 pentagram)   *211. sunflower (4 pentagrams)*

Of course, the combination of 4 pentagrams reminds us of the "Lesser Pentagram Ritual", which consists of a circle and 4 pentagrams on a mandala – but whether that is what is meant here is questionable.

154

- * ❀ * -

The crop circle 97, that has already been discussed, is also 20-polar: at its edge there are 20 "letters".

III 12. p)   Mandalas – twentytwo-polar

The "22" has no known symbolism – except for the 22 paths on the Kabbalistic Tree of Life and the 22 "Great Arcana" of the Tarot cards derived from it, which are a very special symbolism after all.

- - -

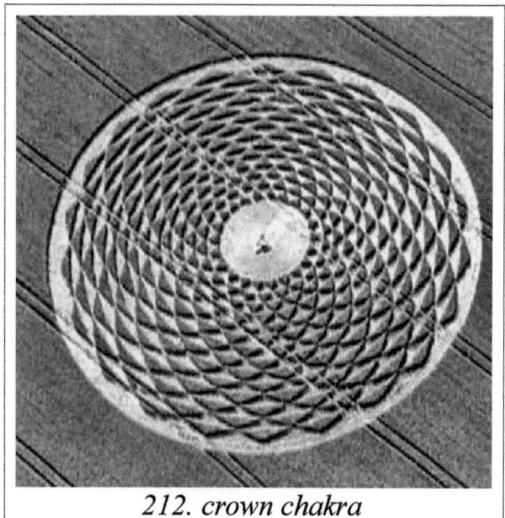

212. crown chakra
(Wiltshire, England, 2000)

This crop circle reminds by its structure of many arc triangles of the representations of the crown chakra.

This "great flower" consists of 14 rows of 22 triangles each, thus of 308 triangles in total.

III 13. Cubic forms

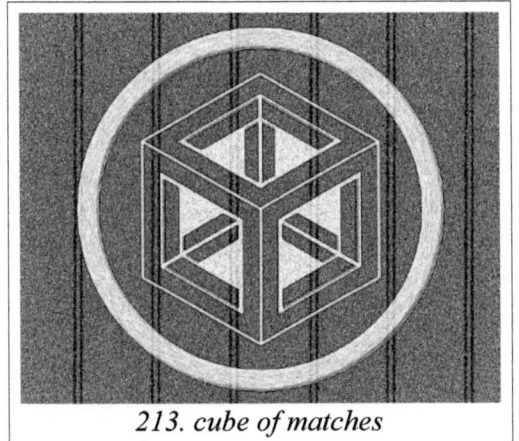

213. cube of matches
(Cambridgeshire, England, 1999)

There are a number of 3D representations. Whether they have a deeper meaning is questionable. The probability that they are man-made is quite high – unless the collective subconscious of mankind enjoys playing games, which, however, it has not yet shown up to now …

- *  * -

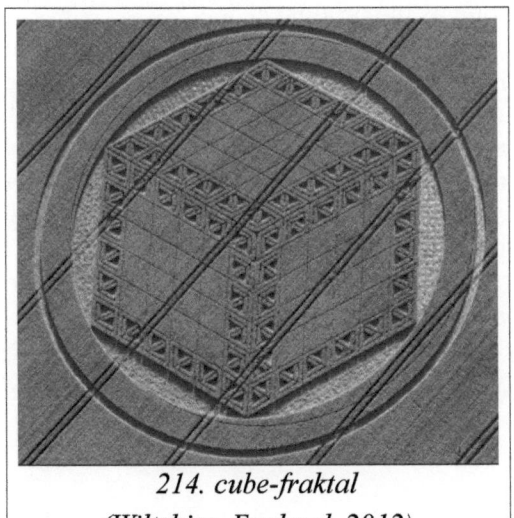

214. cube-fraktal
(Wiltshire, England, 2012)

Here the cube has become a fractal: The edges of the cube are cubes again.

- * ❋ * -

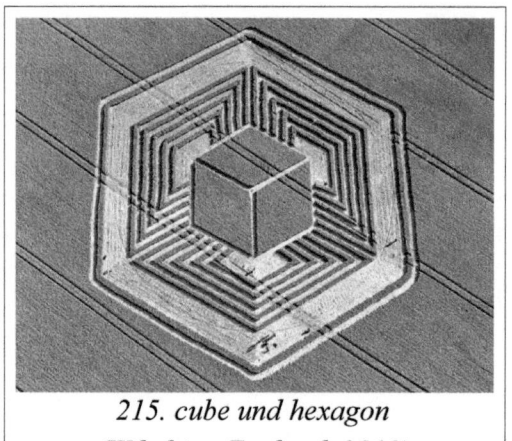

215. cube und hexagon
(Wiltshire, England, 2010)

Here we find the popular plying with 2D and 3D: the 2D outer lines of a 3D cube form a hexagon.

Between the 3D cube and the 2D hexagon, three groups of 5 concentric diamond lines each have been inserted here as a transition – they are already 2D, but still emphasize the three directions of the 3D.

This is a clever graphic solution for the transition from 3D to 2D.

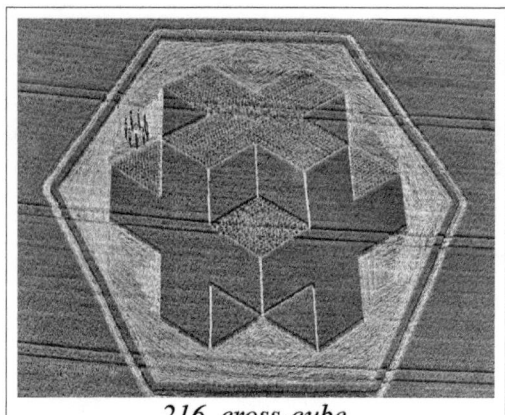

216. cross-cube
(Wiltshire, England, 2010)

This crop circle is also a simple fractal: at each corner of the cube, a cube is removed whose side length is one-third as long as the original cube.

Interestingly, there is a 3-color solution here, which at first does not seem possible with the two possibilities "grain stands" and "grain lies". The 3rd color, i.e. the gray tone, results from the fact that only a part of the grain is laid flat, but rows of tiny grain circles remain standing.

On the upper left is a circle of nine people.

III 14.   Sun-like forms

The symbolism of the sun was already found in the birds and the insects in quite a pronounced way. Also the simple central circle can be seen as a sun. However, the sun also appears in a clearly more direct form in the crop circles.

- - -

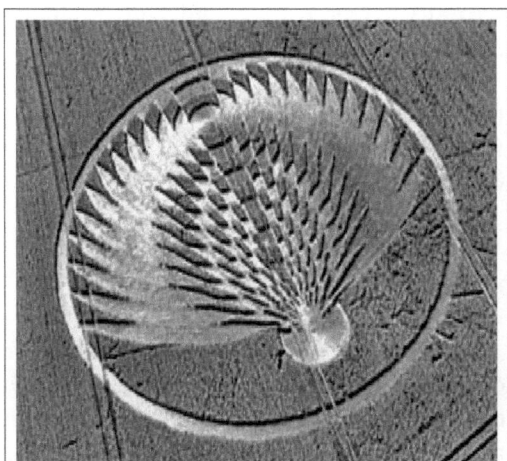

217. sun and magnetic field
(Oxfordshire, England 2006)

Here a circular surface is to be seen, from which a central stripe runs upwards, as well as 12 rays that run to the left above and to the right above. The middle part consists of 11, 9, 7, 5 and probably still 3 and 1 rays seen from the outside to the inside.

This could be a rising sun, an explosion or a chakra (then the middle strip would be the sushumna). Is this supposed to be the root chakra from which the sushumna, as well as the kundalini within it, rises upward?

However, the 2·12=24 rays indicate the sun – or the heart chakra ("sun chakra"), which has 12 petals.

- *  * -

159

In this crop circle, the basic pattern is a central circle with probably 52 rays, 46 of which can be seen. It could be related to the 52 weeks of the year, but this is very uncertain.

The rays are cut off at an angle at their tips, giving the impression of rotation.

The center circle and the rays are partially covered by a "lid with a handle hole" that lies on its side.

Is this supposed to represent the things that prevent the inner sun (heart chakra) from radiating and would need to be dissolved?

218. decentralized sun
(Ravenna, Italy, 2015)

- * ❁ * -

A circle in the the center of the outer circle, is surrounded by a crescent, which covers a part of the rays. The little sun in the central circle ist moved a little to the left of the centre of the central circle.

The total of 12 rays indicate a sun symbolism. They change their color (light/-dark) when passing over the crescent.

Is the crescent a kind of transformer?

Or is this crop circle showing sun and moon?

219. sunrays
(Wiltshire, England, 2017)

- * ❁ * -

160

220. sun
(Hampshire, England, 2000)

Here the "principle of decentralized circles" has been changed a bit in the solar crop circles. The circle in the center and the two rings around it, which form the basic structure, are centered. However, the different sized, half-filled rings on the two rings give the impression of a shift away from the center.

There are 12 rings on the inner ring and 12 rings on the outer ring as well. Since the largest rings on these two rings are on opposite sides and, in addition, the filled halves of the circle also point once outward and once inward, this crop circle, although so systematically constructed, appears very restless – it somewhat confuses the geometric orientation when first viewed …

The twelve outer rings look like suns rising above the horizon.

- *  * -

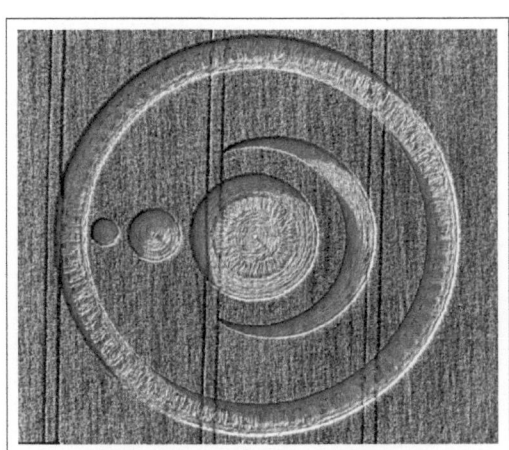

221. sun and crescent moon
(Wiltshire, England, 2019)

Here you can see a central circle, a crescent and two smaller circles in a ring.

In this crop circle, the sickle gives the impression of a foundation. The three circles could be the development "impulse – form – contact".

The area of the circular ring is carefully laid out in about 80 "U" shapes with the fun-dament on the inside and the two tips pointing outward. The corn stalks are also laid down very precisely and artistically in the other areas of this crop circle.

Overall, this crop circle looks very clear and precise.

- *  * -

161

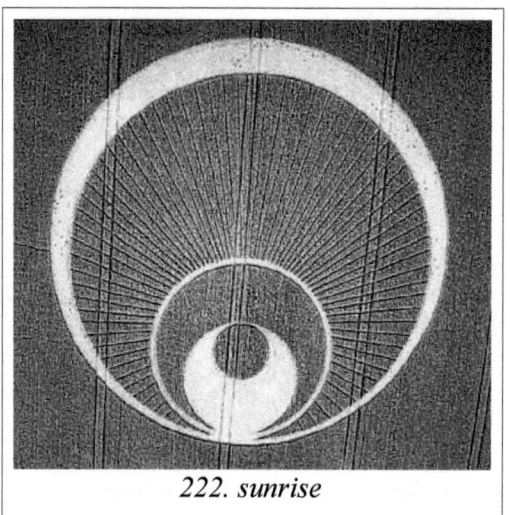

222. sunrise

(Cambridgeshire, England, 2001)

A radiant sun is partially obscured by a dark circle as well as a crescent.

The dark circle seems here like a necessary part of the arrangement and not like a hindrance to be removed like in the crop circle 218. The crescent here seems to be the foundation of the approx. 74 rays. Also the outer ring is again a sickle.

If you turn the crop circle around, you can also see it as an angel: The small dark circle is then the head, the crescent the arms, the rays the body and wings, and the light crescent either a halo or the sun – in the second case it would be a sun angel, probably Raphael, the archangel of the sun.

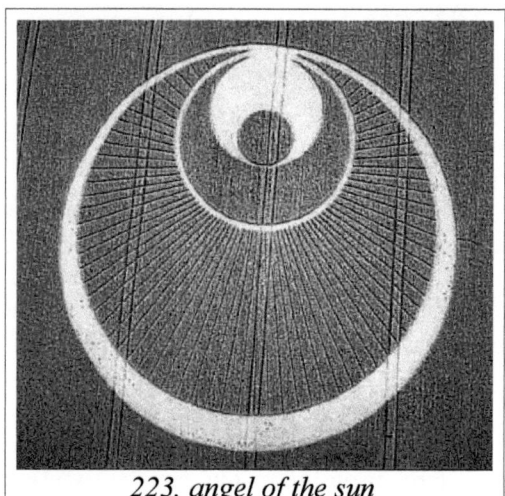

223. angel of the sun

- * ❀ * -

162

224. sun god
(Wiltshire, England, 2009)

xlxlllo	lxloloo	lxloloo	xlxlllo
xxlolo			xxlxlo
xxllo			xlxlo
xl			xllo
llo			llo
lo			lo

sun god
(symbol of headdress of feathers)

This crop circle follows the representations of the sun bird in the chapter "Birds".

There is a face with 2 eyes and beak surrounded by 2 spirals at the bottom left and bottom right, reminiscent of the Chinese lucky symbol.

The face is surrounded by a sickle, which seems to be the holder for the 2·7=14 large feathers.

Should one also regard the two crop circles 221 and 222 as such sun faces? This is at least suggested by their structure (circle, crescent, rays) …

On the 2·7=14 "feathers" in this crop circle there are symbols which are almost symmetrical. The blanks are marked as "x" in the diagram on the left (225), the dashes as "l" and the dots as "o". The symmetrical character series have a dark background. The meaning of this "code" is again unclear …

Next to the cheeks of the bird's face there are 7 small feathers each on the left and on the right – the "7" is obviously important here: the chakras?

The large and the small feathers form together with the two long triangles at the lower end of the small feathers a crescent. Are the feathers here also the rays of the rising sun?

Below this sunbird face there is another crescent consisting of 5 double spirals that rotate in the opposite directions – thus forming 5 "S"s. The bow triangles at the two ends contain three points each. This is flowing power ("S") as well as expansion ("3 points"). This crescent is from its position the foundation and the support of the sunbird face and its "ray feathers".

Between this crescent and the outer circle there are 9 jags on top, which have only been indicated by the position of the lying grain, as well as two "elongated drops". However, these drops seem only to give stability to the overall impression.

The "optical center" of this crop circle is the small circular area on the upper part of

163

the beak. In relation to the beak, the two eye-dots look like the attachment points on some crop circles considered earlier.

Overall, this crop circle appears powerful-radiant and at the same time very organical and hardly technical-geometric. Its style is reminiscent of the art of the Mayas, Aztecs and Toltecs in Central America.

This crop circle was located in a field in front of Silbury Hill, the largest artificial Neolithic mound in Europe.

225. abstract sun god *(Oxfordshire, England, 2005)*	*226. abstract sun god*

In this picture it is not quite clear what side is the top and what side is the base: Is there a crescent in the center with rays down and a circle in the middle, the crescent forming a "drop" with the circle and the bright area above it (Figure 225)? Or are the two triangles of arcs at the bottom and a sun rising from a valley is meant, which is at the same time a face with hair and a feather adornment (= sun rays) (Figure 226)? The second possibility seems to be more plausible, because it agrees with other crop circles.

There are 2·8=16 rays – "8" and "16" are the numbers of perfection.

On the very outside there are 20 rectangles, in each of which a spiral is indicated by 6 straight lines – turning and unfolding. These spirals all turn in the same direction. In the middle of each spiral is a point, which makes the spiral look more organic. Whether the "20" has any meaning is unclear.

164

In the crop circle 225/226 considered here, the 20 spirals consist of 8 straight lines each.

In crop circle 162, the 12 spirals also consist of 8 straight lines each.

In crop circle 173, the 14 spirals consist of 6 straight lines each.

Between the sun face in the center and the spiral outer circle there is another ring interrupted by a cross – the symbol of the four cardinal points in the center of which the sun is located. This ring is divided between each of the four rays of the cross into four fields, which have 16 "inscriptions" when viewed clockwise from the cross ray below. Reading them from the inside out and marking the dark fields with "o" and the light fields with "x" gives the following series:

```
O O O X    O O X O    O X O O    X O O O
X O X O    O X O X    X O X O    O X O X
O X O O    X O O O    O O O X    O O X O
X O X O    O X O X    X O X O    O X O X
O O O X    O O X O    O X O O    X O O O
```

Each of these 4 fields of 20 characters (the same number as the spirals) has 3 "errors" (light instead of dark characters). If these "errors" are changed, a regular pattern of light and dark fields is created. These changes have been grayed out in the following illustration.

```
O O O X    O O X O    O X O O    X O O O
X O X O    O X O X    X O X O    O X O X
O X O O    X O O O    O O O X    O O X O
X O X O    O X O X    X O X O    O X O X
O O O X    O O X O    O X O O    X O O O
```

As you can see, the "errors" are arranged systematically, forming a triangle each time.

Between each of the four fields of 20 characters in the crop circle there is one of the cross rays, which are as wide as the fields. If one imagines in these gaps, thus "behind the rays" also the alternating light/dark fields, the symmetry becomes still clearer:

```
O O O X O O O X O X O X O O O X O O O X
X O X O X O X O X O X O X O X O X O X O
O X O O O X O O O X O O O X O O O X O X
X O X O X O X O X O X O X O X O X O X O
O O O X O O O X O X O X O O O X O O O X
```

165

So the light and the dark fields form a net as background for the rays. But what are the 4 "systematic errors"? Are these 4 crescents?

It is also interesting that both sides of the vertical axis of this "sun bird crop circle" are smmetrical. In figure 225 the error field crescents point with their tops downwards – in the probably correct view of the crop circle on figure 226 the error field crescents point with their top upwards. Are these then, so to speak, 4 very strongly stylized mountains over which the sun rises?

This crop circle is also stylistically Central American.

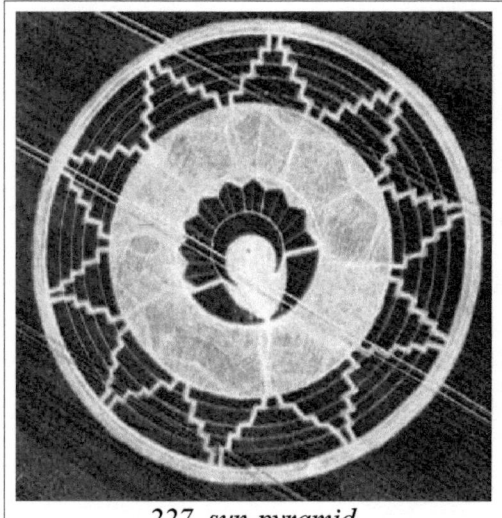

227. sun-pyramid

(Wiltshire, England, 2011)

Here is exactly the same central element as on the previous crop circle: Sun, crescent, two arc triangles and feather sun rays. Here, curiously, there are 8.5 rays … On the right side, there seems to be half a ray too much … Why?

On the broad, bright ring 10 broad rays have been indicated by the laying of the grain.

These 10 rays are then found on the dark ring as 10 5-step pyramids. Do they correspond to the 4 "mountains" in the previous crop circle, as which one could interpret the 4 sickle-shaped groups of fields?

Also this sun-corn-circle has again the style of the Mayas, Aztecs and Toltecs – including the step-pyramids.

The drop-shape, which results from the circle, the crescent and the arc triangle under them in these "sun-faces", appears later still often as the drop-shaped faces of the "crop circle aliens".

166

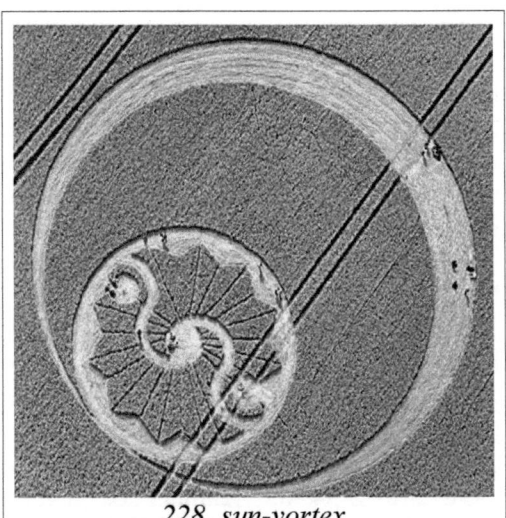

228. sun-vortex
(Wiltshire, England, 2010)

Again a circle with a crescent – the circle here is decentralized as in crop circles 217, 222 and 224.

The circle area contains two strange signs. They become better understandable, if one understands the bright line, which separates them, as two "S"s, thus as two energy flows, which go out from the circle surface in its center. Seen in this way, this symbol is a variant of the Yin/Yang symbol.

There are 24 lines emanating from the center of this symbol, forming a total of 12 rays in pairs – obviously a sun symbolism.

- * ❀ * -

167

229. winged sun
(Wiltshire, England, 2004)

The center is a winged sun, although it has been depicted in an unusual way. Instead of the sun being a "body" with two horizontal wings on it (as in the winged suns of the Egyptians, Persians, and Greeks), the two wings form a kind of vortex – a sunfire vortex?

Here the style is no longer so clearly Middle American.

In their first part, the wings consist of 1 long feather, 1 bipartite feather and 4 tripartite feathers – together 15 "feather parts". In their second part, the wings consist of 19 long, thin feathers. In total there are 2·34=68 feathers or feather parts. If you count the 2 or 3 feather parts each only as 1 feather, you get 24 feathers per side, so a total of 48 feathers – a well known "sun number": 4 directions · 12 zodiac signs = 48 units.

The outer circle is completely identical with the outer circle of crop circle 102, in which there is a complex three-polar vortex – in the crop circle 229 considered here, however, there is a two-polar vortex. So the structure of the outer circular ring could have something to do with the vortex in the center – although the polarity of the vortex apparently doesn't matter.

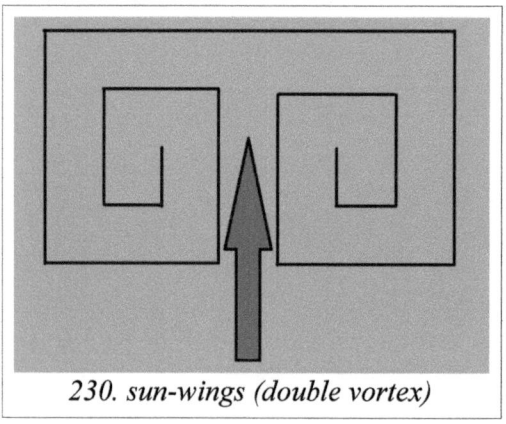

230. sun-wings (double vortex)

The ring is divided into four equal areas by two thick areas each – similar to the four rays at crop circle 225/226. Each quarter contains 2·12=24 stripes, 2·2=4 squares and 4 double spirals – the complex symbols are in the center.

What do these double spirals mean? Are they really the Chinese lucky symbols – simply traditional characters? There is a second possible explanation: When the water of a stream flows into a lake, double spirals are formed – the same is true wherever an impulse enters a still medium. The penis and ovaries also have this shape. On the figure 230 the double spiral is angular drawn like on the crop

168

circle 229 and not round like in nature.

So we can assume that this double spiral indicates that an impulse is going from the inside to the outside, creating this double vortex. The position of the double spirals on the outer circle shows that the impulse comes from the inside and goes to the outside.

If the 4 double spirals are the double vortices caused by the incoming impulse, then the 12 strokes to the left and right of it would be waves coming from it, and the 2 squares in the two corners would be surfaces that remain mostly still. So the ornaments on the outer circle are a flow pattern.

231. spiral-sun
(Wiltshire, England, 2005)

Here, the 12 rays emanating from the center circle are represented in an interesting way: They too are the double vortices described in the previous crop circle – except that here they are very elongated.

The sun's rays in the center therefore go into a surrounding medium similar to themselves, in which they then produce these 12 double vortices. One can at least assume that both the rays of the sun and the surrounding medium are the life force.

The small dots in the center and top right of the outer circle are people.

169

232. sun-heart
(Wiltshire, England, 2020)

Here is a crop circle with a sun that has two wings, each with 9 ray feathers, sending a wide ray downward towards a heart.

This heart symbol is already found in the Paleolithic cave paintings, where it was painted on the chest of a mammoth, but nevertheless there is a slight suspicion that this crop circle could have been made by humans.

The grain in the heart has been laid flat in two circles and then completed by a triangle.

- *  * -

233. pentagram-sun
(Dorset, England, 2018)

Here the sun contains a pentagram and rests in a crescent at the bottom of a large ring: the general arrangement of the "rising sun".

However, the pentagram is unusual in this context. From the 5-polar crop circle mandalas no clear symbolism results, so that one has only the traditional interpretation as a human being with body (pentagon), legs (lower points) arms (lateral points) and head (upper point).

Should this be a man in a rising sun? So a man who sees the sun rising in himself, that is, who has found his own soul? This would fit to the other interpretations of the sun crop circles, but it is questionable whether one may take the interpretation "pentagram = man" put forward here as a basis for the interpretation of this crop circle.

However, the "man in the sun" could be also simply the sun god or derived from it the sun angel.

170

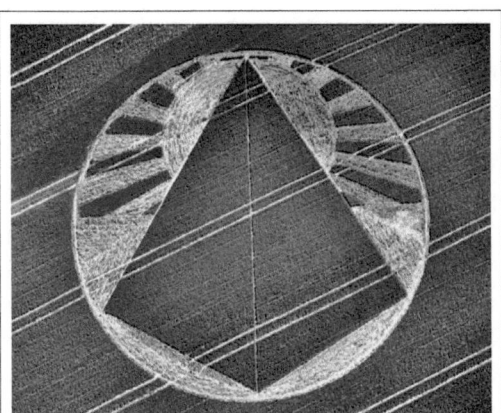

234. pyramid
(Wiltshire, England, 2001)

This 3D image of a sunrise over a pyramid seems a bit man-made …

There are 12 bright rays to be seen, which would fit the sun. But if you would count the rays behind the pyramid, you would get about 16-17 rays – but this is not a compelling argument.

This pyramid is very steep – even steeper than the pyramids in Central America … Only the very small pyramids on Egyptian tombs, which are only 3-5 meters high, are thus steep.

III 15. Organic forms

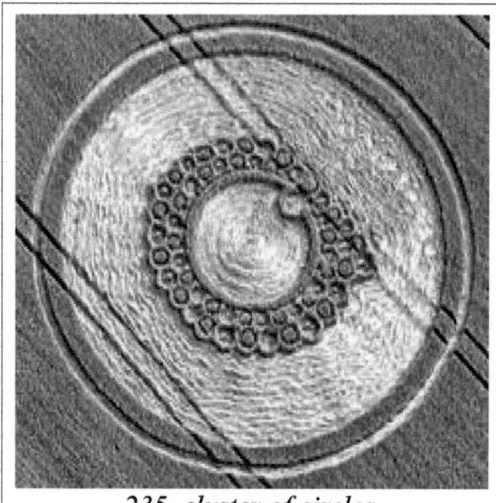

235. cluster of circles
(Wiltshire, England, 2011)

This ring is a bit curious, because on the one hand it is quite regular in shape, but on the other hand it is quite irregular.

It has an inner and an outer narrow ring. The inner ring has an indentation that looks like a gate (top right).

To the left of the gate, first half, then "bubbles with filling" appear, which look a bit like frogspawn. These "bubbles" run counter-clockwise in a circle around the center circle and then a second time as a second, outer "bubble layer". It ends shortly before the gate, where the beginnings of a third "bubble layer" can be seen – but already before the gate, where it looks a bit chaotic. There seem to be a total of 56 half and whole "bubbles".

The "bubbles with filling" seem to come out of the gate and then attach themselves to the ring. This looks like a mother circle with many children circles. Is this the female counterpart to crop circle 172, in which sperm or worms have been depicted? Then the gate would be either the exit of the ovary or the womb.

In the white area of the wide circle ring, the grain has been placed in such a way that it appears soft like waves or wool – this would fit the interpretation of this circle ring as the womb.

- * ❀ * -

172

236. molekule

(Wiltshire, England, 2020)

Is this a fungus? Or a molecule? Or a complex chemical compound?

Below is a circular area with 8 small circles that looks like a stone circle, a nucleus, or a seed.

If the plant interpretation should be correct, the straight line, which goes out from the core, would be the stalk of the plant.

At the top joins a shape in which there are 3 large circles, 3 medium circles and outside in 3 bulges 3 small circles. These 3·3 circles symbolize self-expression and growth (impulse → structure → contact). The development is seen from the inside to the outside from the large to the medium to the small circles.

On the very outside, 8 lines with circular areas at their end then join – they repeat in the large shape, what is laid out in the germ in the small shape below (8 points).

The forms in this crop circle all merge into each other, i.e. all corners have been rounded and thus appear organic.

This crop circle plant seems much more convincing and archetypal than the blossom tree in crop circle 80 and therefore much less man-made.

173

III 16.   Structured areas

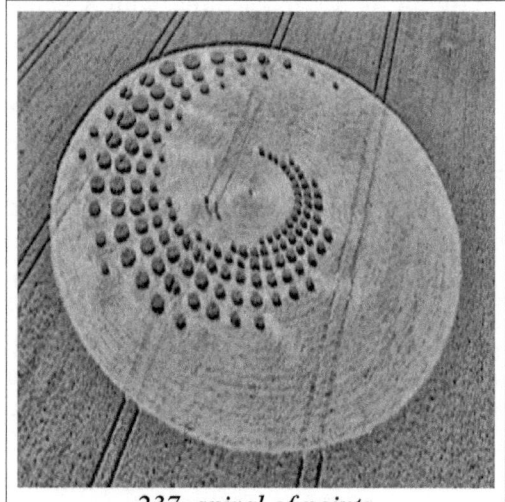

237. spiral of points
(Wiltshire, England, 2014)

Here you can see a spiral of dots. It consists of 9 rows of dots. From the inside out, these rows consist of the following number of dots: 16, 16, 16, 15, 15, 15, 14, 13 – a total of 145 dots.

The 13 times approx. 16 points in the 9 rows are arranged in such a way that they lie one behind the other as seen from the center of the circle and thus form 36 "rays of the centre".

The numbers are obviously not chosen at random: The $3 \cdot 12 = 36$ combines the "3" of the development (spiral) with the "12" of the circumference (zodiac) – it is consequently the "development into the circumference". The "16" is like the "8" the number of the perfection.

The "9" is either (seen from its structure symbolism) the $3 \cdot 3 = 9$ therefore the triple development (like on the kabbalistic tree of life) or (seen from its traditional symbolism) the transformation or the death – here the first possibility fits clearly better.

So here the perfect self-development is represented. It also fits extremely well that the throat chakra, which is responsible for unrestrained and uninhibited self-expression, has 16 petals.

- * ❁ * -

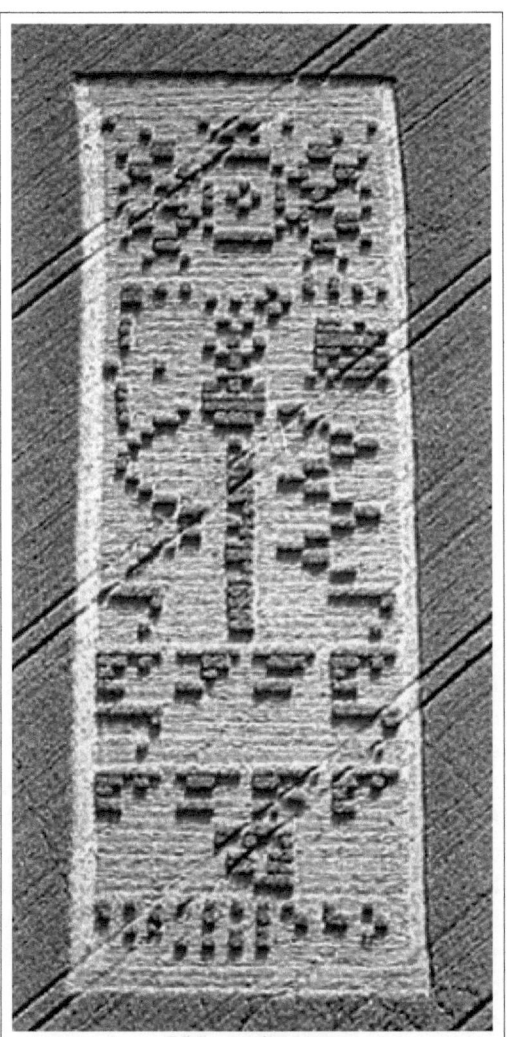

238. code-strip
(Hampshire, England, 2001)

This crop circle is hard to interpret … Is it a binary code? Or a tree with a star above it? Is the "star" a winged sun?

It is easy to see different areas or sections: three horizontal stripes at the bottom, a kind of fir tree above, then a square below under a horizontal line (sun in the sky?) and at the very top the "winged sun".

The lowest of the three stripes consists of 10 vertical lines of dots containing a maximum of 4 dots, the middle stripe consists of 5 symbols or similar, and the topmost consists of 4 symbols or similar.

The "fir tree" has a "trunk" with two circles on top.

Opposite the dark square on the right below the horizontal line, there is a vertical line of 7 dots with two companion dots (?).

So there is a triple foundation on which something grows upwards and unfolds above.

This is still rather abstractly formulated, but at least it represents a basic structure.

This crop circle belongs to the "crop circle photo" of an alien with which it appeared together.

175

239. code-strip and „alien-photo"

240. „alien-photo"

- * ❀ * -

241. circle code

(Hampshire, England, 2002)

242. UFO visit

What to say about it? A spiral with 12 turns – that would have to be the unfolding of a center: the sun with the zodiac.

The spiral begins with a central point and a slightly longer line that starts the spiral. Then follow rectangles of different lengths, between which are gaps of different sizes. On the very outside, the spiral is terminated by a spiral ring.

The "code" consists of 213 rectangles of 4 different lengths. Also the gaps have 5 or 6 different lengths. So it is not a simple binary code, which would consist only of the characters "0" and "1". Because of the variable length each position gets another quality – this "code" can therefore contain quite a lot of information – if it is indeed a code. With $2 \cdot 213 = 426$ characters (rectangles and gaps), which can have 4 or 5 properties, this is $213 \cdot 4 + 213 \cdot 5 = 1917$ informations.

This crop circle is part of a larger arrangement "with photo" – which raises big doubts about the "authenticity" of this crop circle. Why would aliens look so human?

176

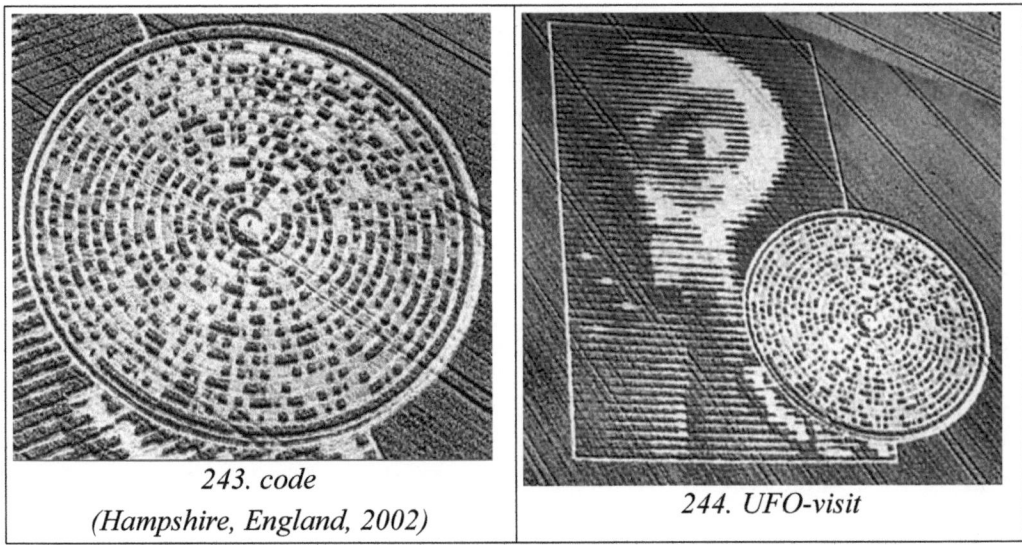

243. code
(Hampshire, England, 2002)

244. UFO-visit

Here is another variant of the previous crop circle – the "code" is even longer, but the alien looks just as human …

All 3 "alien crop circles" are from Hampshire … one from 2001 and two, very similar to each other, from 2002. Presumably the rather human crop circle artist who created these three crop circles loved in Hampshire … The two faces from 2002 are really well done technically.

- * ❀ * -

245. code
(place and year unknown)

This is another very plain binary code on $12 \cdot 12 = 144$ squares – possibly man-made.

- * ❀ * -

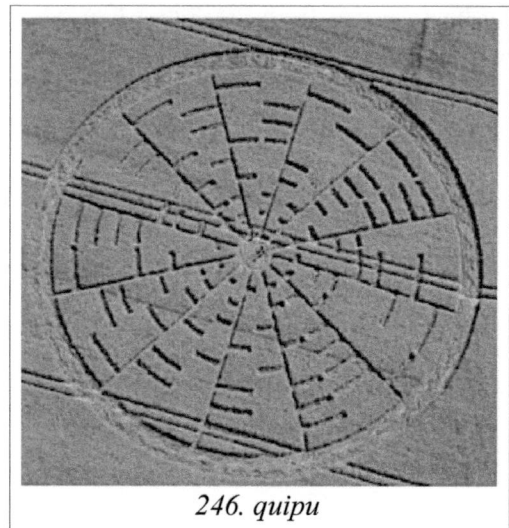

246. quipu
(Wiltshire, England, 2010)

This code is very reminiscent of the Ogham script of Great Britain and Ireland, and also somewhat reminiscent of the Quipu script of the Quetchuas ("Incas").

The similarity with the Ogham is so great that one can assume that this crop circle was "written" by humans.

- * ❀ * -

178

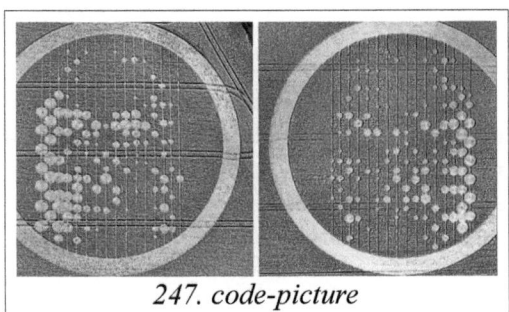

247. code-picture
(Berkshire, England, 2010)

Are these supposed to be two codes or two heavily pixelated images? As with the other code crop circles, the likelihood of human origins is decidedly high.

- * ❁ * -

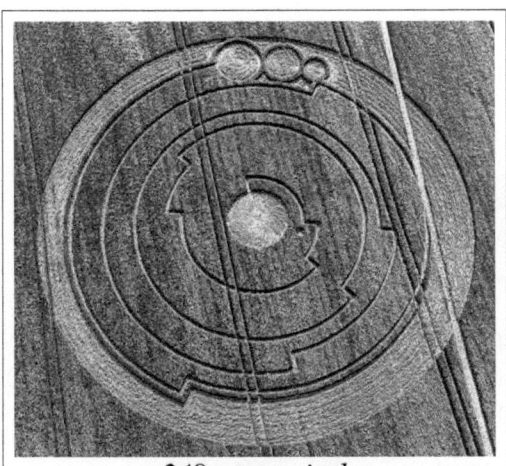

248. step-spiral
(Wiltshire, England, 2008)

This crop circle shows a "step-spiral" It turns outward from the central circle in 10 steps and ends in three circles ("3" = "development").

The arcs between each step are of different lengths: 110°, 40°, 140°, 40°, 180°, 330°, 70°, 220°, 180°, 130°. In total, these are exactly 4 circles around the center point, i.e. $4 \cdot 360° = 1440°$. A regularity is not evident.

Next to the 2nd step a small dot can be seen.

Possibly this is also a man-made crop circle.

179

III 17.   Complex forms

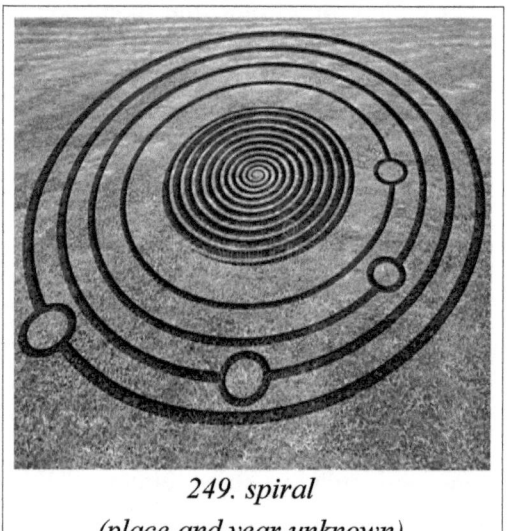

249. spiral
(place and year unknown)

In the center, a spiral with 12 turns can be seen, which is continued outside by 4 rings on 4 circular rings. Here we find again the classical combination of the "4" with the "12".

- * ❀ * -

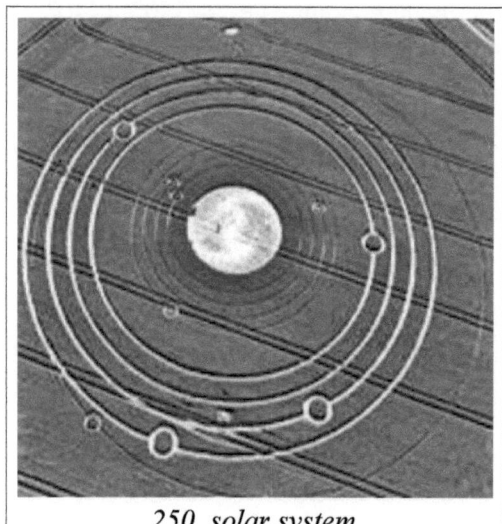

250. solar system
(Wiltshire, England, 2008)

Here, a circular area is surrounded by a group of 5 circular rings, followed by another 4 rings after a gap. On the very outside there is another excentric ring which intersects the outer ring. On all 10 circular rings there is a circle.

Obviously our solar system with the 10 planets has been depicted here – even the eccentric orbit of Pluto has been shown.

Above the whole there is still a single "observer circle".

Man-made?

This is a variant of the "polar motor": two polar circles and a rotating central circle. These three circles have been represented here as three gears or paddle wheels.

The connection between the three "wheels" is emphasized by the three outer rings, which are an endless loop, so to say two "S"s combined with each other.

251. gear
(Oxfordshire, England, 2008)

The three "cogwheels" have 18 "teeth" each, thus altogether 54. The inner ring of the large wheel has inside 14 dark points (standing grain sheaves). The numbers in this crop circle have no apparent symbolism.

- * ❀ * -

This crop circle consists of 24 small circles arranged in a square with square corner spaces.

Their connecting lines form a striking pattern that gives the impression of tension and resembles a condensator.

The circular area in the background seems hidden. Is it caught by the system of lines? Is it protected by it? Are the lines an expression of the circle?

If you look at the combination of circle and square in this crop circle graphic there are two elements that will signify stability: the four circles in each corner and the two diagonals that end in two circles each. Then on four lines there is a pair of circles at the top and bottom: polarity.

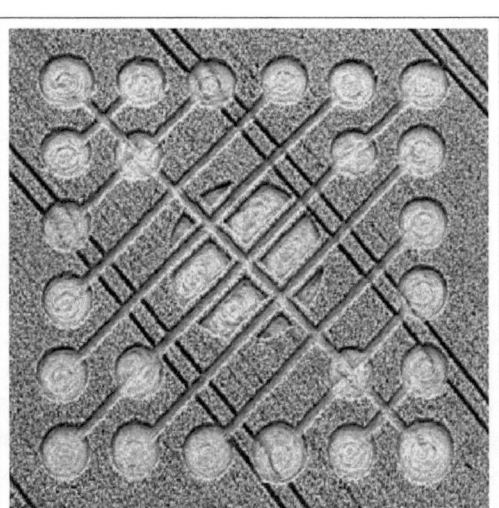

252. square of circles
(Oxfordshire, England, 2012)

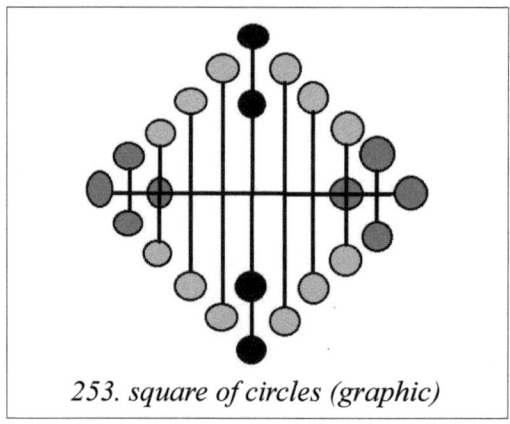

253. square of circles (graphic)

This gets clearer if you draw this as a graph (see left).

The two pairs of black polar circles would be in this graphic the "motor", the two dark grey groups of 4 circles the stabilizing "housing" and the 4 groups of 3 light grey circles the "gear", in which the movement is converted.

The 2·2=4 black circles together with the 2·4=8 dark gray circles are the motor in its housing = 12 balls. The 4·3 light gray balls are the gear = also 12 balls.

It seems as if here the "12" as the surrounding space and the conversion of the potential of the "1" in the center (circle in the background) has been represented in a rather creative way. Of course it's rather unsure, if this interpretation is really that what was intended by the maker of the crop circle …

- * ❀ * -

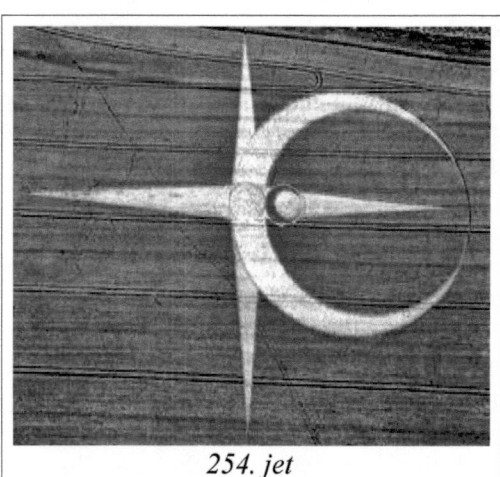

254. jet
(Wiltshire, England, 2012)

Here a pointed cross has been combined with a large crescent as well as with two circular areas and a dark crescent in the center – an unusual composition.

The cross as a structure of 4 is stability. The 4 sharp points of the cross give this cross something fortified. The circle in the center of the cross centers it – the sun and the four directions.

The crescent rests in the central circle where it has its widest point, which is exactly the same as the diameter of the central circle. Consequently, both the pointed cross and the crescent are an expression of this central circle.

The second circle to the right of the central circle repeats the crescent: Both the large light crescent and the small dark crescent are created by placing a second, slightly smaller circle inside one circle, touching the right edge of the larger circle. The small circle with the dark crescent is an image of the large circle – it is its "seed" or "baby".

182

So a development to the right has been depicted – which is also a development from "pointed" to "round".

- *  * -

255. bow-system

(Netherlands, 1999)

A strange "knot" has been depicted here, with arcs running in three different directions. The arc sections with the larger circles are each in front of the arc sections with the smaller circles. The arc sections with the larger circles are also located in front of the ring and the arc sections with the smaller circles are located behind the ring. The main function of this ring is to facilitate the spatial location of this arc system.

Such complex arcs are found in the organ of equilibrium in the ear (vestibular organ), that can sense the movement of the body in the three directions.

In Waldorf schools, it is common to have students bend such arches out of thin copper tubing to help develop spatial awareness.

Is this just a sophisticated 3D representation or is this more? The arc shape seems to be made of $3 \cdot 36 = 108$ circles – that would be $9 \cdot 12$ circles, which is probably not a coincidence.

In India and with the Teutons and consequently already with the original Indo-Europeans the "108" has been a sacred number. It is composed of the factors "$2 \cdot 2 \cdot 3 \cdot 3 \cdot 3$", which can be completed by a "1" to "$1 \cdot 2 \cdot 2 \cdot 3 \cdot 3 \cdot 3$" and then can be written elegantly as power factors: "1^1-2^2-3^3" The Indo-Europeans have obviously liked to play with numbers …

The "108" summarizes the three powers of the three most important numbers: $1 =$ identity, $2 =$ polarity, and $3 =$ development/cycle.

The "108" has been connected with the sun and with the sungod-godfather (Dhyaus, Tyr) by the Indians as well as by the Teutons. The bow system in this crop circle can therefore also be understood as a sun representation – even if this would then be a rather "exotic" version of a sun representation.

- *  * -

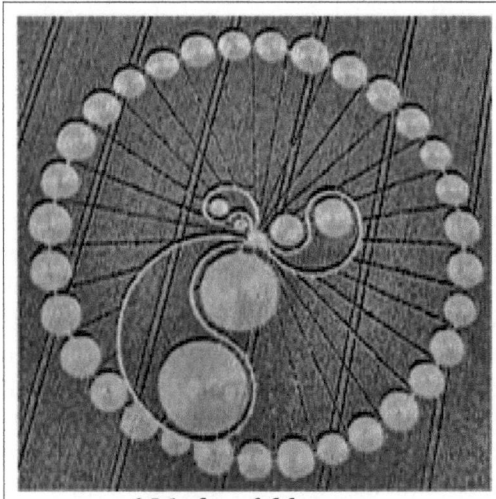

256. threefold vortex
(Wiltshire, England, 2003)

This is a crop circle that at first seems a bit confusing and complex. However, on closer inspection, it is quite simple, but at the same time even more complex than it appears to be at first glance.

The crop circle is simpler because the shape in the center consists of three equal parts, which arise in three different sizes from the center.

These three shapes are composed of two circles and an "arc-drop". This "bow-drop" is a "half yin/yang sign without a point in the center". This form, which consists of a half circle and an "S", is usually called "Miribota" (Persian: "tuft of leaves, shrub").

The two circles are the polarity – the Miribota is formed by the combination of these two circles and the large rotating circle. The rotating central circle, the "S" and the Miribota are thus largely identical in their symbolism.

A threefold polarity sounds like the usual symbolism of the "3": Expansion, Development and Unfolding.

The outer ring consists of 32 circles, to which 32 rays lead from the center – this confirms the expansion and at the same time shows that this circle should be perfect, since the "32" like the "16" shares the symbolism of the "8", of which it is the 2-fold or the 2·2-fold.

The largest of the 3 Miribotas overlaps three of the circles of the outer circular ring. Does this mean that the Miribota goes beyond the boundary? Is this aggression or simply joy of discovery?

The crop circle is also more complex than meets the eye because the circles that make up the outer ring are of different sizes. There appear to be three sizes, but they are irregularly distributed.

- * ✾ * -

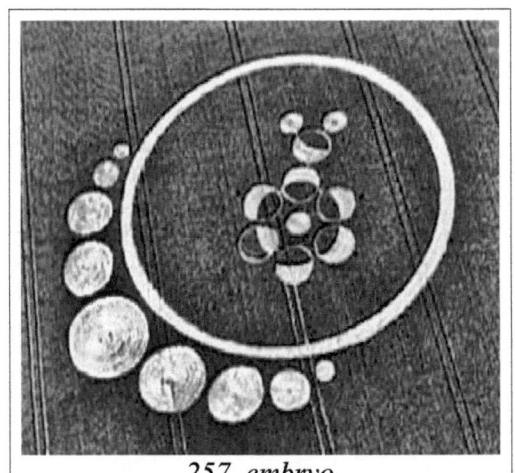

257. embryo
(Wiltshire, England, 2013)

This crop circle has a striking structure. Like many crop circles, it has an outer ring, but inside this ring "floats" a structure that has no relation to either the ring or the center of the ring.

This structure consists of a medium sized central ring with a circular area in the center. On this ring lie the centers of six half-sized circular rings, all of which are half light and half dark.

Since all the light halves except one point outwards, they act like a ray, like an expression of the center of the middle-sized circular ring.

In one of these circles, however, the light side has been exchanged with the dark side. This circle looks inward, so to speak, and not outward. This circle points to the middle, largest of the 9 circles that are on the outside of the large ring. The effect therefore goes from this large, middle circle of the 9 circles to the "reversed" circle on the middle-sized ring.

This just dreates the impression that this is an uterus with a fetus being nourished from the mother or from the placenta by umbilical cord (which is not shown here). The shape of the 9 circles also corresponds very well to the shape of a human placenta. The umbilical cord, which is not shown, runs from the largest of the 9 circles on the outside (mother) to the "inverted circle" on the inside (embryo).

On the "embryo" "swimming" in the large ring there is another appendix. It consists of a circle, which is polar colored to the circle, on which it hangs.

Is this the head of the embryo?

The lines from the center of the appendix circle to the two small circles and to the circle to which it is attached all have a distance of 120°. The appendix circle acts actively through the two small circles. Is it a sperm that just fertilizes an egg in the uterus? "Sex in a crop circle," so to speak?

- * ❀ * -

185

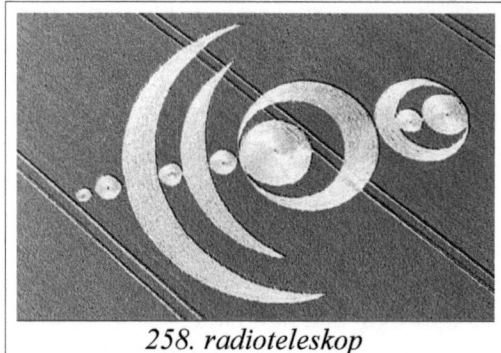

258. radioteleskop
(Moiselles, France, 2019)

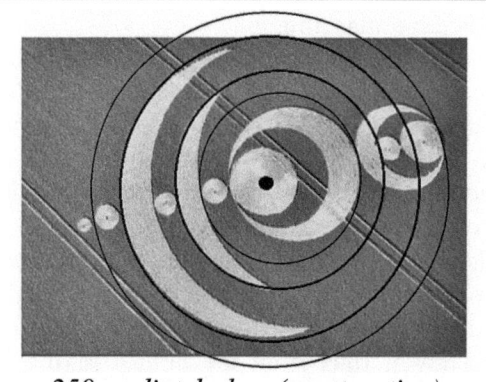

259. radioteleskop (construction)

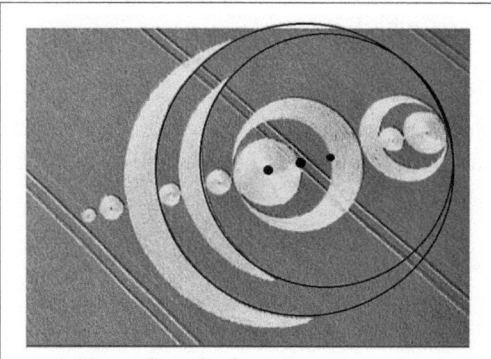

260. radioteleskop (construction)

This crop circle is reminiscent of a radio telescope.

All 13 symbols are on the same axis, which shows that an effect in one of the directions of this axis has been represented here.

The big circle with the crescent and the smaller circle in it is the focal point of the system as sketch 259 shows - almost all measurements refer to this big bright circle.

The inner arcs of the two large crescents have their centers at regular intervals to the right of this main center. These shapes have been laid out systematically and regularly.

The outer arcs of the crescents refer to the main center, while the inner arcs refer to points to the right of this center. The two focal points (centers of the inner arcs) shift the attention in two equal steps towards the right. Thus, a development from left to right along the axis is shown.

The three circles of the same size, which separate and surround the two crescents, are thus something like "spacers". The small dot on the far left is apparently simply something like an end point - a plug, a nut, a lock, or the like.

The dark and the light crescent on the right of the main circle are therefore the development of the main circle – the size of these two development steps is determined by the two focal points of the two crescents.

Finally, on the far right, a somewhat smaller circle can be seen, which contains a medium sized circle, a small circle and two crescents. If one understands the small circle as a spacer, this circle is an exact reflection of the circle to the left of it.

This right circle is, so to speak, a self-image that the main circle sends out to the right.

- *  * -

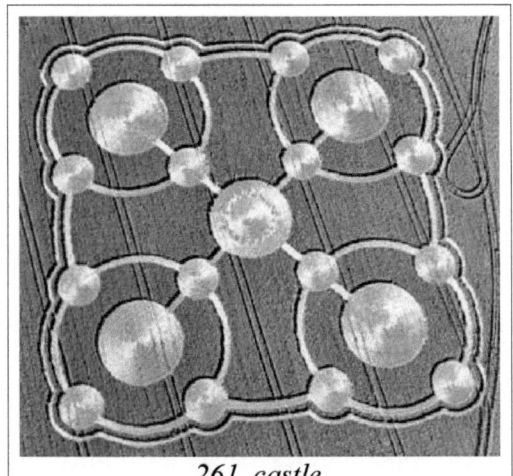

261. castle

(Wiltshire, England, 2005)

This crop circle has a very regular structure:

4 large rings in the corners;
5 medium circles in these circular rings and in their center;
each of the five rings is surrounded by 4 small circles – since the 4 outer circles each share a small circle with the middle circle, this makes 16 small circles;
the five circles are connected by 8 short straight lines;
the 4 outer circles are surrounded by a ring that passes through the centers of the four small circles around it;
around the middle circle runs a much larger ring, of which only a small piece can be seen at the centers of the four sides – it runs through the centers of the four outer circles;
the whole is surrounded by an "arc-square" consisting of 24 sections – 12 lage ones and 12 small ones.

This crop circle is so regularly constructed that it is almost a simple fractal – only the straight lines have not been multiplied in a fractal-like manner.

This crop circle mandala spans a space by emphasizing the "4" and keeps it stable. The straight lines mark the 4 outer circles as 2 polar circles – which gives power to the whole. The whole shape is held together by the outer line as by a skin and centered by the middle circle and the cross.

- *  * -

262. triskelis
(Wiltshire, England, 2008)

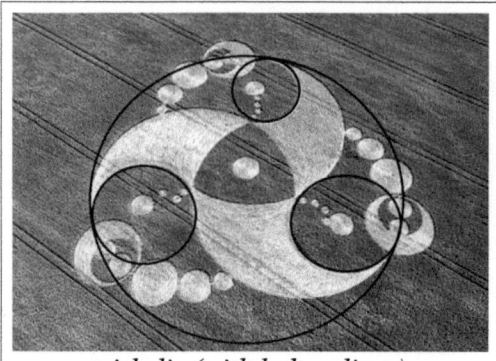

triskelis (with ledger lines)

Here, apparently, a triskelis has been depicted as a crop circle. A triskelis is a "tripod", a "three-leg" – the face of the sun, which has three legs and is thus identified as a celestial wanderer. The "3" is the number of development, of the cycle and therefore also of the migration of the sun and the course of the sun. This motif is known throughout Eurasia from the Celts and the Greeks to the Mesopotamian peoples and the Japanese.

The central arc triangle is the face of the sun, the dot in its center is the sun's eye, and the three bright, curved arc triangles are the three legs of the sun.

The three crescent circles, which contain two small circles and from which three wider circles hang, are either the "wake" of the "sun-legs" or the propulsion of the legs – the first variant seems to be more plausible.

At the three points of contact between two "sun-legs" a small circle can be seen, which is connected to the central circle "under" each "sun-leg" by 2 or 3 points. On closer inspection, it can be seen that this makes the triskelis a 3-polar yin/yang sign (3 "drops"). In Japan, the triskelis, which is called "tomoe" there, is represented in exactly this way.

The different size of the three small ledger line circles is only due to a perspective distortion.

- * ❀ * -

188

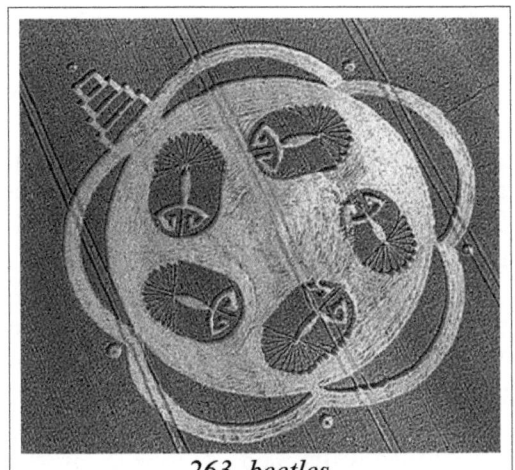

263. beetles
(Wiltshire, England, 2011)

The 5 strange shapes in this crop circle look like crawling animals. The double spiral looks like mouth and eyes – according to the rotation of the double spiral in the "head" of the animal, something is picked up there by the "mouth" of the animal.

The "almonds" in the middle of the animals give the impression of back-spirals or similar.

The 12-15 rays at the back look almost like a drive. The base line of the 12 rays of each animal corresponds to the central axis of the animal following it. From the central axis of an animal, about 5 rays are on the left and about 7 rays are on the right.

What could 5 animals crawling behind each other in a circle mean?

The circle is surrounded by 5 crescents, which are not exactly the same width. In the angles and on the tower there are small circle areas with center – but not always exactly in the angle. The four-tiered tower is also a bit crooked.

The inaccuracies in the number of rays, the different thicknesses of the crescents as well as the crooked tower suggest that this crop circle was made by humans.

Moreover, this crop circle was made in two consecutive nights, which is quite a sure indication of human work. After the first night, in the lower third of the bright circle area, the crop had not yet been flattened. In case of an emergence by collective telekinesis, one would assume a symmetrical division of the process into two phases (e.g. the emergence of the details of the animals in the 2nd night) – although it is completely unclear why a crop circle should emerge in two instead of one phase by collective telekinesis.

- * ❀ * -

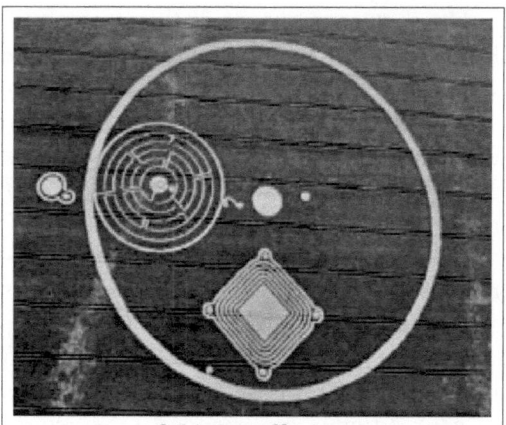

264. installation

(Cambridgeshire, England, 2001)

The first thing to notice about this crop circle is that many of its shapes are not quite precise – suggesting manufacture by untrained people.

The basic structure consists of a central circle, a very large ring, a labyrinth-like circle, a square at right angles to the labyrinth and some "appendages".

The labyrinth is very unsystematic – neither a real "search labyrinth" nor a Neolithic symmetrical labyrinth representing the way to the otherworld.

The square looks like a fortress with 6 concentric walls and 4 towers at the corners.

The various "appendages" are not arranged very coherently.

All in all, this crop circle seems to be a "sculptor's installation" without too much concept, conclusiveness and depth – so it is quite certainly man-made ...

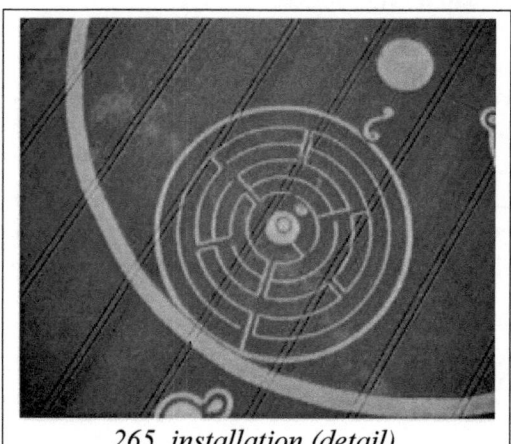

265. installation (detail)

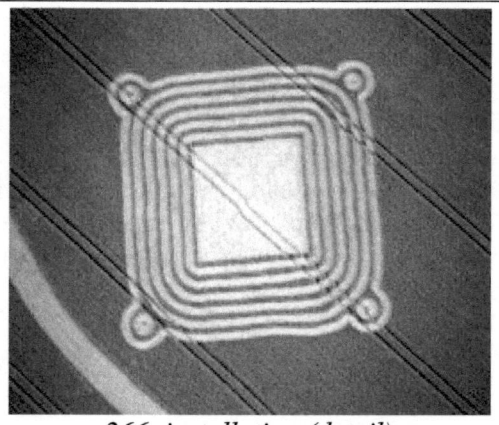

266. installation (detail)

- * ❀ * -

190

267. cross with roots
(Wiltshire, England, 2017)

First of all, this is a simple 4-polar mandala.

However, it is noticeable that the four outer circles have a small dark center, but the central circle does not – possibly the 4 elements have already been gathered in the 4 outer circles, but the quintessence has not yet been called into the central circle.

But why is there a quarter circle at the outer end of one of the circles with 7 semicircles hanging from its arc? Is this a hint that one can find one's own center only when one has awakened his 7 chakras? Then the central circle would also be connected with the heart chakra, which would be quite conclusive. However, the representation of this connection by a quarter circle attached to an outer circle is quite strange, since it emphasizes one of the four elements and not the balance of the four elements or the like.

268. dumbbell
(Wiltshire, England, 2007)

In this crop circle, two very different circular areas have been connected by a line – so it is obviously the polarity principle.

In the right circle there is a light octagram in the center, around it 8 dark diamonds, which together with 8 light triangles then form an octagon, which is then completed by 8 dark triangles (which form squares with the light triangles) again to an octagram.

This shape lies in a circular area, creating 8 arc triangles. This circular area is connected to 8 dark arcs, which are interrupted by light stripes. These light stripes begin at the tips of the dark triangles, are continued by a dark square in the light outer circle, and then end in a "defense triangle" on the outside of this outer circle.

This crop circle, composed mainly of straight lines, is orderly, stable, static, extroverted, and defensive.

The left crop circle, on the other hand, is round and characterized by the "3": 1 center circle, adjoining it 3 rings, in which lies another circle, drawn towards the center and connected to it by a short axis, and 3 circles between the 3 circle rings, pushing outwards towards the outer ring.

This crop circle is round, dynamic, designed to evolve, and both introverted and extroverted.

The right static-cornered crop circle and the left round-dynamic crop circle are obviously contrast-complements – both are however well centered. There should be a connecting tension between them, which is also expressed by the straight line.

The two long lines next to the straight line, each having an angle at its two ends, look like a tube or a pipe or a stabilizing and protecting structure. The short straight lines next to the long straight lines seem to be some kind of reinforcement of the long straight lines.

On the far right there is still a circular area with a small dot pointing to the complex crop circle. One could think that the left crop circle is a "generator", the straight line is a kind of tube, the right crop circle is an optical lens and the circle on the far right is what the generator emitted through the tube and focused through the lens.

Finally, a small companion circle can be seen in the lower right.

- * ❀ * -

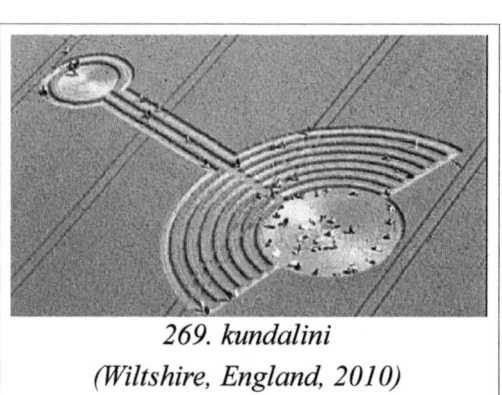

269. *kundalini*
(Wiltshire, England, 2010)

This crop circle is plain, but it has an unusual shape.

On the left is a bright circular area with a dark ring. It looks like a round vessel.

Then follows a straight line with a bright inward space connected to the circular area. The dark ring merges seamlessly into the "envelope" of the bright straight line. This straight line acts like a conduit.

To the right is a large circular area, half open and half protected and held by 7 half rings. The outer half ring is the continuation of the circular ring of the left circle and the "envelope of the line". These half circles are actually quarter circles, since the bright straight line originating in the bright circular area on the left runs without interruption through the 7 half circles into the large bright circular area.

One could understand the left circle as the origin, the line as the dynamic, the 7 semicircles as the unfolding and the great circle as the creation or the crowning.

This would correspond to the Kundalini in the root chakra (left circle), its rising

192

(channel of life force), the 7 chakras (half circles) as well as the awakened crown chakra (right circle). In this interpretation, the root chakra and the crown chakra would have been cited twice (as a circle and as a chakra semicircle) – but since they, together with the conduction, represent the basic dynamics of the chakra awakening, this would be quite plausible.

270. „parachute"
(Dorset, England, 2014)

Judging from the direction of rotation of the two spirals in the semicircle on the right, there is a movement here from right to left. However, the surface of a semicircle as a "receiver" is quite unusual – one would rather expect a bowl (crescent) as a receiver. However, the direction of the rotation of the two spirals is clear.

The arc-triangle on the right between the two spirals is therefore the one that receives and picks up that what comes from the right to this crop circle. Is the arc-triangle between the two spirals therefore something like a lens or an eye? The received collects in the big circle in the center of this semicircle.

From this circle onward there is a forwarding to the focal point which follows next on the long straight line (longitudinal axis) seen from the center of the semicircle. This point lies on the circumference circle of the semicircle, if you add the missing half to it. The distance of this point from the focal point is therefore exactly as large as the radius of this semicircle. This circle is the point of a triangle with its baseline on the diameter of the halfcircle.

From this central point two further straight lines go to the two corners of the semicircle. On these two straight lines there are two small and one large circle – a polar construction?

The radius of the semicircle occurs three times on the longitudinal axis:

    1. from the outer arc of the arc triangle to the center of the semicircle,
    2. from the center of the semicircle to the focal point where the three straight lines from the semicircle meet, and
    3. from the focal point to the circle in the center of the crescent.

From the crescent circle two "supports" go to the two large circles on the two semicircle corner straight lines. On each of them is a circle where the tips of the crescent end.

What are the dynamics of this crop circle?

- Something arrives from the right and is taken up over the arc triangle and creates thereby left and right a vortex (spiral) each.

- What is picked up is concentrated in the center circle and then passed on to the focal circle.

- Between the semicircle corners and the focal point circle there is a polar circle construction in each case. This means that a voltage is built up between the focal point circle and the corners of the semicircle. Is it to stabilize the focal point circle and its position?

- The taken up now flows further into the crescent center circle, whereby this flow is stabilized by two further straight lines, which starts from the center circle of the two polar circle constructions and consequently has energy.

- On each of the two lines just mentioned there is another circle which holds the ends of the crescent and thus stabilizes its position.

- The crescent forms the space which takes up the received.

Altogether a receiving and integrating is represented here. An optical perception with the eye? A radio telescope? A conception?

- *  * -

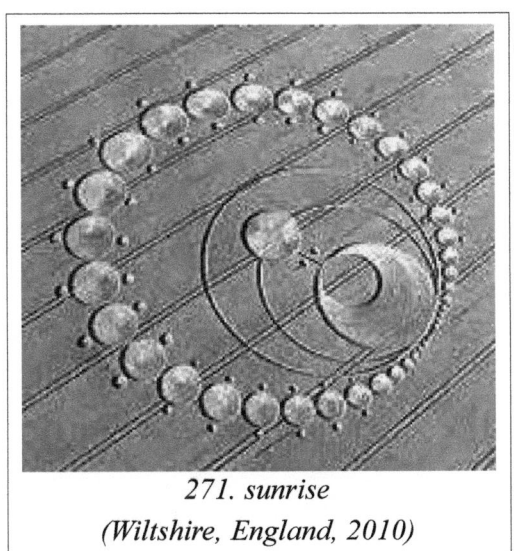

271. sunrise
(Wiltshire, England, 2010)

This crop circle bears a distinct resemblance to the solar crop circles.

The smaller ring on the right contains a small, dark circular area in a light crescent that looks like a mouth; the short straight line is the nose and the two attachment points next to it are the eyes. They are surrounded by a "hair" crescent like the sun-faces on the crop circles already considered.

Interesting here is the circular area on top of the head – the crown chakra?

At the same time, the "mouth" and the "crown chakra" (which are equal-sized circles of opposite color) together with the "nose" are a polarity system that brings the basic tension into this crop circle.

The outer circle, which acts like a ray aureole, consists of 40 circles, of which 23 have two companion points and 17 are without companions. A strange number – 24 (2·12 zodiac signs) and 16 ("perfection") would have been much more plausible …

- * ❀ * -

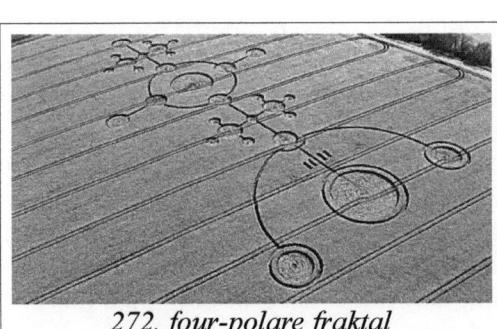

272. four-polare fraktal
(Wiltshire, England, 2009)

This crop circle seems at first sight very different from the previous circles.

Its starting point is the ring on the upper left, which has a center and one circle in each of the four directions – the 4-point mandala already well known from other crop circles.

Each of these four points forms an "offshoot": a line at the end of which is another circle.

Two of these circles (top left and bottom right) now again form the center of four circles, which are connected to the central circle by lines.

Here, too, each two circles again send out four lines ending in points – so this crop circle has been partly constructed according to the fractal principle.

This quite static fractal part rests in the "dent" of a semicircle ending in two circular areas with ring. In the extension of the fractal axis lies a straight line, which leads to a third, larger circular area with ring. This straight line is accompanied by two double lines, which act like a stabilization or like a capacitor.

The fractal works by the fact that it is not completely 4-symmetrical, but develops alternately a 4 circles and 2 circles. The fractal would be then on the one hand very stable by the 4-polarity and would produce on the other hand a tension by the 2-polarity.

The relationship of the semicircle construction to the fractal is not quite apparent. Is it a support? Or an energy-storage device? The semicircle doesn't look like an energy recycler. Or is this again an eye, a radio telescop or a conception?

One of the two circles at the end of the semicircle seems to protrudes further to the right than the other – but this is not true, for this is just an optical effect created by the angel of approx. 75° (and not 90°) between the axis of the the crop circle and the traktor tracks.

- * ✿ * -

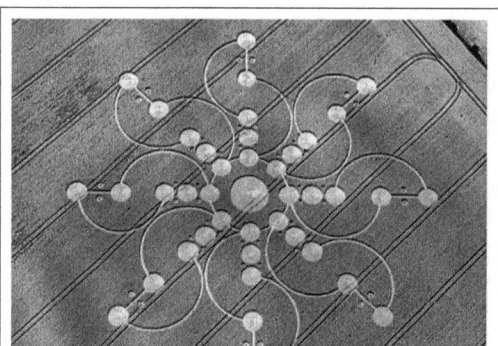

273. vortex

(Wiltshire, England, 2009)

An interesting construction can be seen here.

In the center there is a circular surface and around it there is a ring with **8** smaller circular surfaces, each of which is the beginning of a row of three such circular surfaces: The center (1) radiates (3) out ward in the relaxed ordered form (8).

These eight rows of three circles have been stabilized by two pairs of fixing points.

From the 1st circle as well as from the 3rd circle a half ring starts, which ends at two circles of the same size as the circles in the rows of three. This pair of circles is exactly as long as the row of three circles, but they are connected only by a line and not by a third, middle circle. To the left and right of this line, a small ring with a central dot can be seen – probably two attachment points.

On the inside a developing row of three, on the outside a tension pair – what does this result in? In any case, this construction causes a flow of energy, which is represented by two semicircles each, which together with the circle-rows result in the meanwhile well known "S".

What is the purpose of the tension at the outer edge? Is this the necessary distinction between inside and outside and thus the readiness for self-defense?

196

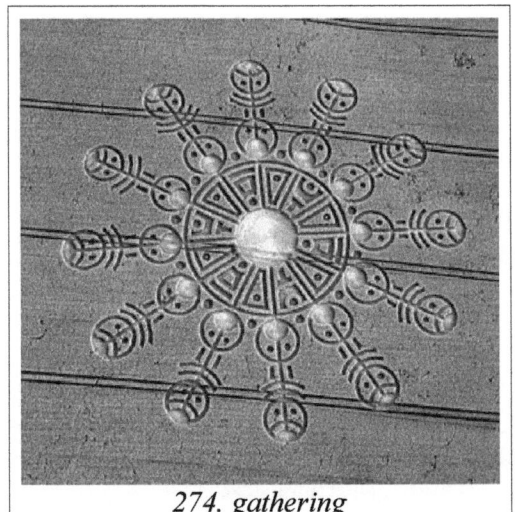

274. gathering

(Wiltshire, England, 2009)

Here, a gathering of 12 "people" seems to have been depicted sitting around a round "table".

This table is quite interesting. Every other of the 12 table segments contains a triangle with a dot in the center. The remaining 6 segments alternately contain two more characters, so there are 3 of each. This is an unusual division, since it does not correspond to the elements of the zodiac, their dynamics or the planets.

Each segment contains a circle – the triangle segments still contain a small light dot in their center. So these 6 triangle segments are more "active" than the 6 other segments.

The 6 triangle segments act as if the triangle merely fills this segment, but does not add any other property. Are these 6 segments therefore neutral in this crop circle? Do only the other 6 segments have an effect?

3 of these segments consist of a "T" and a "U". This looks like a pedestal and a support in which the core point is located. This makes the impression as if it could be the element "earth". From the arrangement of the four elements in the zodiak then the 6 triangles would have to correspond then to the elements "fire" and "air" – which are possibly inactive here.

The 3 other segments consist of the point below, an arc-square above and a horizontal straight line at the top. This seems to be very passive – the centre has sunk down to the bottom. This could well represent the element of water.

The 12 "people" sitting at the table have a complex structure: 2 polar circles connected by a line, separated by two arcs and stabilized by two short straight lines.

The inner circle has a circular surface as "mouth", the outer circle has an "almond" as mouth – otherwise these two circles are the same, which speaks for their interpretation as polar circles. Also the two stabilization lines have appeared so far only between two polar circles. The faces of these "double-people" look in opposite directions.

The faces are interestingly not in front of one of the 12 segments, but always exactly between two segments. In front of each segment there is a stabilization point. Therefore the twelve people cannot be thwelce signs of the zodiac.

197

The straight line between two segments is continued as a line in the "faces" and as their connecting line. In the faces, they form the "nose". The two "eyes" will be stabilization points.

The two arcs could represent a concentration on the outside, but also a protection against the outside.

The inner face is the contact to the inside, the outer circle is the contact to the outside – inner perception/action and outer perception/action.

These 12 "double people" correspond apparently to the polar circles in the previous crop circle (273). Both crop circles apparently represent a person (central circle, ring of 8 or 12) as well as their external relationship (8 or 12 polar circles).

A b C   D   EF g h IJKlMNop q

275. long crop circle
(St. Hippolyte, France, 2019)

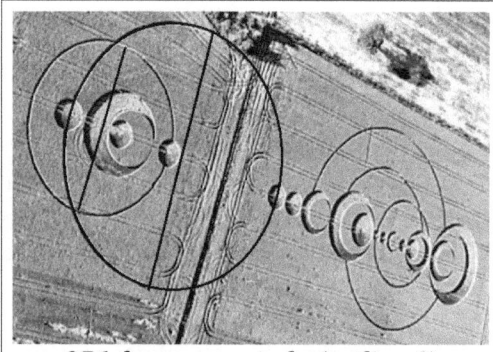

276. long crop circle (outline 1)

This is a crop circle in the style of "long crop circles", most of which occurred in 1999.

There are 10 circles, 2 rings, 6 crescents, and 4 semicircles with the center points all on the same axis.

The circles are labeled below the image on the left with capital letters and the crescents with lower case letters.

At first, it looks as if there are two parts, despite the common longitudinal axis. But if you complete the large semicircle on the left side and add its diameter transverse to the longitudinal axis, two things become clear: On the one hand, the center of the first circle "E" lies on this ring, and on the other hand, the center of this semicircle completed to a ring lies exactly to the right of the circle "D".

Actually one would expect that the center of this large ring lies in the center of the circle "D" and not at its edge, but this is not so. The semicircle is exactly half a circle and not 48% or 53% of a circle – the connecting line of the two ends of the semicircle intersects the longitudinal axis exactly next to circle "D" and

198

not in circle "D".

Circle "C" is exactly in the middle of circle "A" and circle "D" – so one could consider these 3 circles as a polar system. However, the left ring does not really fit to this assumption, because its center is in the crescent and not in the central circle. Moreover, one should expect crescents rather at the outer circles and not at the central circle.

E F g h I J K l M N o p   q

277. long crop circle (detail)

The right part of the complex crop circle 276 has a clear center: the circle "M" in the center of the small ring. This ring intersects the longitudinal axis in the center of circle "J" and in the center of sickle "o". One could consider the circle "N" and the sickle "l" as the two poles of the circle "M", but the shapes adjoining them do not make much sense, i.e. they do not show symmetries consistent with the previous observations of other crop circles.

The three semicircles in the right part of the crop circle can be connected to a spiral, which would have its center approximately in circle "M" (see sketch 2). It goes through the center of the circle of the crescent "p" and along the left side of the crescent "h".

The centers of the three semicircles do not lie in the center of circles on the longitudinal axis (see sketch 3). Moreover, the ring with the circle "M" in its center does not seem to be completely circular.

199

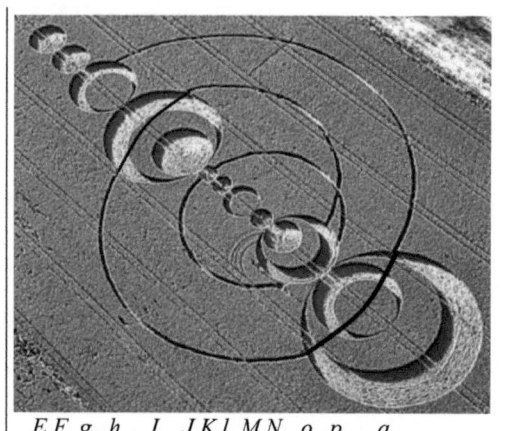

E F g h I J K l M N o p q

278. long crop circle (outline 2)

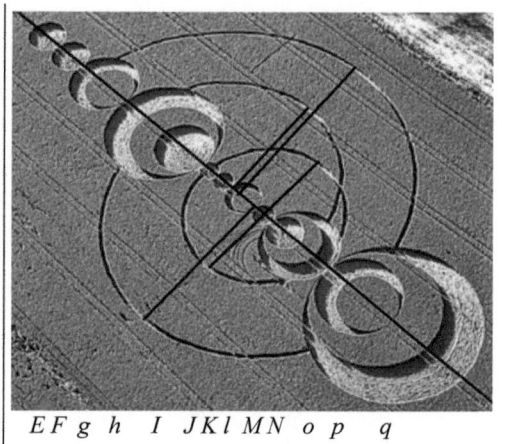

E F g h I J K l M N o p q

279. long crop circle (outline 3)

All in all, it seems as if this crop circle looks like a crop circle, but does not adhere to the usual rules of symmetry, which give these crop circles their special appearance. Therefore the assumption is obvious that this crop circle has been made by people who have not been too much connected with the "crop circle inspiration" either.

This crop circle also does not come from the "crop circle center" in Wiltshire, but from the south of France – which of course does not mean that only Wiltshire crop circles can be "real".

- *  * -

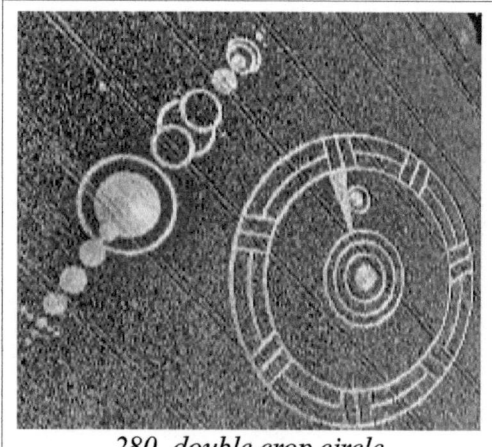

280. double crop circle
(Essex, England, 2014)

Two crop circles whose distance is less than their diameter should probably be considered together – here the distance is less than 1/4 of the diameter or length of the two crop circles.

The curious thing about this constellation is that there are no conspicuous axes or the like in these two crop circles which refer to elements in the other crop circle.

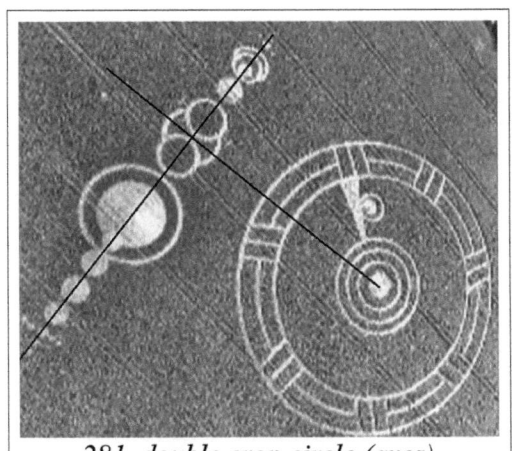

281. double crop circle (axes)

There is only one reference between the two: To the right of the center of the long crop circle (large light circle) is a polarity system consisting of two small rings and a large ring between them, with the centers of the small circles lying on the large ring. If you put a straight line through the center of the large circular ring, which intersects the connecting line between the two small circular rings at right angles, this line meets the center of the round crop circle.

The center of the long crop circle is a circular surface with a ring – a self-sufficient, in itself resting, protected element. On the edge of this circular area there is a small circle whose center is exactly on the edge of the circular area – a kind of "offshoot" of the large circular area moving to the left. There follow 3 circles of the same size – a development. It ends in a very small circular area, which has 2 small points each in the direction of the axis as well as to the left and to the right, thus forming a cross – this seems to be the end point of the development in this direction – a seal, a lid, a screw plug or similar.

In the other direction, the polar system is connected to the central circle – here, a voltage is generated and with it, the large ring is made to rotate. The polar system is followed by a small circular area and then a second, even smaller circular area with two attached crescents – the first crescent completely surrounds the circular area, the other crescent only half. This circular area reminds of the sun face. The end is a very small circular area with one point each in the direction of the axis as well as on the left and on the right. They form the end again – but why are here only $3 \cdot 1$ points and not $3 \cdot 2$ points as at the other end of the axis?

On the left and on the right of the central circle there are 4 circles each: on the left the offshoot and the 3 development circles, on the right the polar system, the single circle and the sun face. If these two sequences of 4 circles each should be equivalent, the forming of an offshoot, which then develops, would have to correspond to the building of a tension, an intermediate circle and the sun-face. One could say that a tension is needed, so that an offshoot can develop to a sun-face. The sun-face is probably something like the "complete unfolding of a seed".

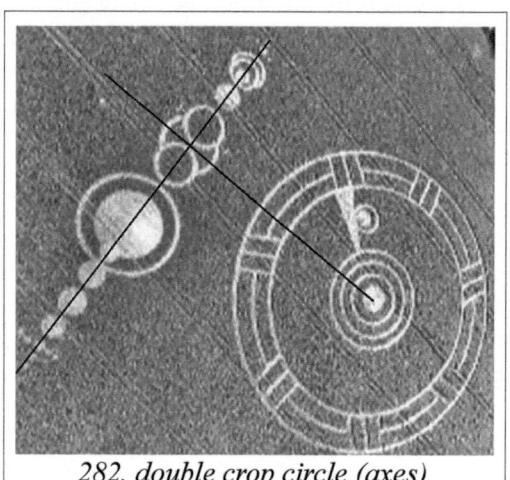

282. double crop circle (axes)

Now there is still the round crop circle. It consists in the inside of a small, central circle surface which is surrounded by 3 circle rings: an unfolding (3) center. It is surrounded from the very outside by two dark circular rings, from which 2 rays emerge diagonally (not at 90°) at 7 places – the round crop circle seems to rotate. If the "7" should refer to the chakras, the central circular area would obviously develop in all 7 chakras (3 rings).

On the wide, dark ring, a ray can be seen at the top, next to which is a circular area with an enveloping crescent (sun face). The axis of this ray points past the long crop circle.

Both crop circles seem to send something out or to hold something ready: the round crop circle the small circular area with sickle and the long crop circle the small circular area with 2 sickles. The long crop circle wants to expand or emit something and the round crop circle wants to radiate. The only noticeable elongated element in the round crop circle is the wide beam from which the crescent circle hangs.

Should the round circle represent a woman with vagina and ovum and the long crop circle a man with sperm? Then the conceived child would arise from the two sun faces. In the crop circle 270 probably also a procreation has been represented and in the crop circle 257 an embryo.

- *  * -

202

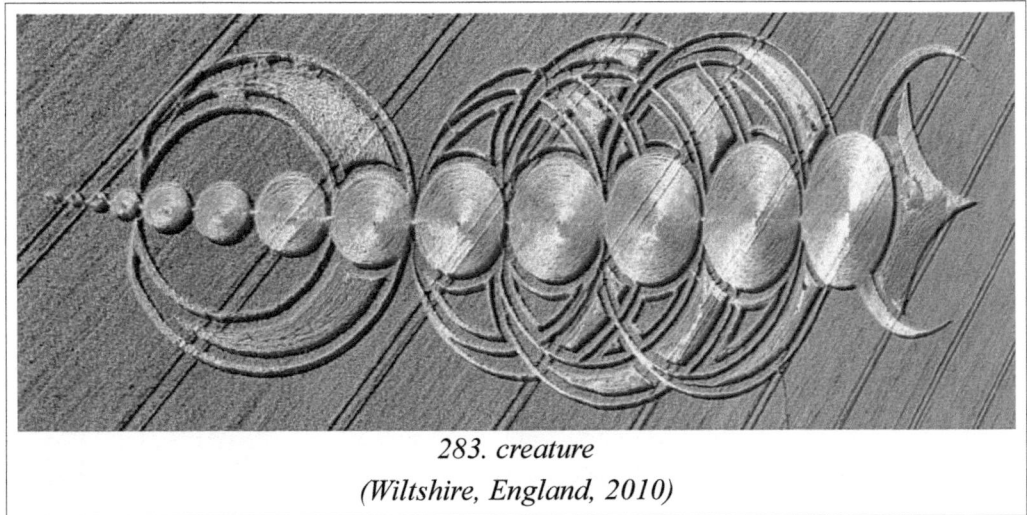

283. creature
(Wiltshire, England, 2010)

This is quite a long crop circle with many elements. The axis of this crop circle is formed by 13 circular spaces. 1 circle belongs to the "head/neck", 4 circles belong to the "chest", 4 circles belong to the "abdomen" and 4 circles belong to the "tail" – apparently a systematic structure. This diameter of circles is getting steadily smaller towards the tail – it is like the vertebrae of this creature.

Through the head runs a narrow, long crescent, whose outer arc runs through the center of the circle – they look like horns or grasping pincers. In front of the circle, there is another small circle with two more smaller crescents in front of it, which together look like a horn or a snout.

On each of the first 3 of the 4 chest circles is a narrow crescent whose tips meet behind the next circle – this looks like ribs: a closed, protected area.

The 4 abdominal circles are enclosed by a crescent that starts from the first abdominal circle and is as wide as this circle – this acts like the abdominal space. This crescent has been cut off at its narrow end with a straight line – a very unusual element.

The 4 tail circles have no special features.

These 4 groups could represent an unfolding:

1. head   = center, origin, seed
2. chest   = impulse, expansion
3. abdomen   = form, structure
4. tail   = contact

However, these assignments don't quite fit, since the second area has the most

203

structure and the 4th area has no indication of contact.

Has the basic structure of a living creature simply been depicted here?

- *  * -

284. long complex form
(Wiltshire, England, 2004)

This long crop circle has a completely different structure than the previous one.

On its axis there are 27 circles, 1 ring, 3 crescents and 1 horizontal line. This shape can be divided into 6 parts:

1. the 3 "antennas",
2. the head with the crescents,
3. the neck with ring and circle,
4. the 1st abdominal segment with 5 circles of increasing size,
5. the 2nd abdominal segment with 5 circles of increasing size,
6. the 3rd body segment with 4 circles with increasing size.

285. long complex form (outline 1)

286. long complex form (outline 2)

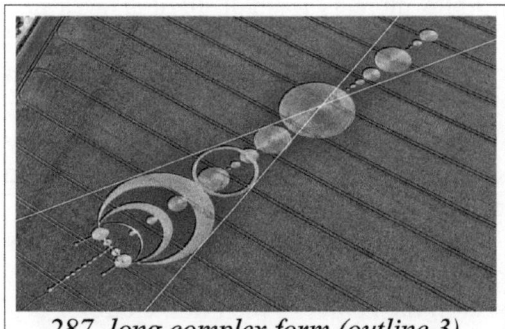

287. long complex form (outline 3)

At first, not much can be said about the 3 body segments. If you connect the outer edges of the circles with a line (tangent), you can see that the lines of the 3 segments are exactly parallel. Obviously these 3 segments strengthen each other and push towards the head.

The 4 circles of the head and the neck also have 2 common tangents, but they are not parallel with the tangents of the body spheres – obviously they have an independent dynamic. However, they involve the largest body circle – which is plausible, since the head and the neck are independent, but not completely independent of the rest of the body.

Also the outer edges of the 3 big circles of the 3 body segments can be connected with a common tangent.

The head/neck tangents and the other tangents, which are adjacent to the 3 largest body circles, intersect at the largest body sphere.

Furthermore, there are two common tangents at the largest crescent, at the neck circle and at the second largest circle of the first body segment, which then intersect in the center of the largest body circle.

There are some more tangents which are adjacent to several circles and then intersect in the center of another circle.

The neck ring with the crescent in it seems to be something like a forwarding organ. Similar shapes can be found, for example, in the dragonfly crop circle.

First of all, unfortunately, all this only shows how carefully this crop circle has been constructed and laid out. At least it becomes clear that it represents something organic, since such multiple connections and multiple symmetries are a characteristic of all living creatures.

205

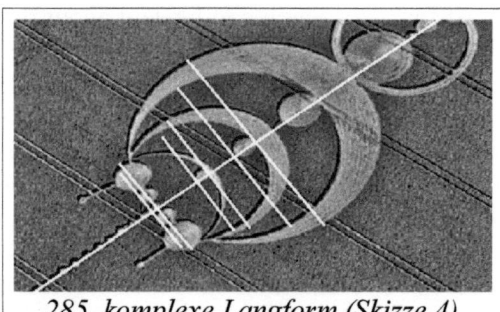

285. komplexe Langform (Skizze 4)

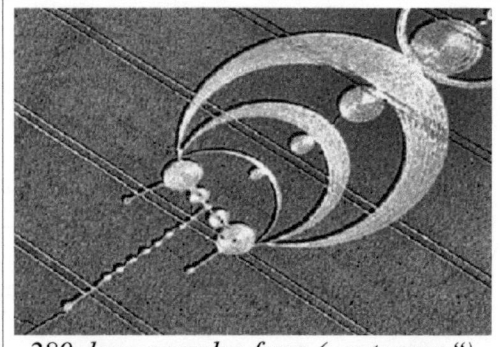

289. long complex form („antennae")

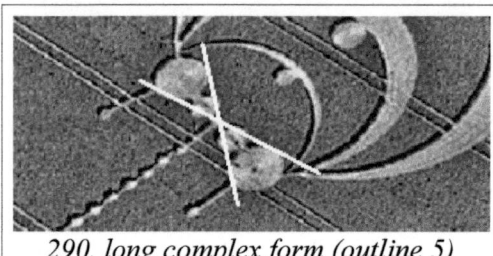

290. long complex form (outline 5)

Similar structures are also found in the head. If one intersects the longitudinal axis in the center of the crescent arcs at right angles with a transverse line, the distance between the line belonging to the outer arc and the line belonging to the inner arc corresponds to the small circle in the next crescent.

Thus, both the 3 body segments and the 3 head crescents have been conctructed fractally.

The antennas of this "insect" are at a "crossbar", which connects the endpoints of the three head-sickles on both sides. Obviously, everything that is sent from the body via the circular rows in the direction of the head is bundled by the crescents and then directed into the "antenna bar".

On this beam there are two large circular areas on the outside, in the middle there is a small circular area and in between there are 2 medium sized circular areas. Is this a concentration on the center? This is similarly constructed to the circle sequences in the 3 body segments, which also become smaller and smaller in a regular way.

Also the 4 outer 4 transverse circles have two common tangents which intersect in the center of the middle circle.

The middle one of the 3 antennas starts with the small point on the crossbar. Then follows a straight line, on which 7 points follow in equal distance. At the end, there is another slightly longer straight line with a final point.

The two outer antennas simply consist of a straight line with a dot at the end. They look as if they should only help to align the impulses of the middle antenna safely.

One has the impression that an impulse is sent out through the entire crop circle by the antenna.

206

Here, as with crop circles 268 and 282, two different crop circles have been combined: A kind of "palace" at the bottom and a round crop circle at the top. Both contain unusual shapes.

The round crop circle has a diamond as center, from which four connections start:

1. To the left, a line leads to a diamond with a vertical line and furtheron to a half diamond that ends at the ring. The sides of these diamonds are rounded.

2. The same is found on the right side.

3. At the top there is a circular space with two crescents. This could be a sun face.

4. At the bottom a straight line leads to a circular area with one crescent. This circular area is rounded upwards in the same way as the diamonds, so that the circular area without a corner merges into the line.

At the bottom of the outer ring there is a small triangle that sends a straight line downward, in which there is again an arc diamond with a cross line.

This diamond sits like a star on the middle "tower" of the "palace". Each of these 5 towers consists of a hollow rectangle with an elongated triangle divided in the middle as a "pointed roof".

On the two outer sides, the walls of the tower merge into a arched half-diamond.

291. palace and sun
(Wiltshire, England, 2012)

Below each of the 5 towers hangs a "drop" on a "thread" that is fastened to the tower by a half diamnond.

The lines, the drops, and the interiors of the rectangles have been executed rather carelessly and inaccurately. Together with the unusual arched checks and the equally unusual "palace", one can assume that this crop circle was created by humans. It is

207

also noticeable that although the round crop circle contains two circular faces with crescents, they do not form a polarity as is usually the case – the "sun heads" face the same direction instead of opposite directions.

But all this is nevertheless not a completely sure indication that this crop circle was man-made.

- * ☸ * -

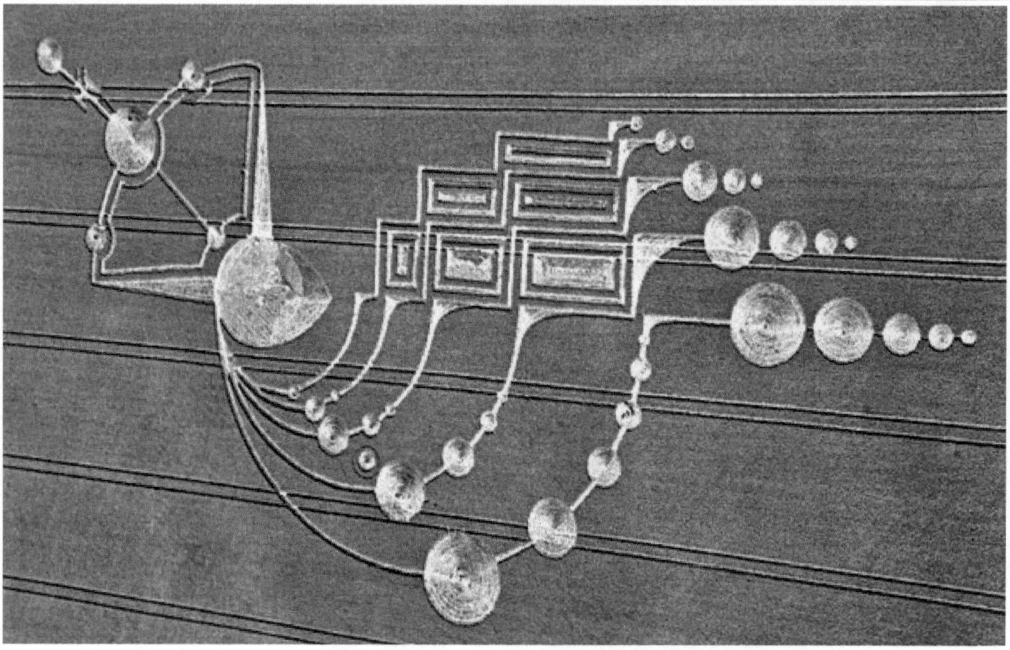

292. radioteleskop
(Wiltshire, England, 2009)

This is one of the most complex crop circles that have appeared so far. At first glance, one has the impression that a radio telescope has been depicted here.

The arrangement of circles, rectangles and lines on the right and below is simpler than it first appears: There are 5 lines starting at the left center at the "drop".

The top one goes through 1 circular area, goes through an arc angle, then has 3 steps and ends after an arc angle in 1 circular area.

The second top one goes through 2 circular areas, goes through an arc angle, then has 2 steps and ends after an arc angle in 2 circular areas.

The middle one goes through 3 circular surfaces, goes through an arc angle, then

208

has 1 step and ends after an arc angle in 3 circular surfaces.

The second lowest goes through 4 circular faces, goes through an arc angle, through another arc angle, and then ends in 4 circular faces.

The lowest one goes through 5 circular surfaces, goes through an arc angle, and ends in 5 circular surfaces.

This will be clearer if depicted as a list:

Structure of the right part of the crop circle						
Arc	*Drop*	*Circles*	*Angle*	*Steps*	*Angle*	*Circles*
upper one		1	1	3	1	1
2nd from above		2	1	2	1	2
central one	1	3	1	1	1	3
2nd from below		4	1	-	-	4
lowest		5	1	-	-	5

The areas between the steps have been filled by rectangles. The three lower rectangles are filled, the two middle ones have a center line, the upper one is empty.

Between the first circle of each of the 3rd and 4th arcs there is a small circular area with a ring. It gives the impression of a person who directs the processes in this part of the crop circle – a kind of lock-keeper?

In this part of the crop circle apparently the qualities of the "1", the "2", the "3", the "4" and the "5" are mixed. This is an unusual process – what is meant by it?

The "drop" is the link between the two parts of this crop circle. Its axis lies on the 5 first angles and the 5 second circles of the outer arc. It gives the impression of a "collecting basin".

The "device" that can be seen at the top left of the "drop" looks (as said) like a radio telescope. The central circle and the two secondary circles could be a polar system – but the centers of the three circles would not lie on one axis. The central axis of the telescope starts and ends with a small circular area. Between the main point and the point at the tip are two short straight lines, which could be stabilizers.

The overall impression is clear: something is produced in the 5 arcs, which is then emitted.

However, there are 6 elements which suggest that this crop circle is also man-made:

- 5 qualities are mixed instead of combined.
- The structure of the 5 arcs is regular, but it does not reveal a logical over-all system.

- The axis of the drop does not coincide with the axis of the telescope, which should be the case if the drop contains what the telescope emits.

- The function of the steps and the rectangles is not apparent.

- The centers of the 3 circles of the polar system are not on the same axis.

- The 3 circles on the telescope axis should actually be a polarity with center circle, but the two outer circles are not marked as such – which does happen quite often.

- *  * -

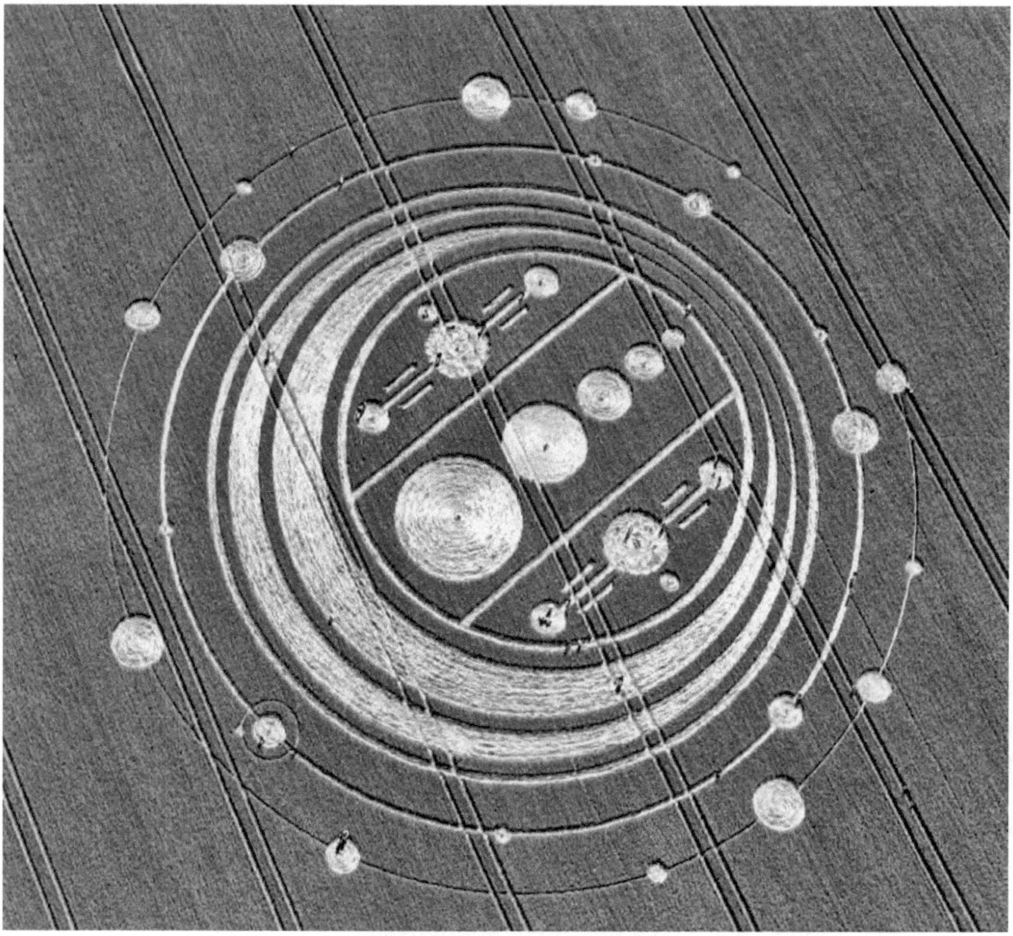

293. solar system machine
(Wiltshire, England, 2009)

210

Here, apparently, a more or less normal crop circle has been combined with a kind of planetary system.

On the outer, thin ring there are 12 differently sized "planets" in different distances.

On the inner, thick ring there are 9 differently sized "planets" at different distances, one of which also has a "moon".

The circle in the center, divided into three parts by two straight lines, is surrounded by two crescents, the inner one twice as thick as the outer one. The whole is enclosed by a ring. The combination of ring and crescents and the direction of the two straight lines gives the impression that the circle is moving towards the top right.

Viewed from the top right, this circle would be a variation of the "sun face".

The division of a circle into 3 stripes does not occur otherwise.

The sequence of 5 circles with evenly decreasing size is known from other crop circles. This series of circles symbolizes a thrust in the direction of the largest circle – that would be here, however, contrary to the assumed "flight direction" of the circle.

The two 3-circle-systems are polar-circles, which make the middle circle rotate by their tension. The 4 straight lines of the 2 polar circles are stabilized by 2 short straight lines each.

On the outside of the center circle there is a small circle each. Such a small single circle is unusual – one should expect 2 attachment points. Does this circle direct the energy from the polar circles to the center?

This UFO-like crop circle undoubtedly looks very aesthetic and fascinating, but a clear inner logic is not recognizable. Therefore, this crop circle will probably be man-made, too. What a pity …

III 18. Details

294. bent stems
(Wiltshire, England, 2012)

Here it can be clearly seen that the stalks in some crop circles have not been torn out or broken off with the root, but have been bent over in the stalk nodes. If one tries to do this purely mechanically, the stalk breaks. Moreover, the nodes are the most stable parts of a culm.

- * ❁ * -

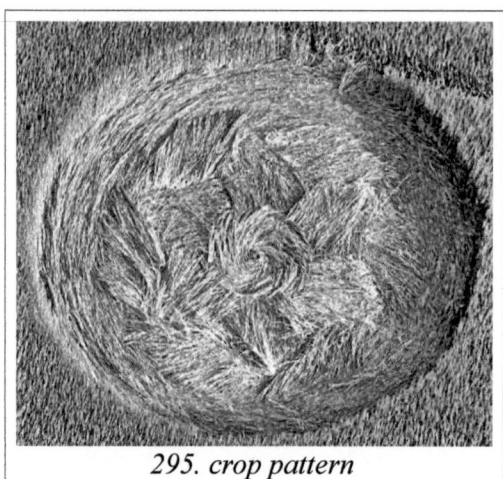

295. crop pattern
(Wiltshire, England, 2012)

In some crop circles, the grain is laid into elaborate patterns. Here you can see a central circle, a hexagram, six arched diamonds and an outer circle.

- * ❁ * -

212

296. weaving technique
(Italy, 2011)

In this crop circle, the grain has been woven, so to speak.

- * ❀ * -

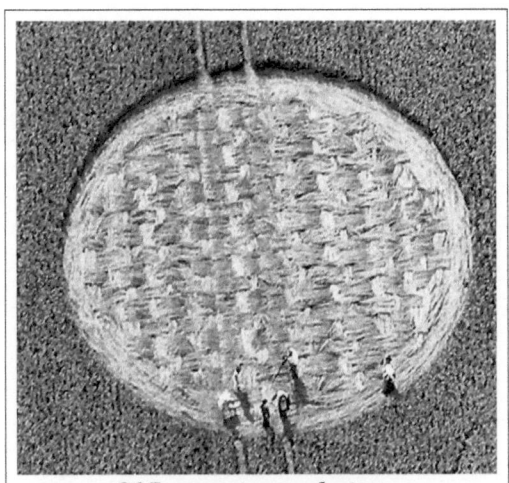

297. weaving technique
(place and year unknown)

Here this grain-weaving technique has been used on a large scale.

213

III 19.   Man-made shapes

298. Coca Cola
(place and year unknown)

With crop circles like this one, it is obvious that they have been man-made – and possibly commissioned by the Coca Cola Company.

The quality of workmanship on this crop circle, and on many of those yet to follow, is truly remarkable.

- *  * -

The competitors do not sleep …

299. Afri Cola
(place and year unknown)

- *  * -

214

300. Bacardi-Rum
(New Jersey, USA, 2005)

Colleagues from the high-precentage beverage dividion have also commissioned a crop circle.

- * ❀ * -

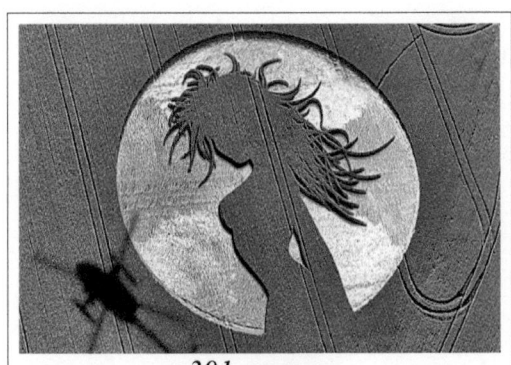

301. woman
(place and year unknown)

Obviously, Casanova also enjoys making crop circles – and has a lot of expertise.

- * ❀ * -

215

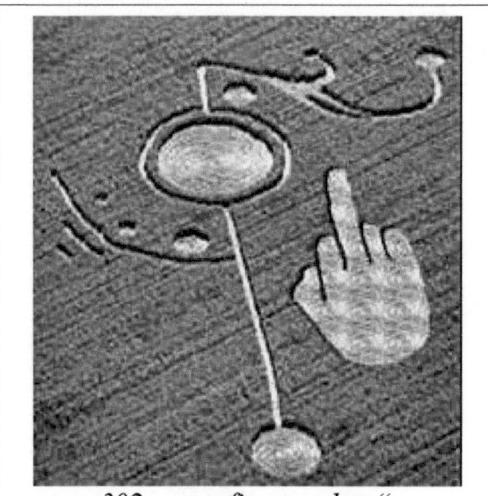

A very human gesture next to a very crooked crop circle.

302. „one-finger salute"
(place and year unknown)

- * ❀ * -

Is this supposed to be an alien in an UFO ???

303. bicycle
(France, year unknown)

- * ❀ * -

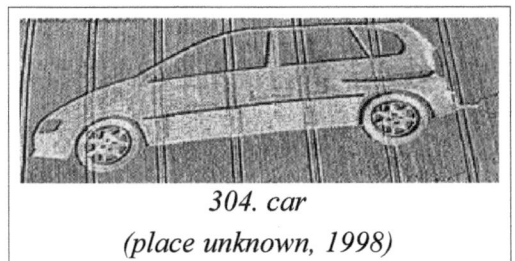

304. car
(place unknown, 1998)

It took the "Satan" crop circle team 10 hours to make this "Honda" crop circle. However, the car has been stretched too much – this is not because of the photographic perspective or distortion of the image.

- * ❀ * -

305. Mini
(place unknown, 2010)

This is a "Mini Countryman" as written underneath – a Morris Mini model.

The idea for this crop circle came from the "Osnabrück Anzeiger" – they apparently wanted to make an ecological car advertisement based on grass ...

- * ❀ * -

306. Audi
(Wiltshire, England, 2016)

Audi also apparently thought advertising by grain was worthwhile. Or was that just a fan? Ironman, perhaps, who often drives Audi, after all?

(The crop circle, however, was quite unsensationally made by Julian Richardson).

217

This crop circle, which is the logo of the Firefox browser, was made by the "Linux user group" at Oregon State University.

307. Firefox
(Orgon, USA, 2006)

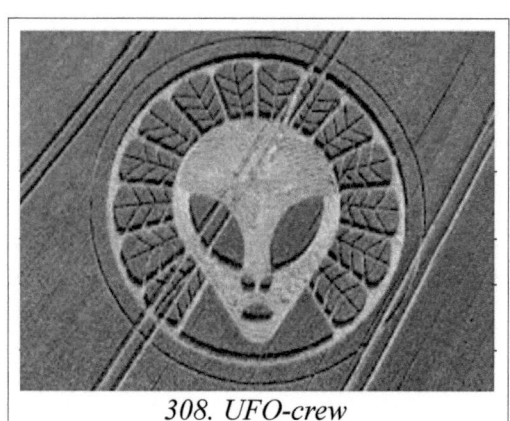

So this is how people imagine aliens – distinctly earthly and human ... and with a 14-piece fether crown – what do aliens have to do with Native Americans?

308. UFO-crew
(Surrey, England, 2016)

309. UFO-crew

(England, 2013)

Here's another colleague from the previous UFO pilot – this time in a quite stylishly rendered crop circle.

- * ❀ * -

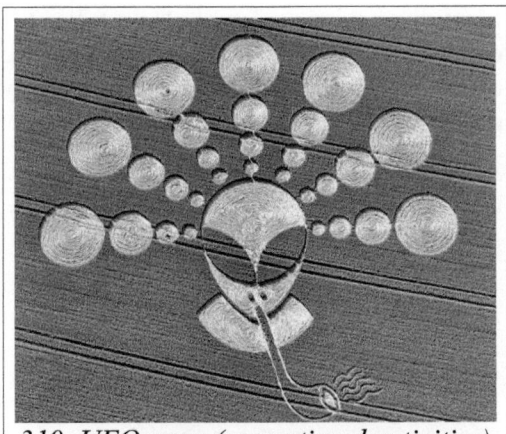

310. UFO-crew (recreational activities)

(Wiltshire, England, 2011)

Um – do the aliens come to Earth perhaps to import very specific herbs? In any case, the effect on the consciousness of this UFO pilot is remarkable …

What about the airworthiness? Is this pilot possibly responsible for some of the not-quite-successful crop circles?

- * ❀ * -

311. leaf of hemp
(place and year unknown)

This is probably the article that the UFO pilots want to import from Earth ....

- * ❀ * -

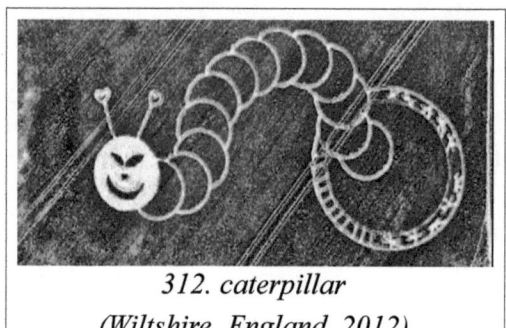

312. caterpillar
(Wiltshire, England, 2012)

Did the UFO crew bring caterpillars from their home planet? Hopefully the caterpillars don't like cannabis, because otherwise the aliens would get a delivery problem (see crop circle 310 and 311).

- * ❀ * -

313. man with protective deity
(place unknown, 2008)

A slightly older, largely bald man in front of Buddha Manjushri, holding his usual sword and Tibetan book in his hands. As an addition, parts of a hexagram and a hexagon can also be seen.

The man's head represents Ken Wilber, of whom there is also a painting together with the Buddha Manjushri, who has been depicted here.
The quality of the execution is really impressive.

- * ❈ * -

314. greeting
(Buckinghamshire, England, 2018)

This crop circle was placed in the approach path of the airport where President Donald Trump landed in England.
In allusion to his connections to Russia, the first word has been written in Cyrillic. The inscription reads "Fuck Trump!"

- * ❈ * -

221

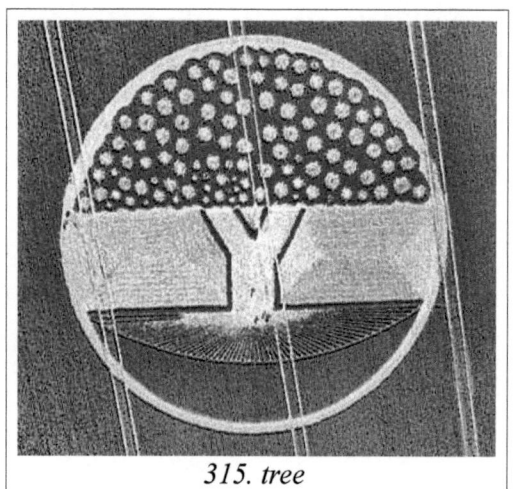

315. tree
(Wiltshire, England, 2002)

What to make of this tree? It is the only representation of a plant (apart from the fractal tree) and it contains none of the elements known from the crop circles considered so far.

The naive-simple and at the same time plump style in which this tree has been executed suggests that the person who made it has a Taurus-ascendent in his horoscope.

- * ❀ * -

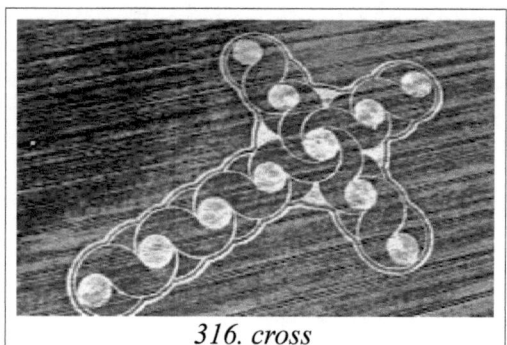

316. cross
(Wiltshire, England, 2008)

A Christian cross made of 11 circles and 20 "S"s …

This crop circle was probably made by an artistically talented Christian. The quality of the technical execution is quite good.

- * ❀ * -

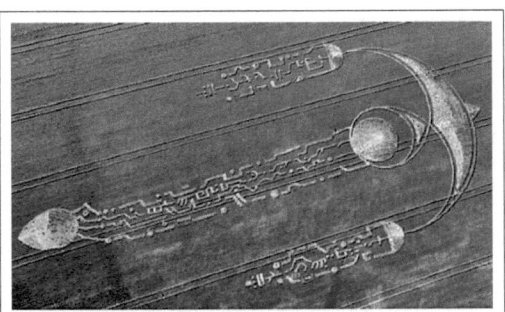

317. swallow-jellyfish
(Wiltshire, England, 2009)

This crop circle combines elements of the swallow crop circles with elements of the jellyfish crop circle.

However, since the elements are oblique and unprecise, and also a large amount of fancy characters have been used for the "tentacles", this crop circle is unlikely to be "genuine".

The "drop" is also found in crop circle 292 – are both made by the same artist?

III 20.   The crop circle alphabet

With the help of the previous considerations, we can now describe about 100 elements that make up the crop circles. Among these elements, four categories can be distinguished:

- polarities
- structures
- dynamics
- complex structures

Much has already been said about these crop circle elements in the various crop circles, but in the compilations the properties of these elements and their differences to other elements become even clearer.

III 20 a)   The polarity elements

Here are listed only the polarities in the crop circle mandalas which have a recognizable symbolism, which are due to structures in nature and thus have a structural, i.e. natural symbolism.

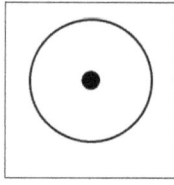

The **unipole** is the simplest form of a crop circle. In it, all the elements are arranged concentrically and are therefore to be considered aspects of identity. In astrology it corresponds to the aspect of conjunction (0° angle; symbol: ☌), which binds all elements involved tightly together as in a marriage. In nature, this structure corresponds to the unipolar gravity that pulls all things together. The unipol creates cohesion.

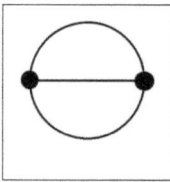

The **bipole** is a complementary opposition. It consists of two "charges": "+" and "−" or "north pole" and "south pole". It is known mainly by the Yin/Yang symbol (☯), but also by the astrological symbol of the opposition aspect (180° angle; symbol: ☍), both of which describe an eternal change like a swing. This structure corresponds in nature to the bipolar electromagnetic force. It creates attraction and repulsion as well as rhythmic and circular movements.

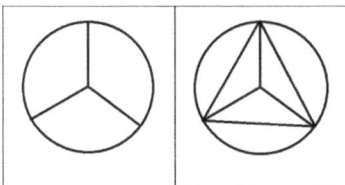

The **three-pole** has three charges, which only together result in the neutral state: "red" + "yellow" + "blue" = "white". In nature it is found as the three-polar "strong interaction", which, among other things, shapes the processes in protons and neutrons. Because of the color-metaphor for its three-polarity it is also called "color-power". It corresponds to the astrological aspect of the trine (120°-angle; symbol: ▲), which connects all elements involved in a friendship. The three-polarity is also associated with the circular course through several constantly recurring cycles. In astrology, a trine connects the three phases of the same element such as the creating fire of Aries, the shaping fire of Leo, and the moving fire of Sagittarius.

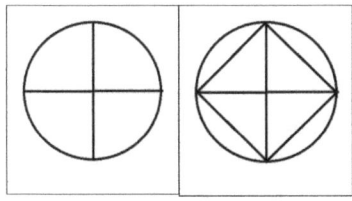

The **quadripole** is found in nature, among other things, between the electric wave and the magnetic wave in a photon – both waves always cross at right angles. In astrology the square separates two things and thereby spans a space (90° angle; symbol: □). The quadripole also corresponds to the four directions with the sun in the center, as well as the four elements with the quintessence in their center. In astrology, the square connects the same phase of the four elements such as the creating fire of Aries, the creating water of Cancer, the creating air of Libra, and the creating earth of Capricorn.

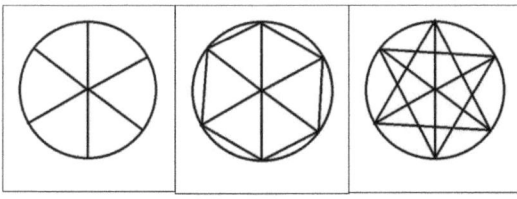

The **six-pole** occurs in many places in nature: as a snowflake, as a honey-comb, as the arrangement of equal-sized spheres, as six moons on the same orbit, all of which have the same distance from each other, and so on. In astrology, the six-polarity is found in the sextile, which binds the same elements together into a group (60° angle; symbol: ✱). This polarity has recently become somewhat better known as the "flower of life". The six-pole, which is a differentiation of the three-pole and thus the interaction of two forces, appears as the more dormant hexagon ("honeycomb") and the more active hexagram ("six-pointed star"). In astrology, the two forces that interact here are either the three phases of fire and the three phases of air, or the three phases of water and the three phases of earth.

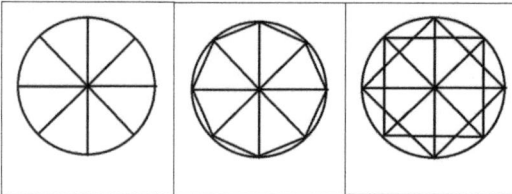

The **eight pole** is a differentiation of the four pole – it represents a complex order and the interaction of two forms. There is the more resting variant of the octagon and the more active variant of the octagram. Traditionally, the "8" has the symbolism of completeness and perfection, which can be found in many places: Buddha's eightfold path, the eight trigrams of the I Ching, the groups of eight deities of the Egyptians, the eightfold calendar of the Mayas, etc. The eight-polarity results also purely geometrically e.g. by the addition of the four cardinal directions by the four intermediate directions.

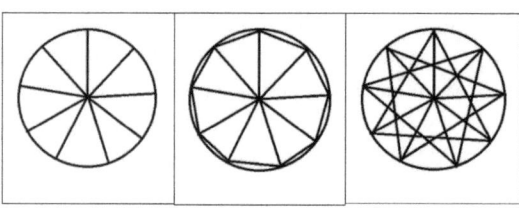

The **nine-pole** is a differentiation of the three-pole by a further three-division. One can understand it therefore as a differentiated consideration of the development quality of the "3". This differentiation can be found e.g. in the Kabbalistic tree of life, which first consists of unity, development and multiplicity. The development is then divided into three parts and each of these three elements is then divided into three parts again, which then results in the eleven (1+9+1) areas ("Sephiroth") of the Tree of Life. In the case of the crop circles, however, this polarity hardly plays a role. The nonagon is again more passive than the nonagram.

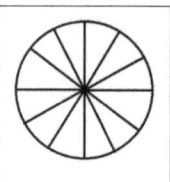

The **twelve-pole** results from the combination of the one-polarity with the two-polarity, the three-polarity and the four-polarity. It is found in nature as the 12 basic elementary particles, as the twelve-part superstring (the basic element of physics today), and as the zodiac. The surrounding space of a center is twelve-divided. This polarity is very common in crop circles.

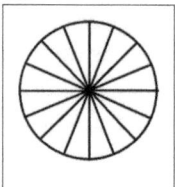

The **sixteen pole** occurs only very rarely. It can be seen as a further differentiation of the eight-pole.

III 20. b)   The structure elements

In this section all elements are listed which have mainly a structure like the circle, the triangle, the square, the line and the like, but also more complex structure elements like the arc rhombus.

The **circle**, sometimes called the "circular area" for better distinction, is a center and therefore the area of identity. He is an individual and therefore also the basic building block of the crop circles which have been at the beginning only such circular spaces for a long time.

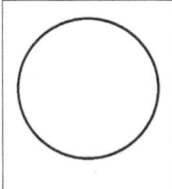

The **ring** is a surrounding space, an environment, a skin, a city wall, a radiation etc.. It can be static, but it can also rotate or something can flow in it like in a pipe. The ring is often twelve-divided like the zodiac or the superstring, in which also something flows in the circle. This twelve-division is not always drawn into the crop circle as a structure, but this structure is, so to speak, always present in all rings without expression.

The symbolism of the **straight line** is simple: Either it is as a straight line the shortest connection between two points or it is a ray which leads out from a point into the surrounding space.

An **arc** is a part of a ring. These are mostly semicircles, more rarely quarter circles and very rarely three-quarter circles. The semicircle is an opening to something else: a fixture, a transmitter or a receiver – it is like a parabol mirror. The quarter circle is more like a point of contact. The three-quarter circle is an open vessel.

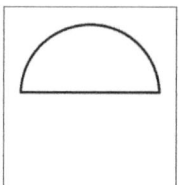

The **closed semicircle** is quite a rare shape. It is the closed half of a whole and thus one of the two poles of a complementary opposition.

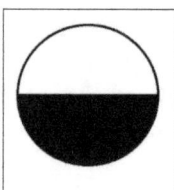

The **color-coded bisected circle**, on the other hand, shows both poles lying within a whole. However, this structure often appears simply for geometric reasons when a ring intersects a circle. In this case, the polarity of the circle is that one half is inside the ring and one half is outside the ring - the color bisected circle connects inside and outside. Such a circle is therefore like a sense organ that perceives the outside world, or like the legs with which one moves in the world, or like the arms and hands with which one shapes the outside world. So this structure represents perception, participation, involvement and shaping.

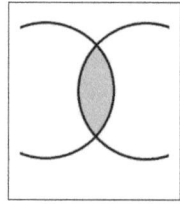

The **almond** is the intersection of two circles. Its longitudinal axis lies at right angles to the line connecting the centers of the two circles. Thus, the almond lies transversely between two individuals and is shaped by them. It therefore expresses something that both circles have in common: the area in which two individuals (circles) coincide. One can also look at the almond in a second way: The centers of the two circles exert pressure on each other, creating a flat shape that moves between this pressure – like fish, which are also usually approximately almond-shaped and can most easily move because of this shape through water almost without resistance. Which of the two interpretations is more suitable in each case, one must decide from case to case.

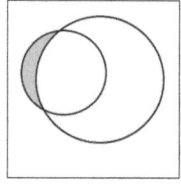

The **sickle-crescent** is in a way the counterpart of the almond: it is the part of the area of two circles that is not common to both. Therefore, the crescent is something attached to something else, something that supports or protects something else. It can also be something receiving. The crescent, unlike the almond, also has a clear alignment because it has two different sides: The inner arc receives and seeks contact; the outer arc repels and protects.

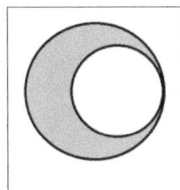

The **crescent circle** has a slightly different meaning than the sickle-crescent, since the crescent circle describes an internal process, while the sickle-crescent describes an external process. The sickle circle shows that the inner circle moves from the center to the edge – a movement impulse. When several crescent circles appear one after the other, they form a conduit, so to speak, for this movement impulse – they are then both the movement itself and the envelope of this movement. Therefore, a series of sickle circles is also well suited for the representation of the vertebrae and the like.

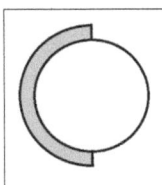

In contrast to the crescent, the **semicircle magnet** has a partially angular shape – it is a kind of extension or reinforcement of one side of the circle. This can be a restraint, a protective wall or even an attached pole, so in a sense a battery or a magnet.

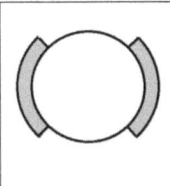

In the case of the **quartercircle magnet**, both poles have been shown, so it is more certain here that they are to be understood as poles and thus as the drive of the circle. This structure corresponds to the structure of an electric motor, which is essentially also a rotary motion caused by two poles (see also the company logo of the German electrical appliance company Bosch).

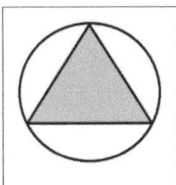

An **equilateral triangle** is a three-pole, i.e. the combination of three poles into one unit. The triangle thus stands for a dynamic entity that moves and develops. In crop circles, however, the arc triangle is found much more often than the triangle with straight sides.

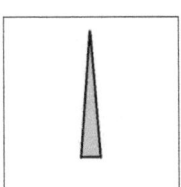

The **pointed triangle** is a ray, an impulse, an attack, a defensive structure, or the like. Its interpretation depends largely on the context in which it appears.

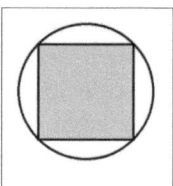

The **square** appears very rarely in crop circles. It is very static, solid, hard and spans a space. It can therefore be a foundation or a protective wall.

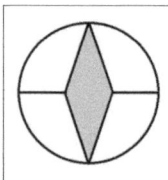

A **rhombus** is a square without right angles or with two diagonals of different length. It appears as an area between two groups of parallel lines. If these lines are straight lines, the classical rhombus with straight sides is created; if these lines are arcs, however, the arc rhombus is created, which will be discussed later on. Because the rhombus is created as a space between overlapping parallel lines, it is almost always an indication of force fields, i.e. of the relationship between two impulses that meet.

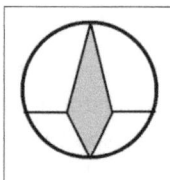

The **pointed rhombus** is a rather rare shape, although it is actually quite interesting. It is created in the same way as the normal rhombus, but also has the quality of a ray, i.e. it has a direction: it moves in the direction of the narrower tip, i.e. in the direction of the longer end.

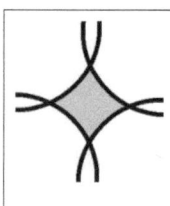

An arc rhombus with four arcs pointing inward is called a **diamond**. It is created as a space between four circles whose centers form a square. Thus, the diamond is the space in the center left by four individuals (circles) of equal size (= equal strength) when they span a space. A diamond is thus a shape that is under pressure from all four sides. It tends to implode, that is, to collapse in on itself – it is a rather passiv shape.

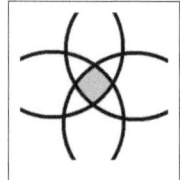

The **arc diamond with four outward arcs** is the common intersection of four circles whose centers form the corners of a square. A diamond is the space formed when the outer lines of these four circles do not reach the center between them. The arc diamond, on the other hand, is formed when the outer lines of the four circles extend beyond their common center. While the diamond is under pressure from four sides, i.e. from the outside, the arc rhombus contains the combined pressure of four circles in its interior, since it is the intersection of four circles. The arc rhombus is therefore an extremely expansive element – it is the "anti-square". It works well as the center of a complex form.

The arc rhombus, which has two inward arcs and two outward arcs, might be called a **bud**. The two inward arcs (in the sketch below) make pressure on the bud from inside, which in turn makes pressure outward with its two outward arcs (in the sketch above). So this rhombus of arcs is something that wants to move, that wants to progress, to grow, to come out of something - just a bud, a germ, a penis, an unborn child, a new thought, a strong impulse and so on.

Arched four-sided diamonds with 3 inner arcs and 1 outer arc or with 1 outer arc and 3 inner arcs are also conceivable, but they do not seem to occur in the crop circles.

Likewise, there do not seem to be any asymmetrical arched rhomboids with sides of different length.

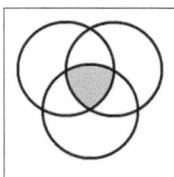

The **arc-triangle with 3 outer arcs** is, like the arc-rhombus, an expansive surface, because it is the common intersection of three circles, which interact in this intersection. This arc-triangle, like the arc-rhombus, is therefore well suited as the center of a complex form.

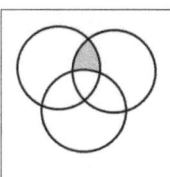

The **arc-triangle with 2 outer arcs** corresponds roughly to the "bud". However, it is somewhat weaker because it only has the power of one circle and not two circles at its disposal – only one arc projects into this shape and not two as in the "bud". The shape this arc-triangle wants to take on the outside (two outside arcs) is twice as big as the force it has available (one inside arc) – so the expansion is weak.

In the case of the **arc-triangle with 1 outer arc**, it is the other way round as in the case of the previous arc-triangle: It is virtually "squeezed" towards the outside by two inner arcs. There is a strong expansion pressure here.

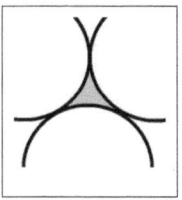

The **arc triangle without outer arcs** is, so to speak, the "three-cornered diamond". This area is left between three circles which do not overlap at all or only a little. Like the diamond, this shape is a passive surface that tends to be obliterated by the expansion of the three circles around it.

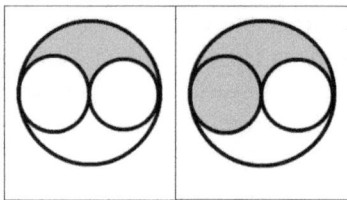

The **three-cornered crescent** is a rather special shape. It is formed when there are two small circles next to each other in a larger circle, whose radii are half as large as the radius of the large circle. In the three-cornered crescent, the forces of the two small circles combine to form the shape and force of the large circle. So this shape is the common shape of two allies. This form usually occurs only together with one of the two circles, with which it then forms the "curved drop" known from the Yin/Yang sign and usually called "Miribota". This combined form is considered in more detail under the dynamic forms.

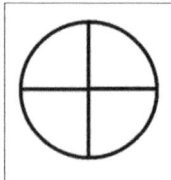

The **cross** occurs relatively rarely in crop circles. It is formed when two straight lines cross at right angles. Such lines are usually the connection between two poles – so there must be two poles twice in a cross.

This is the case e.g. with a photon, which is physically an electromagnetic wave. If you look at such a wave from the front, as if the light comes flying towards you and you would be able to recognize this light in its structure, you would see the following picture: The electric wave, for example, could be the horizontal line – since it is a wave, it would be constantly changing back and forth from the "+" on one side to the "–" on the other side. The magnetic wave would then be the vertical line and would be there constantly changing between the "north" at one end and the "south" at the other end from up to down and back. The angle between these two waves is always a right angle (90°). This angle is the maximum distance between the four poles involved. Such a cross is therefore a very stable construction.

Also in astrology, the 90° aspect ("square") is a very stable angle that spans a space. So, a cross is rigid, fixed, stable and gives rise to shapes that have two longitudinal axes and polarities.

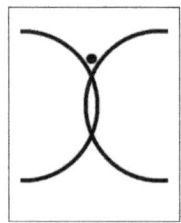

The **fixing point** in the angle between two shapes just seems to fill the "empty angle", but it also gives this place a greater stability.

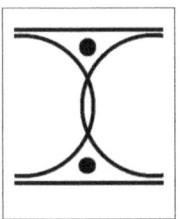

In the case of the **pair of attachment points**, both the aspect of filling space and the aspect of stabilization are even more evident than in the case of the single point. Sometimes one has the impression that these pairs of points are something like the intervertebral discs between two vertebrae. These pairs of points make most of the crop circles in which they appear appear more "round" and more organic than they would be without these points.

The **companion line pair** seems to be something like a shell, i.e. a conduit. These lines almost always occur in pairs – to my knowledge they appear only next to straight lines, but not next to arcs. This suggests that they also have the function of aligning the straight line between them. They are, so to speak, what makes a normal light beam become a laser beam.

The **double companion line pair** is rarer than the single companion line pair. The function seems to be the same – probably just a little stronger.

The **double "L" companion line** with additional line appears only once. Presumably it is supposed to be a particularly effective stabilizer.

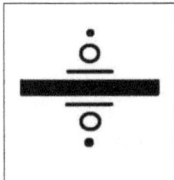

The **companion line/ring/dot pair** has, as far as can be seen, the same function as the three previously described companion forms. The dots let assume that here the line was fixed by the dots, since the dots are stabilizers. This form has occurred only once.

No crop circle feature is recognizable, from which would be evident, which form of the line pairs is used in what places.

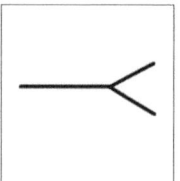

The **line bifurcation** is extremely rare and seems to appear only in three crop circles, which are moreover so inaccurately made that one could assume that they were created by humans. If this bifurcation has the angle of 90° or 120°, it could have a meaning – the creating of space (90°) or the binding to a unit (120°).

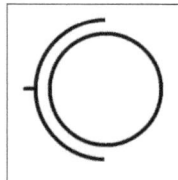

The **simple semicircle holder** is obviously exactly that: the holder of the circle which is in this semicircle. This holder is also a contact point between the line ending in the semicircle and the circle.

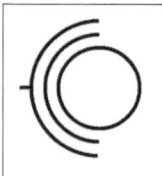

Presumably, there is no difference between the single and the **double semicircle holder**. The double bracket is merely more emphasized and therefore probably more important within the overall structure of the crop circle.

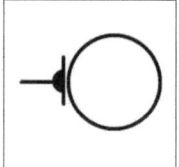

The **"T"** and similar shapes are sometimes a base or similar for circles. There doesn't seem to be much difference from the half circle mount – except that the half circle gives more support to the circle, while the "T" is limited to contact. This element is very rare.

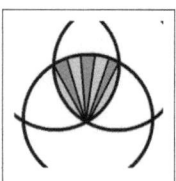

The **feathers** are often indistinguishable from rays – what is meant by these elongated shapes can often only be discerned from the context. But since they are either the representation of a movement (ray) or of the thing that causes a movement (feathers), this distinction is not so important either, since this shape indicates a movement in both cases.

The **small circle with center** is a conspicuous element that appears especially at some fixing points. Presumably, it is meant to emphasize the stability of these points. It seems to appear on more static shapes such as 4-polar mandalas, but not on moving shapes such as snakes, where simple points tend to appear as companions.

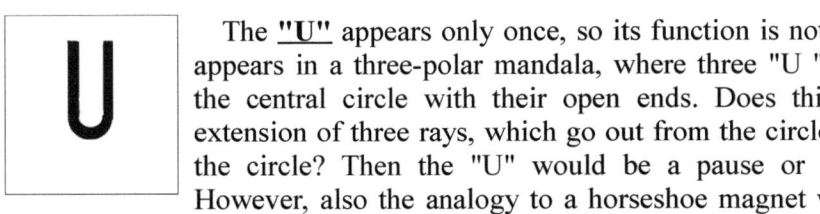

The **"U"** appears only once, so its function is not entirely clear. It appears in a three-polar mandala, where three "U "s are adjacent to the central circle with their open ends. Does this mean that the extension of three rays, which go out from the circle, are led back to the circle? Then the "U" would be a pause or a contemplation. However, also the analogy to a horseshoe magnet would be conceivable – but also then the interpretation would be a self-reference and a self-reflection, because then both poles of the magnet would point to the center.

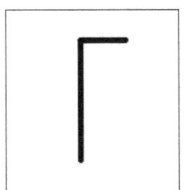

The **"L"** appears only as an "appendage" to complex crop circles. The right angle suggests a ray which ends at this angle and changes. Sometimes this "L" also looks like an antenna or a signature.

The same is true for the **"F"** which appears in the same position. However, the impression of a transformation at the end of a line is even stronger because of the two transverse strokes. Is something being sent out there?

The **"3-dash F"** is once again an increase of the "L" and the "F". It seems almost like an apparatus with a very specific purpose. If the number of horizontal lines is related to the symbolism of their number, the "L" would indicate the sending of a simple, unchanged message, the "F" would indicate the sending of a message containing a polarity, and the "3-dash-F" would indicate the sending of a dynamic, developing, cyclic message. However, this interpretation is uncertain.

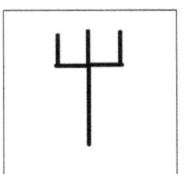

The **trident** is a variant of the "3-dash-F" in which the three parallel strokes point not to the side, but in the direction of the original ray. Here the message could have been less reshaped. But here, too, the interpretation is uncertain.

The **"F" pair** seems to have the same meaning as the holding semicircle: It holds a circle, has contact with it, and conveys to it the quality of the system from which the "F" emanates. In the "F" pair, the aspect of holding is largely dropped, while the transmission of an information is emphasized.

III 20. c)   The dynamic elements

The distinction between structure elements and dynamics elements is not always easy. A circle is a structure element and an "S" is a dynamics element, but what is a drop that has both a center and a direction?

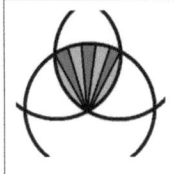 Such an ambiguous case is the group of **rays**, which are often indistinguishable from fethers. However, since they are either the representation of a movement (ray) or of that which causes a movement (feathers), this distinction is not so important, since this form indicates a movement in both cases.

 The **"S"** is formed on the outer edge of two polar circles and is also an element found in the Yin/Yang sign. It represents a tension and a movement. It is a more direct and independent version of the rotating and pulsating large ring between two smaller polar circles.

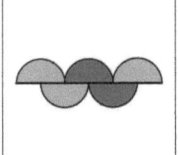 The **semicircle series**, i.e. a straight line with semicircles on either side, each end of which meets the center of the semicircle on the other side, is a second way of constructing an "S" (the single dark gray shape). Here a longer movement is shown than with a simple "S". Therefore, the semicircle series can also be seen as a sequence of several "S"s.

 The **snake line** is nothing else than a semicircle series, where the inner angles between the semicircles have been rounded. It also represents a longer movement.

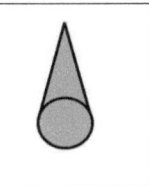 The **straight drop** is the movement of a circle in a certain, straight direction – thus the "falling" or "being pulled" towards something else.

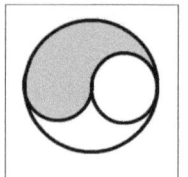 The **curved drop**, also called "Miribota", is also a movement, but in a circle. Such a movement occurs when the impulse of the drop (which would move it in a straight direction) is joined by an attraction from the side. This principle is found e.g. in the circular orbits of the planets around the sun or of the electrons around an atomic nucleus. The Yin/Yang sign also represents this principle. The Miribota thus indicates the movement of a unit (circle) within a system. In most cases, this system consists of two units: the two polar circles representing "+" and "–", "north" and "south", Yin and Yang, and so on. These two poles revolve around each other, giving rise to the movement of the curved drop.

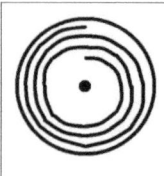 The **spiral** is either a development from inside to outside or a development from outside to inside. Here the ray is superimposed with a circular movement. So one can conclude from a spiral that the system in question radiates, i.e. expands or shines, and that the system in question rotates, i.e. rests in itself. The spiral is, so to speak, the pirouette of a dancer who rests completely in himself and thus has a great radiance.

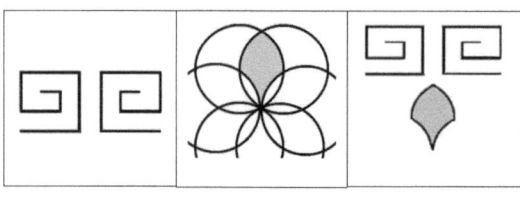 The **symmetrical double spiral**, which is also known as the Chinese luck symbol, is created when an impulse enters a system. This is the case, for example, when a stream flows into a pond. In right one of the three sketches the impulse comes from below. This form can be found in many places like for example in the ovaries of a woman (left sketch). The symmetrical double spiral is formed in the system where an impulse enters – the impulse itself takes the form of the "bud", which is found, among others, in the penis of the man (middle sketch). The bud and the symmetrical double spiral thus belong together and are the two forms that arise when two systems combine.

 The **asymmetrical double "S"** can also be seen as a short asymmetrical double spiral. Here either a movement flows in two directions from the inside to the outside or from two directions from the outside to the inside. Either something gathers in the center or something flows out from the center.

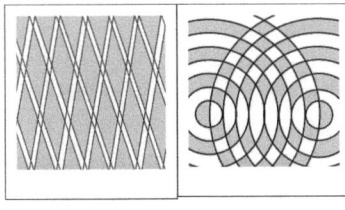

The **force field of rhombuses** results from the superposition of parallel straight lines or arcs, which are again waves, which go out from two active centers. These centers are mostly circles (right sketch). By superimposing the concentric circles starting from two different points or of the rows of straight lines starting from two straight surfaces (left sketch), a pattern is created in which these lines cross each other. This results either in rhombuses with straight edges or in arc rhombuses.

The rhombus pattern thus represents a force field in which the influences of both "transmitters" are combined and graphically represented. The shape of the rhombuses depends on four influences:

1. on the number of transmitters,
2. on the shape of the transmitters,
3. on their distance from each other, and
4. on the considered section of the common force field.

III 20. d) The complex elements

There are some more complex forms, thar form units, which are frequent in the crop circles. They are, so to speak, not cells, but organs – or if one prefers to look at it technically, not individual screws and the like, but machine parts, such as an electric motor.

To these complex elements belong also two structures, which are not geometric forms:

One of them is the multiplication of numbers. For example, if you combine the polarity of "2" with the dynamics of "3", you get the "2·3=6" of the creative group. On the other hand, if you combine the polarity of "2" with the space of "4", you get the "2·4=8" of the differentiated space division. The most famous is certainly the combination of the dynamics of the "3" with the space of the "4", which gives the "3·4=12" of the circumspace, i.e. zodiac and the superstring, which are a stable ("4") rotating circle because of the "3".

Multiplication is the mathematical form of combining two quantities – for example, multiplying the length of a field by the width of a field gives the area of that field.

The second of these non-geometric structures is self-similarity and the closely related fractal.

In all living beings, its basic properties are found in all of its constituent parts. A living being develops by a "construction plan" which always uses the same procedure for all similar places, whereby all places which have a similar function also have a similar appearance with this living being. This principle is also found in crop circles and contributes to their coherent, harmonious appearance. In art, this self-similarity would be called "stylishness".

The fractal is a simple form of self-similarity. From a starting point, the same developmental step is applied over and over again, resulting in the same forms appearing over and over again. Also this element is to be found with the crop circles of the frequent.

The essence of this self-similarity ist desribed by the horoscope of the person or thing in question.

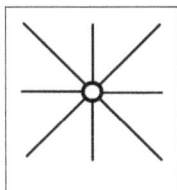

The **lines, which start from a center point**, represent a radiating, expanding system, which shapes its surrounding space.

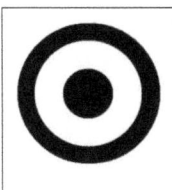

The **circular area with a ring** is an individual that has protected itself well. However, the impression of this structure depends very much on the size of the circle, the thickness of the ring and the distance between them.

The **small central circle area** in a large circle area centres this area and gives the impression of consciousness and determination.

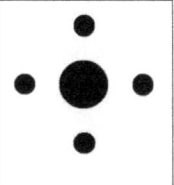

The **central circle with 4 peripheral circles** is a center with an organic surrounding space: the sun with the four directions, the quintessence with the four elements, etc. So this form is a structured organism.

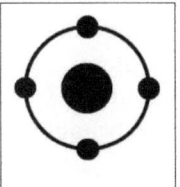

The **central circle with ring and 4 circles** corresponds to the previous form. It is however more stable by the ring and and it is outwardly delimited. Therefore, almost only this form occurs – the previous, ring-less form is extremely rare.

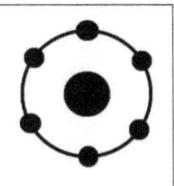

The **central circle with a circular ring and 6 circles** is even more organic than the two previous forms, because the "6" represents an organic group and not only a space like the "4".

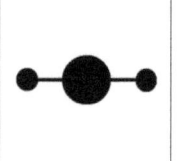

The **center circle with two pole circles** is, so to speak, the motor or the heart of very many crop circles. The two poles cause the pulsation or rotation of the central circle – like an electric motor or a heart. One can understand this form also as a magnet or as a battery.

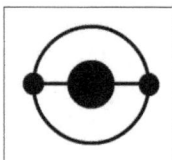

The **central circle with two pole circles and ring** emphasizes the unity of the system by the ring. The ring also represents the rotation and pulsation of energy in the system.

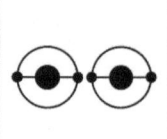

The **rows of polar circles** that sometimes occur are, so to speak, magnets, batteries or electric motors connected in series, which together have a greater force than a single polar element. This structure occurs almost exclusively in the long crop circles.

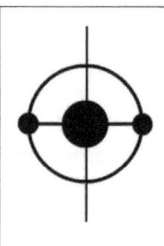

Surprisingly, the **jets at polar circles** are quite a rare element at the grain circles, although these jets play a big role in nature. For example, the jet is the axis of the magnetic field created by a rotating electric charge. The Earth's magnetic field also has two such jets: the north pole and the south pole.

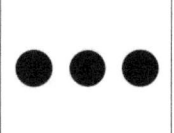

Triple shapes of the same size are an indication of the symbolism of the "3": unfolding, development, contact – thus creating rhythm and cycle. As a rule, it is circles that are represented in triples – other triple shapes are very rare. Their symbolism corresponds to the symbolism of triangular shapes such as the triangle and the arc-triangle.

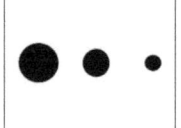

In **triple shapes with decreasing or increasing size**, in addition to the cycle, a direction in which this cycle develops (towards the largest form) is emphasized. Again, circles are most often used.

 The **almond three-star**, like the previous two forms, is indicative of an unfolding, a development, or a cycle. This three-star is created by the intersections of three circles whose centers lie on a fourth circle. This structure emphasizes the radiance of the cyclic system.

 The **almond cross**, on the other hand, according to the symbolism of the "4", emphasizes the taking, conquering and shaping of a space.

 The **Almond Six Star** emphasizes the organic design and coordination of all elements with each other in this radiating system.

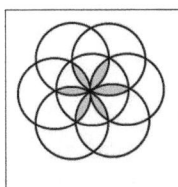 The **almond six-pointed star with central circle** distinguishes the centre from the surrounding space of this structure and is therefore more protective of itself. This form is also called the "flower of life". It is also the representation of the astrological sextile aspect (60° angle), which describes an organic group formation.

 The **circle with 4 triangle indentations** is quite a rare structure. It represents a unity which receives impulses from all four sides. Therefore, this structure can be seen as the way to the center - the 4 elements are united to the quintessence. This structure seems to exist only with 4 triangles, but not with any other number of triangles.

 The **circle with 4 triangle bulges** is also quite rare. This structure represents the self-expression of the quintessence in the center with the help of the 4 elements. It also occurs with other numbers of triangles.

243

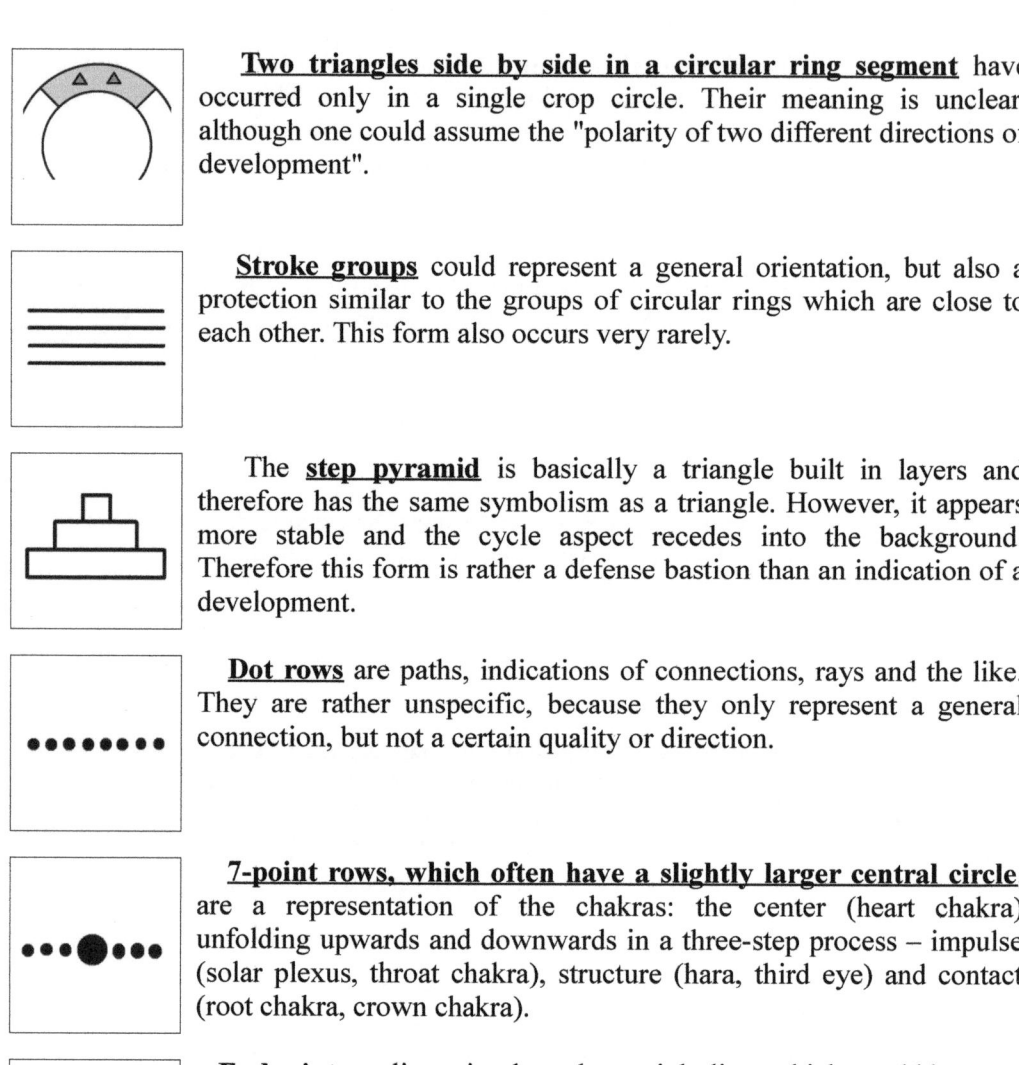

Two triangles side by side in a circular ring segment have occurred only in a single crop circle. Their meaning is unclear, although one could assume the "polarity of two different directions of development".

Stroke groups could represent a general orientation, but also a protection similar to the groups of circular rings which are close to each other. This form also occurs very rarely.

The **step pyramid** is basically a triangle built in layers and therefore has the same symbolism as a triangle. However, it appears more stable and the cycle aspect recedes into the background. Therefore this form is rather a defense bastion than an indication of a development.

Dot rows are paths, indications of connections, rays and the like. They are rather unspecific, because they only represent a general connection, but not a certain quality or direction.

7-point rows, which often have a slightly larger central circle, are a representation of the chakras: the center (heart chakra) unfolding upwards and downwards in a three-step process – impulse (solar plexus, throat chakra), structure (hara, third eye) and contact (root chakra, crown chakra).

Endpoints on lines simply end a straight line, which would be a ray without the point at that end. While a ray goes out from a center endlessly into the distance, a straight line starts at a center (circle) and ends at another centre.

244

Two **points on the end of two lines** are probably a contact point which connects these two lines. At such a point, something new begins, but it is firmly connected to the previous one – a relay, a plug, a passing on, a sending, and so on.

Rows of circles with sickles in circles are almost always the vertebrae of a living creature. However, this structure can also be thought of more generally as a moving, flexible conduit in which energy and information are transmitted. This structure often has a stabilization point in each angle between two circles, i.e. a pair of points between each two circles (one point above and one point below). In the sketch, the impulse in this line moves from left to right.

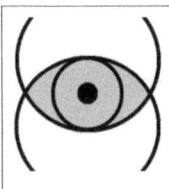

The **eye** is geometrically seen a circle with a ring in an almond. The circle gives autonomy to the almond and the ring gives protection and solidity to this autonomy. The association with an eye, of course, makes this shape much more impressive than it would be without that association.

The **face** appears in several forms. Whether this is anything more than a human association is debatable, as these shapes lack convincing structures.

A **single, small circular area** next to a crop circle is among the "appendages" whose function is not entirely clear. Is it an attendant? Or an observer? Or a passenger? Or a kind of "signature"?

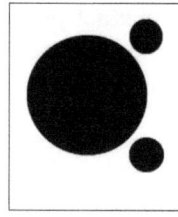 The **occasional two smaller attached circles** with or without contact to the main circle can only be interpreted in individual cases. Their meaning depends mainly on the angle formed by the connecting lines between the three centers of these circles.

If this angle is 180° and the small circles are exactly opposite each other with the large circle between them, this is a simple polar system.

If it is three angles of 120°, it would be a 3-polar system, that is, the representation of a development or a cycle – although it would then be the question why these cycles are not represented by circles of the same size. To my knowledge, this self-contradictory form has not appeared anywhere.

If it is (as in the sketch above) a 90° angle, the two small circles would make room for the large circle, so to speak. They would then be messengers, scouts, feelers, sense organs, eyes, ears, graspers, hands, and the like, that is, paired structures with which the individual can grasp and reach into the space in front of it.

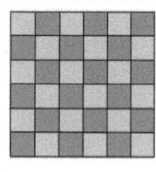 With the **patterns in the grain** there are many different forms, which structure in different way the concerning surface of flat-laid grain once again. The most common are large circular areas, which most likely represent chakras. However, there are also other highlightings and also the weaving or interweaving of grain, which gives the impression of the solid structure of the grain surface in question. These patterns must always be considered on a case-by-case basis.

IV Contemplation

IV 1. The language of crop circles

The previous consideration of crop circles, the elements of which they are composed, and the way these elements are combined, shows that crop circles have a distinct inner logic and are a "geometric language". This inner logic and conclusiveness is found both in the "words" of this language (the meaning of the individual elements) and in the "grammar" of this language (the combination of these elements).

This "geometric language" contains elements of several other domains and is closely related to some other areas. A closer look at the crop circles reveals a simple kind of logic according to which forms develop.

IV 1. a) Music

Music is a universally understandable language because it is based on a simple inner logic that is found in all its elements.

This logic is based on a simple fundamental principle: elements that repeat a form or have an easily grasped relationship to another form are experienced as harmonious – the two forms resonate with each other. This "resonating together" is experienced not only as recognition, but also as joy.

First of all there is the single tone. Its pitch can be indicated by its frequency, i.e. by the vibrations per second which produce this tone. This oscillation is given in "Hz" (oscillations per second).

From this it follows that there are certain tones which vibrate harmonically together. A tone with 400Hz fits well to a tone with 800Hz, because two oscillations of the higher tone (800Hz) fit exactly into one oscillation of the lower tone (400Hz). These two tones therefore complement each other without interfering with each other. This doubling of the frequency is called "octave". This is the simplest harmony. Now other harmonies can be found like "2 waves of one tone = 3 waves of the other tone" – this is a quint (fifth). Another harmony is "3 waves of one tone = 4 waves of the other tone" – this is a quart (fourth).

The octave is the most harmonic because it crosses the baseline together with the fundamental the most times (5 times at the base line – see in the sketch below). Then follows the fifth as the second most harmonious sequence of notes (3 crossings at the

247

base line), and the third is the fourth (2 crossings at the base line).

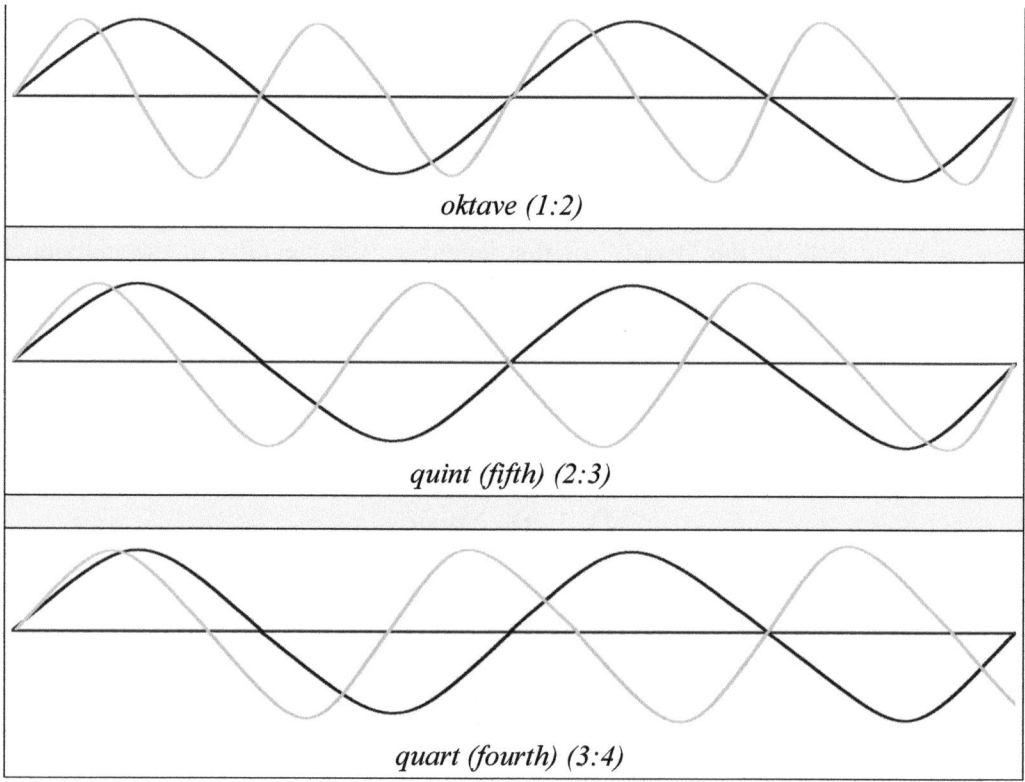

oktave (1:2)

quint (fifth) (2:3)

quart (fourth) (3:4)

These simple numerical ratios can be heard without any previous knowledge and are perceived as pleasant.

Chords consist of three notes that have been put together in such a way that they have simple numerical ratios to each other. For minor chords this is "4 waves + 5 waves + 6 waves" within a certain time interval, for major chords this is "10 waves + 12 waves + 15 waves" within a certain time interval. This may sound like two complicated numerical ratios, but the ear is able to recognize these ratios – and perceives them as harmonic.

The same principle applies to tone length: tones that are the same length repeat the tone length and therefore sound "matching". Tones that are half as long or twice as long also sound "fitting" in this way. With tones that are three times as long or only a third as long, this harmony is still recognizable, but no longer so easy to grasp.

Such repetitions can also occur with groups of tones. For example, if a new note always begins after 4 quarter notes, this is a 4/4 time signature – you can then clap along without knowing the melody. The 4/4 time is the easiest time, the 3/4 time the second easiest.

Now, the certain note can always be stressed in a measure. In classical music this is the first note of a measure, in rock music almost always the first and third note of a 4/4 measure, in reggae the second note of a 4/4 measure and so on. This emphasis gives the rhythm that a measure has.

The music builds itself up thus from elements, which one can hear and feel without any previous knowledge. From the sequence of the tones with their respective pitch and tone length as well as their possible emphasis then the melody results, which one can follow like an energy flow.
Because of this simple structure, music is a universally understandable language – everyone experiences an increase of energy when a melody rises and a decrease of energy when a melody falls. The melody tells the story of a level of energy.

The crop circles use a very similar principle. For example, the same sizes (circle diameters, circle distances) are often repeated – this corresponds to equal tone lengths. The repetition of whole units like the polar system corresponds to the beat. The doubling of the size of a circle corresponds to the octave, which has a frequency twice as high. The overall design of a crop circle corresponds to the composition, i.e. mainly to the melody.
Therefore, the crop circles can be called the "music of geometry".

IV 1. b) Astrology

In astrology, the 12-part zodiac is especially noticeable, which very often shows up in the crop circles as the 12-part surrounding space around a circle – as 12 rays, 12 feathers, 12 triangles or the like. In music these are the 12 notes of a scale.
But also the astrological aspects find their correspondence in the music and in the crop circles:

Astrology, music and crop circles					
Angles	Fractions	Quality	Astrological aspects	Musical intervals	Crop circle forms
0°	12/12 = 1/1	unity	conjunction	first	circle
30°	1/12	step	semisextile	second	-
60°	2/12 = 1/6	group	sextile	third	6 circles on 1 ring
90°	3/12 = 1/4	separation	square	fourth	4 circles on 1 ring
120°	4/12 = 1/3	connection	trine	fifth	3-pole
150°	5/12	transformation	quincunx	sixth	-
180°	6/12 = 1/2	opposition	opposition	octave	2-Pole

The different possibilities to change a quantity always have the same quality in each area: the doubling is always harmonious, the halving creates an opposition, the quartering separates and spans a space, the thirding creates a development cycle, etc.

The crop circles are therefore not only a "music of geometry", but also a "geometrical representation of astrological aspects", i.e. an "astrological geometry".

IV 1. c) Physics

Also in physics the same qualities of numbers and fractions can be found: the "12" of the number of elementary particles, the "12" of the oscillations of the super-strings, the "1" of the gravitation which pulls everything together, the "2" of the bipolar electromagnetic force, the "3" of the tripolar color force, the "4" of the right angle between electric and magnetic wave, and so on.

Another important element of physics are the conservation laws, which lead to the fact that nowhere something is added out of nothingness or is lost into nothingness. In the case of crop circles this element can be found in the conclusiveness of the structure of a crop circle: Each element ideally has a meaningful relation to all other elements – no impulse of a crop circle element is lost. However, this connection is not as obvious as e.g. the number analogies.

IV 1. d)   The Three-Step

The three-step is a principle which can be observed wherever an impulse acts out from a center into a medium surrounding this center. Such a center is e.g. the sun – the associated medium is the stardust in the universe, which consists of finest dust and gases.

The sun emits not only light but also ions, i.e. electrically charged particles. These particles fly away from the sun in all directions and collide with the stardust, which is thereby pushed away from the sun. In this way a hollow sphere has gradually formed, which consists of stardust and solar ions and which is extended by the ions constantly bouncing on it from the sun. This hollow sphere, which is called "impact front", consists only of "dense stardust", but it has nevertheless a total mass as large as the earth.

- The sun is in the center.

-Around it there is the area which has been completely emptied by the solar ions, so that the ions can fly unhindered up to the shock front. This area is called the "solar wind area".

- Next follows the "shock front" – the stardust hollow sphere.

- At the very outside comes the "bow wave", which is caused by the shock front moving through the stardust due to its constant expansion – this has the same effect as a ship sailing through water.

So, around a radiating center in a medium there are three areas with distinctive features, which describe the radiation of this center:

1. solar wind: the unobstructed expansion
2. shock front: the shape created by the encounter with the world
3. bow wave: the movement which arises from the contact with the world

These three steps, i.e. impulse, form and contact, are the dynamics found in every expansion.

251

IV 1. e) The Chakras

The chakras are the combination of a polar system with the developmental dynamics of the three-step.

The center is the heart chakra and the two poles are one's own body (three chakras below the heart chakra) and the rest of the world (three chakras above the heart chakra).

At the bottom, the three developmental steps are the solar plexus (unrestrained physical self-expression), the hara (physical posture), and the root chakra (physical contact). Above, these are the throat chakra (uninhibited social self-expression), the third eye (orientation and posture in the world), and the crown chakra (social and mental contact).

IV 1. f) Polarity

The principle of polarity, i.e. the consideration of the interaction of two complementary opposites, is found in many systems: in the Yin/Yang system, in Hegelian dialectics (thesis – antithesis – synthesis), in Steiner's threefold system (expansion – contraction – rhythm), and so on.

IV 1. g) Polarization

Polarization is the separation of a healthy state into two suffering extremes. There are three basic forms of this polarization:

1. the polarization of contact: It can happen in Freud's "oral phase" (age: 0-1 year). Thereby the security splits into a renouncing ascetic and a greedy addict.

2. The polarization of the form: It can happen in Freud's "anal phase" (age: 1-3 years). Here the force splits into a dominant perpetrator and a submissive victim.

3. Polarization of the impulse: This can happen in Freud's "phallic phase" (age: 3-12 years). Here, self-love splits into a fan with an inferiority complex

252

and a star with delusions of grandeur.

This polarization, however, is not relevant for the crop circles, because through the crop circles only wholesome states are represented.

IV 1. h) The Kabbalistic Tree of Life

The Kabbalistic Tree of Life is a structure that can be found in all things – from the structure of a vacuum cleaner or a cell, to the German constitution and the organization of a bee colony, to the evolution of living beings on earth and the possibilities of experience in meditation.

This structure is so universal because it is based on a simple principle that is developed step by step:

1. the world is a unified whole. Therefore, it can be represented by a circle:

o

2. the world is both a unity and a multiplicity. Between the two, there is the unfolding of unity to multiplicity, or the return of multiplicity to unity. The unity expresses itself quite simply in the uniform laws of nature in the whole universe. These three steps can be represented by three circles, where the upper one represents the unity, the lower one the multiplicity and the middle one the differentiation:

3. this development, i.e. the circle in the center, can be represented as a three-step, i.e. as impulse, form and contact:

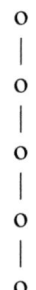

4. each of these three development steps (the three middle circles) can be divided again into three development steps (three triangles of three circles each):

```
     o
   o | o
   | o |
   o | o
   | o |
   o | o
     o
     |
     o
```

5. the classical representation of this structure looks as follows:

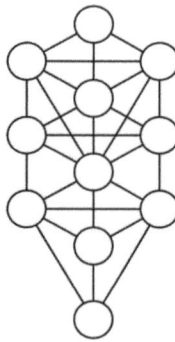

This structure appears in the crop circles 1. as a Tree of Life graphic, 2. as a 9-polarity and 3. as a three-step development.

(A detailed presentation of the Tree of Life may be found in my book "Blüten des Lebensbaunes I, II, III").

IV 1. i) The Dynamics of Development

There are seven developmental phases in both biography and history. They are based on three three-steps, where the last step of one three-step is at the same time the first step of the following three-step.

The developmental phases						
Phase	*Three three-steps*		*Biography*	*History*	*Quality*	*Essence*
1st phase	1st three-step, 1st part		baby (oral phase)	Paleolithic	living as part of the whole in the whole	„Yes"
2nd phase	1st three-step, 2nd part		infant (anal phase)	Neolithic	distinguish pleasant and unpleasant	"No!"
3rd phase	1st three-step, 3rd part	2nd three-step, 1st part	child (phallic phase)	Kingship	thinking, seeing and doing everything out of the centre	"Yes" + "No!" = "I!!!"
4th phase		2nd three-step, 2nd part	adolescent (genital phase)	Materia-lism	exploring and using the outside world	"You?"
5th phase	3rd three-step, 1st part	2nd three-step, 3rd part	adult (adult phase)	Globali-zation	creating a stable system (family)	"Me!!!" + "You?" = "We"
6th phase	3rd three-step, 2nd part		age (tutorial phase)	Future I	exploring the new and tea-ching the known	"Other …"
7th phase	3rd three-step, 3rd part		old age (venerable phase)	Future II	wisdom of old age	"We" + "Other …" = "All".

In the crop circles almost only the single three-step is found, but not this sequence of 7. Possibly there is a connection to the isolated 7 circles, but this is rather uncertain.

(A detailed account can be found in my book "Die sieben Schritte des Lebens").

IV 1. j) Self-similarity and fractals

All living systems are characterized by self-similarity – all parts of a system are designed according to the same basic principles (among other things, they all have the same horoscope). This is also true for crop circles and also for any convincing work of art.

The fractal is, so to speak, the manufacturing instruction for self-similarity: the same principle is applied at all places and at every level of differentiation.

IV 1. k)   The golden section

The golden section is a mathematical relation between two lengths. The golden ratio is defined in the following way: "a:b = b:c" and "a+b=c". The size ratio for which these two formulas apply is "a:b=b:c=1.618".

Graphically, the golden section looks like this:

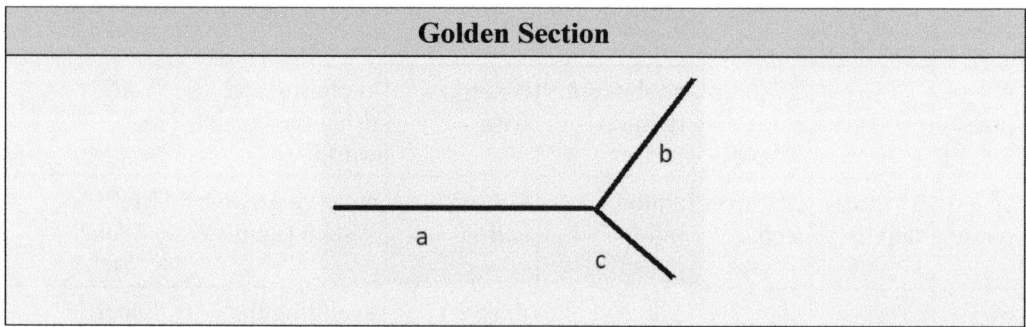

If you add the length of the straight line "c" with the length of the straight line "b", you get the length "c". If you divide the length "b" by the length "c", you get "1.618". If you divide the length "a" by the length "b", you also get "1.618".

So, with the Golden Ratio, there is a set of quantities whose ratio to each other always remains the same, which causes the harmonic effect that this ratio has.

One can approach the golden ratio as follows:

$$
\begin{aligned}
1+ 1&= 2 \Rightarrow \ 2: 1= 2,000 \\
1+ 2&= 3 \Rightarrow \ 3: 2= 1,500 \\
2+ 3&= 5 \Rightarrow \ 5: 3= 1,667 \\
3+ 5&= 8 \Rightarrow \ 8: 5= 1,600 \\
5+ 8&=13 \Rightarrow 13: 8= 1,625 \\
8+13&=21 \Rightarrow 21:13= 1,615 \\
13+21&=34 \Rightarrow 34:21= 1,619 \\
21+34&=55 \Rightarrow 55:34= 1,617 \\
34+55&=89 \Rightarrow 89:55= 1,618
\end{aligned}
$$

First of all, it sounds son as if it is quite easy to check the presence of the Golden Section in the crop circles – after all, you only need to look for whether two sizes in the crop circle have the ratio "1:1.618". However, because of the many sizes that normally occur in a crop circle, this is not as easy as it seems at first.

I don't know of any crop circle which consists e.g. of a series of 5 circles whose sizes all decrease in the golden ratio, which thus have e.g. the diameters 10.00m, 6.18m, 3.82m, 2.36m and 1.46m. With such a crop circle the golden section would be clearly intended.

This crop circle, if it consisted of concentric circles, would look like the following:

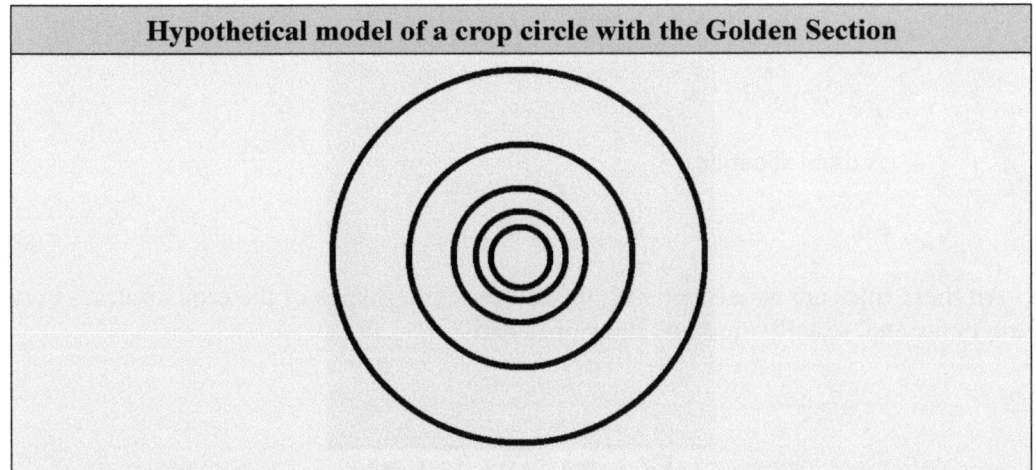

Hypothetical model of a crop circle with the Golden Section

Such a crop circle is not known so far. Nevertheless one finds in the books and articles about the crop circles again and again the quite unprecise reference "The crop circle seems to contain the Golden Section" or similar.

One can understand the Golden Section as a simple fractal – it is created by multiplying a length again and again by "1.618" or dividing a length again and again by "1.618".

IV 1. l) The Feng-Shui

Feng-Shui also deals with the effects of shapes, among other things. Some simple rules for the effects of shapes from Feng-Shui are:

1. Straight lines focus the flow of life force and give rise to a hard beam ("laser beam").

2. Curved lines, circles, wavy lines, etc. loosen the flow of life force and create a soft flow.

3. The repetition of the same elements creates a rhythm.

4. A curve sucks from its inside (sliding slope of a river in a curve) and radiates towards its outside (bouncing slope of a river in a curve).

5. A mountain centers.

6. A valley collects.

7. A ditch separates.

etc.

All these rules are consistent with the effect of the shapes of the crop circles – they are, in the end, exactly the same rules of shape.

IV 1. m) The Ba-Gua

A special element of Feng-Shui is the Ba-Gua. With its help one can recognize the balance of forces in a place.

The Chinese Ba-Gua, which is also known as "Vastu Purusha" in India, is based on a very simple principle: a division of a surface into three steps twice.

The surface is divided from bottom to top into three stripes: at the bottom is little energy ("valley"), in the middle is medium energy ("plain") and at the top is a lot of energy ("mountain").

The surface is also divided into three stripes from left to right. Since the sun, the moon and the stars for an observer on the northern hemisphere of the earth (where this system originates), always move from left to right, the following division results: on the left the past, in the middle the present and on the right the future.

This results in an area which is divided in a simple way into 3·3=9 fields. If in each case the two qualities are combined, distinctive qualities result:

The Ba-Gua		
much energy in the past: sponsor, donation, help, God, angel, blessing, store-room, meeting-room.	much energy in the present: glory, crown, prestige, office, residence, crown room	much energy in the future: goals, ideals, hope, relation-ships, bedroom (relationship room), tower (wide view)
medium energy in the past: family of origin, parents, living room	medium energy in the present: center, self-image, current main topic, one's own soul, altar	medium energy in the future: one's own family, children, children's room
little energy in the past: studies, work, ignorance, curiosity, departure, origin, workroom	little energy in the present: profession, foundation, acti-vity, workplace, workshop	little energy in the future: rest, exhaustion, failure, toilet, sauna, compost

This structure can be applied to all things. For example, with the help of this structure one can recognize in which condition a painter has painted a picture.

For example, you can also find the different themes in the corresponding places on medieval paintings:

- bottom left: starting point
- left center: helping angel, altar
- top left: God (helps, blesses)
- center bottom: Bible, church
- center middle: Christ, central theme

259

- center top: the ideal
- bottom right: the desperate, the striving, the praying, hell
- center right: a saint as an example
- top right: Heaven, Paradise

Since the crop circles usually stand freely in space and have no clear bottom and top, the Ba-Gua can only very rarely be applied to the crop circles.

IV 1. n)   Tribal tattoos

If you take a closer look at the newer tradition of "Tribal Tattoos", you will notice that many of the forms used in these tattoos have a great dynamic. The tension and dynamics of these tattoos are based, like the aesthetics and fascination of crop circles, on the observation of simple geometric shapes, of number ratios and the like. However, there seems to be no such system to these tattoos as there is to the crop circles – if one disregards the general "spanning of the lines".

However, a well-done tribal tattoo often has a similar aura as a crop circle – they are just much more dynamic and aggressive than crop circles.

IV 1. o)   Places of power and leylines

It seems as if crop circles appear rather often at places of power and on ley-lines, i.e. on the connecting lines between two places of power. However, it is a little difficult to say something more precise about this.

For example, the large field in Alton Barnes is next to the White Horse in Wiltshire the place where probably most regularly crop circles may be found and where also the most crop circles occur. Is that because of the White Horse? Is it a power place? It's hard to say.

Wiltshire as a whole has many places that could be considered power places such as White Horse, Stonehenge, Woodhenge, Silbury Hill, Avebury, barrows, etc. So, at the very least, we can say that the place where the vast majority of all crop circles occur is full of prehistorically significant places.

Whether these places are places of power and whether there is a direct connection between these places and the crop circles is difficult to determine.

IV 1. p) Summary

All in all, the picture that emerges is that there is a simple language of forms, which results from proportions, development dynamics, form origins of forms and the like. It characterizes not only crop circles, but also music and parts of geometry. Also the numbers themselves have the same qualities in the most different areas.

The crop circles are a geometrical expression of these basic qualities and connections. Therefore one can understand the crop circles as the "music of geometry".

IV 2. Life force and crop circles

The previous observations of the crop circles show that they represent fundamental forms and structures. They therefore correspond to the chakra system, the zodiac, the Kabbalistic Tree of Life, the harmony system in music, Feng-Shui, Ba-Gua and similar systems, which also represent fundamental relationships in forms and dynamics.

If one looks at these systems, one notices that they all do not describe physical processes, but rather something like fundamental orders, which in turn then shape the physical processes. They are, so to speak, something like the rules according to which the laws of nature are constructed – the rules behind the rules, so to speak.

Furthermore it is remarkable that all these systems are symmetrical as well as simple.

Finally, it is also noteworthy that the structures that follow these rules look beautiful and exert a fascination on almost all observers. Apparently, such structures remind people of something they carry within themselves and recognize.

Therefore, one can wonder what it is in the human being that is being recognized and what it is that has such a great effect.

If you look at the chakra system, it becomes clear that it stands between consciousness and matter – it is a structure on the border between the two. The "substance" of this boundary is often referred to as the "life force".

Also with the other systems, which were just enumerated, one can say that they do not represent physical connections (except perhaps the music) and are also no pure processes of consciousness, but just at the most something like structures at the transition from consciousness to matter, i.e. "life force structures".

The life force apparently has its own rules, which are similar to the principles of music and the basic laws of physics. The life-force rules are simple principles of symmetry, qualities of form, dynamics of development, laws of conservation and the like. One could say that when looking at these structures, one can watch God constructing this world – one does not see the individual law of nature, but the harmony underlying the laws of nature.

If the crop circles apparently give form to this harmony-preservation, these symmetry-principles, form-qualities and development-dynamics, one wonders how this can come about at all.

Does the collective subconsciousness create the crop circles by collective telekinesis? Then the collective subconsciousness of the people obviously knows these life force structures.

Telepathy and telekinesis are the eye and hand of both the personal subconscious and the collective subconscious – and both the subconsciousness and the telepathy

262

and the telekinesis in it belong to the life force. That means that telepathy and tele-kinesis take place in the area, in which also the structures are resident, which can take shape among other things in the crop circles.

Now one may ask whether really all crop circles, which express these structures, really originated by collective telekinesis. This question is not so important as it may appear at first, because if a single person or a group of people is able to produce crop circles which express these structures, then these people must have had an access to their subconsciousness or to the collective subconsciousness – they were thus inspired, i.e. they perceived something inwardly and then represented this outwardly.

It is of course interesting to know that there are both possibilities of origin – for some crop circles it is known that they were created at night within one hour (which cannot be done by humans), while for others it is known that they were made by humans. However, since only from a tiny part of the 10,000 crop circles it is clearly known how they were created, unfortunately the quality of the telekinetically created crop circles cannot be compared with the quality of the crop circles created by hand – one does not know as a rule how a crop circle was created.

In the end, however, it is enough to know that there are two possible ways of origin for crop circles – if one leaves out the advertising crop circles and the like:

     1. collective telekinesis:
          a) Structures of the life force
      => b) selection of a motive
      => c) collective telekinesis
      => d) crop circle

     2. human work:
          a) structures of the life force
      => b) inspiration of a human being
      => c) craftsmanship
      => d) crop circle

The crop circles have a radiance when they are an expression of the structures and dynamics of the life force. Then they are the "music of geometry".

Crop circles, like astrology, the Kabbalistic Tree of Life, the Ba-Gua, etc., can illustrate the basic rules according to which our world is constructed.

They show the structures in the life force and thus make it easier to orient oneself in the world.

They make it possible to better understand the transition and the connection bet-ween consciousness and matter.

They show a way to understand the rules according to which the structures of the world are built and according to which the dynamics in the world take place. This makes it easier to behave reasonably and effectively in the world.

They are a help both on the way from the outside to the inside, i.e. in self-knowledge, and on the way from the inside to the outside, i.e. in self-actualization. Knowing these structures and dynamics, both meditation on the way from the outside to the inside and magic on the way from the inside to the outside become easier and more effective.

It is obviously worthwhile to learn this "language of the life force" and to keep it in mind in all contemplations and in all actions.

These structures and dynamics of the life force are the central element in the magical-mythological cultures. In them they are called "rightness", "roundness", "poetical metre", "beauty" and the like. This quality is seen in these cultures as the right state from which knowledge, power, love and flourishing arise.

This quality is also conceived as the security with the Mother Goddess. It is symbolized by the roundness of the wheel or by the right tuning of a harp. The personal part of this rightness is one's own soul.

If one acts in accordance with this rightness, one is successful, if one acts in contradiction to this rightness, one reaps failure. It is true that it is also about the general rightness, i.e. about the archetypes in the collective subconsciousness, but it is primarily about the personal rightness, i.e. about the images in the personal subconsciousness. The general rightness shows up in every single human being through the birth horoscope of this human being – for every human being other aspects of the general rightness are in the foreground.

The principle of rightness is found in almost all ancient languages:

Egyptians:	*ma'at*	("mother")
Sumerians:	*me*	("mother")
Chinese:	*tao*	("way")
Teutons:	*sidr*	("ancient way")
Navahos:	*ho'zhong*	("beauty")
Indians (new):	*dharma*	("poetic metre")
Tibetans:	*tashi*	("happy destiny")
Celts:	*fhirinne*	("truth")
Slavs:	*prawda*	("truth")
Romans:	*ritus*	("wheel")
Hittites:	*aya*	("wheel")
Indians (old):	*rita*	("wheel")
Persians:	*asha*	("wheel")
Greeks:	*dikaios*	("justice")
etc.		

The "rules of the life force" are the "roots of truth".

They are the rightness to which behavior is related in the proven, time-honored way and which creates righteousness.

It is the right measure and also the verse measure that gives rise to beauty. It is perfectly round and balanced like a wheel.

It is the gift of the Mother Goddess that helps to go one's own way and find a happy destiny.

These are also the qualities that give the crop circles their fascination.

IV 3. Dream journeys to the crop circles

So far in this book, only observational, analytical, comparative and deductive methods have been used. One stands in the world, contemplates its phenomena and wonders how it all came about …

However, one can also go to the level where these phenomena originate, i.e. to one's own subconsciousness, to the collective subconsciousness, to the life force – which is ultimately all the same realm: the transition between consciousness and matter. This realm can be directly perceived through dream journeys.

A dream journey is nothing exotic: one merely coordinates waking consciousness with dream consciousness. This is something that can be learned quite quickly once you do it with someone who can already do it.

This state of consciousness also occurs spontaneously: on the one hand in the morning when waking up from a dream, when the dream continues to run in its own dynamics for another five seconds, although one is already awake, and on the other hand in a daydream, in which, for example, one relives a vacation scene in a very realistic way.

Such dream journeys can also be used to investigate the crop circles. One can imagine to go through a crop circle like through a door and then to look what one experiences on the other side of the door. You can also imagine sitting inside a crop circle you have once been inside, and then see what happens. One can also simply address a crop circle inwardly and ask it a question. There are no limits to creativity here.

The good thing about such dream journeys is that you never know what will come, and you always find things you didn't expect. In this way, the image you have of the thing to wich you are making a dream journey, can become more complete.

A great advantage of dream journeys is that telepathy is, so to speak, the sensory organ of the subconscious mind and therefore it is much easier to perceive telepathically on a dream journey than in a normal waking state. Therefore one can find out with the help of dream journeys also things about crop circles, which one would discover with the help of his mind only very laboriously (if at all).

To do a dream journey does not mean, of course, to give up one's mind. During the dream journey itself, one should simply look attentively at what one perceives inwardly and first of all not evaluate or reject anything. Afterwards, you can have a look at what you have experienced and what it probably means and what benefit it has for you.

A dream journey is an experiment: one plans it, one carries it out and observes attentively, one analyzes afterwards the observations, one examines the possible applications of the results, and one plans due to the results further experiments.

In the case of dream journeys, the attitude of a researcher makes the most sense …

266

1st dream journey

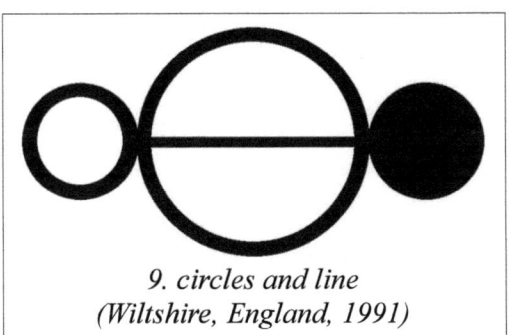

*9. circles and line
(Wiltshire, England, 1991)*

For this dream journey I use the crop circle shown on the left, in which I experienced and understood the polarity tension for the first time. In my imagination I will go to this crop circle and talk to it.

"Hello crop circle. Through you I have seen the inner tension and dynamics of a crop circle for the first time 29 years ago. Would you like to tell me something about yourself or anything else that might be useful to me or for the readers of this book?"
"What do you want to know?"
"I want to know what crop circles are."
"Patterns in grain."
"Hmm – should I speak to you as precisely as possible?"
"I'd like that."
"So: how do crop circles form?"
"By pushing down the stalks."
"What pushes the stalks down?"
"The force."
"What force? Or whose force?"
"The force of the people."
"Physical force or telekinetic force?"
"Both."
"Sometimes this and sometimes that?"
"Yes."
"What was it with you?"
"The telekinetic power of some people near this place."
"Did they do it consciously?"
"No, unconsciously."
"Did I get the meaning of the crop circle right?"
"Yes."
"Did I also recognize it completely?"
"No."
"What did I not recognize?"

"The harmony and the life in the flow."

"Um ... the harmony is in the crop circle as a whole and the life flow is in the tension between the outer circles as well as in the flow, rotation and pulsation in the central circle?"

"Yes."

"And I haven't quite grasped that yet?"

"That is so."

"Why?"

"You still fear the flow of life."

"Um, yes ... that may be ... especially Kundalini maybe? ... Say, Crop Circle, I've made dream journeys to my soul, to deities, to power animals, to healing plants, and much more, but I've never had a dream journey where I had to ask mathematically precise questions, so to speak, and get mathematically precise answers. Why is that?"

"You're asking a geometric shape. My essence is precision. My answers are precise. My answers are formal. My answers are symmetry. If you will take dream journeys to healing stones, you will find something similar."

"Yes, I can see ... that's quite plausible – animals have dynamics, plants have posture, and minerals have structure. ... Does that mean that crop circles appear in grain, but are actually mineral in nature?"

"Geometric – yes, and closely related to mineral. Both are structure-related."

"Why do crop circles actually occur? I mean, what is the impetus that causes the collective telekinesis of the collective subconsciousness of humans to set in motion such complex telekinesis?"

"Desire."

"Um – the collective longing for becoming aware of these fundamental structures and dynamics again?"

"The perception of the state of non-rightness generates the longing for the state of rightness."

"The perception of the state of non-rightness ... yes, that is plausible as a cause ... the Hopis call such a state 'Koyaanisqatsi' – a state that needs to be changed' ... the Egyptians had a goddess of rightness – she was called 'Ma'at' ... and they had a goddess of non-rightness – she was called 'Isfet' ...

So you mean that from about 1975 on people had an increased longing for correctness in a world of non-rightness? This fits well with the other currents of that time: late hippies, environmental protection, first globalization approaches, the 'Limits of Growth', religious-spiritual openness, disarmament demonstrations, etc. And this collective yearning then materialized through collective telekinesis?"

"Yes."

"That's conclusive. It also explains why it happened at that time. At that time, the first people to have the Pluto/Neptune-sextile in their chart turned about 30 years

old. This aspect began around 1945 and continues to this day and further on until 2039. At that time, Pluto was in Leo and Neptune was in Libra, which means that these people were looking for the harmony of individuals – both in the individual and in the community. This harmony in individual and collective self-expression is the most important thing for people with this aspect. So the longing for an image for this harmony fits well with that – and the crop circles are the image for this longing for a harmonious rightness?"

"Yes."

"Um – that makes a lot of sense to me. So far in my considerations the reason has been missing why the crop circles have appeared increasingly from about 1975.

The first people with the Pluto/Neptune-sextile in their horoscope were about 30 years old around 1975, i.e. they had their Saturn phase just behind them, which takes place approximately at the age of 28-29 years. At this age, Saturn is again in the same place as in a person's birth chart. This means that at the age of 28-29 people are confronted with what they have become so far and what they have done with their life so far – this can be a crisis. You can observe this very clearly with soccer players, who almost all have a crisis at this age, only have to sit on the reserve bench, no longer score goals – soccer players are at the appropriate group of persons for these observations because their achievements are publicly displayed.

So this means that the first people with this Pluto/Neptune-sextile around 1975 had their Saturn phase behind them and realized what they find unbearable. As usual after the Saturn phase, a re-orientation and a longing for the right state arose. And this then showed up in the collective crop circle telekinesis ..."

"Pluto is the great force and Neptune is the boundary dissolution ... that together results in the great force in the collective subconsciousbess. This force, this longing for the right state has then materialized, among other things, as the crop circles."

"Now I'm looking on crop circles in this way, it's all much more coherent than it has been so far ... I'm surprised how coherently astrology fits in here ... well, actually it always does, but you don't always see it – and then when you discover it, you wonder why you didn't figure it out sooner ... ... is there anything more you could tell me, crop circle?"

"I only have as many answers as you have questions."

"Yes ... I guess that's the nature of geometric shapes and mathematical structures ..."

"Yes."

"Thank you, crop circle! That was really very helpful!"

"You're welcome."

"Ho!"

I also noticed that in 1975, all people who were 30 years old or younger had the

269

Pluto/Neptune-sextile in their chart. That must have been about 40% of humanity by then. So the longing for rightness of the oldest of them, who had just had their Saturn phase, resonated with 40% of the people. These 40% of the people seem to have been something like a "critical mass", which was necessary to set the emergence of the crop circles in motion.

As Mr. Spock would say: *"Fascinating ..."*

2ⁿᵈ dream journey

19. bow triangles
(Wiltshire, England, 1996)

I use this image as a door and walk through this door.

I see fire and water – red and rather vertical areas of flames and blue, horizontal areas of water. The whole thing is not a landscape or similar, but rather something like a 'qualities-picture' – but it is very beautiful and appealing ...

I greet fire and water with a "Hello." There's something else – a yellow light in the center behind the water and the fire ... something like a golden yellow sun ... radiant ... I'm liking the image more and more ... this is – yes, I almost said 'juicy' ... it's substantial, lively ... um, I can't find the right word ... it's also essential ... it's even more ... it's like life itself ... being in the middle of life ... that's perfect, pure enjoyment – that's really brilliant! These are rich colors, a fulfilling glow – oh boy!

There's also a smile in all of this – it's a bit like that Buddha smile, or like the smile of most ancient Egyptian statues, but it's more joyful, more alive, more dancing, more joyful ... it's just brilliant! What kind of place is this! Life ...

The fire and the water are completely opposite, but they are friends at the same time and dance together and through their dance shines this bright yellow sun ...

The two circles of the crop circle are the fire and the water, the two crescents are their common dance, the big circle is the sun ... the two buds are something like the security that the fire and the water have in their dance ... they are also the joy that comes through this dance ... the two buds are the two tips of an almond and thus the intersection between the fire-circle and the water-circle – so it fits well that it is the joy of the common dance ...

"Can you also flow in me?"

270

This is possible only very gradually ... it is like a groping through my body ... a gradual pushing of things and energies ... but then this broad 'grinning from ear to ear' begins ... that feels good!

The sun is now in my heart chakra and I suspect it is also in my sushumna, fire and water are on the left and right, dancing and blending together – so not water on the left and fire on the right or anything ... it's a joint movement – a joint wafting and flowing ... That feels good! That's the right way! So many worries and fears just stop ... Amazing!

I don't know if this state is permanent in me as of now, but feeling it like this now just feels good!

"Thank you!"

I feel a smile in response ...

"Ho!"

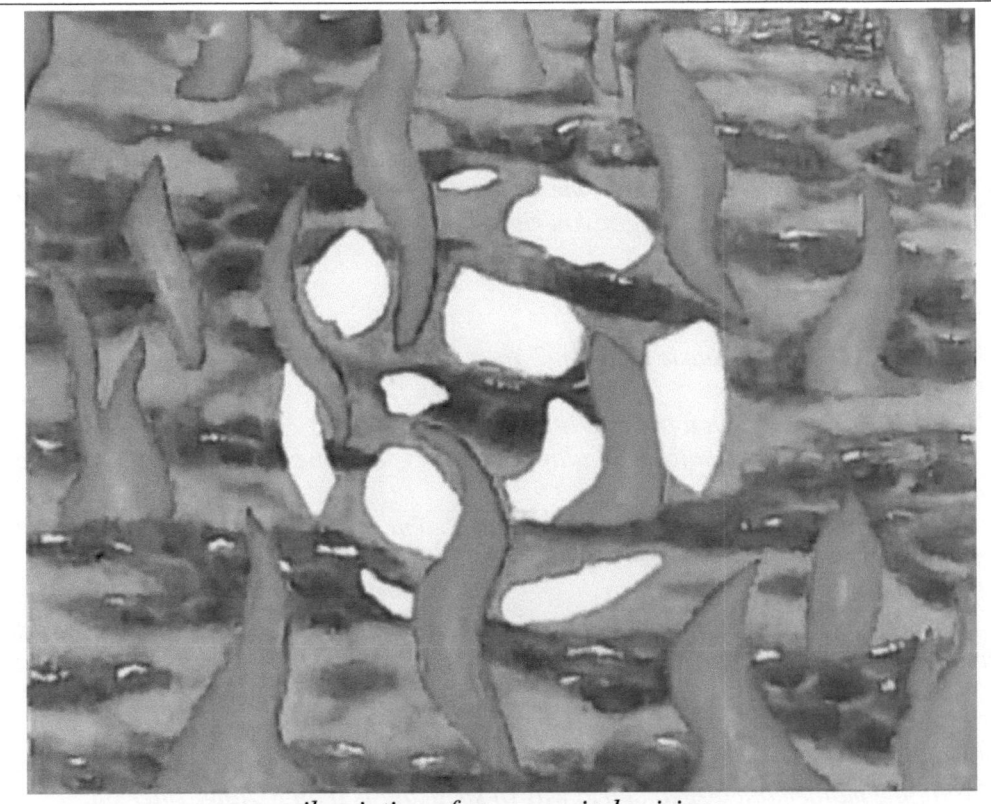

oil-painting of my crop circle vision:
water (blue waves), fire (red flames) and sun (yellow circle)

271

3rd dream journey

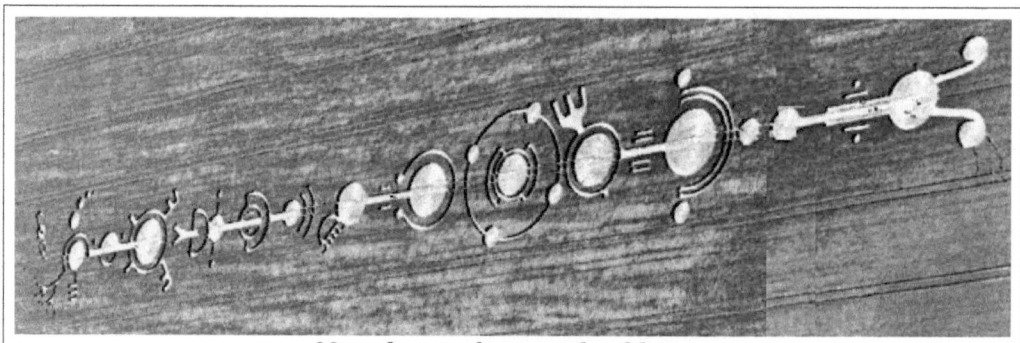

38. polar strukture with additions
(Wiltshire, England, 1999)

What's the best way to proceed with a crop circle like this? To me, asking questions seems to make the most sense ...

"Hello crop circle – can you tell me something about you? Or show me something about you? I'm not so sure I've got you right."
"You didn't."
"Um – not at all or errors in detail?"
"Errors in detail."
"Can you tell me your basic meaning? Your core principle, so to speak?"
"Evolution."
"Um ... ah yes ... can you put in a little more detail?"
"The basic principle unfolds, multiplies, grows, becomes bigger and more effective."
"Yes ... that sounds like life and evolution ... I'm just not quite clear on what can actually undergo evolution in a crop circle."
"The shape."
"Um, yes ... that's what makes a crop circle to begin with. But where does a crop circle evolve to?"
"Variety."
"Um – in a fractal way? Or just more complex? Or bigger?"
"More diverse."
"Well, the mathematical-geometric way of speaking is a bit tedious, after all."
"Formulate precisely."
"All right – I'll give it a try. I'd like to know what you're expressing as a whole."

"Joy."

"Hm ... well ... it's not easy for me to see that as the essence of this crop circle – it does somehow fit the size and the playfulness that this crop circle has ..."

"Why do you speak of me in the third person?"

"Oh, sorry – it's because it's a little unusual for me to be talking to a crop circle. So it's joy ..."

"Yes."

"Does that apply just to you or to all crop circles?"

"For all crop circles."

"Only joy?"

"No, there can be something else mixed in."

"What has been mixed in with you?"

"Complexity and playfulness."

"Yes, that can be seen. ... Can you say that the collective subconscious plays with forms of joy?"

"If you have a longing for rightness – yes."

"Um – showing joy as a response to the search for rightness is plausible, even if I wouldn't have thought of it myself. ... And why so complex?"

"It triggers wonder."

"Yes, it does ... and what does wonder do?"

"To wake up, to pause."

"And that probably helps you see rightness again."

"It opens your eyes."

"O.k. – that's more accurate."

"Thank you."

"Oh – please! ... Is there such a thing as an overall gesture in your forms?"

"Play."

"Hmm ... how does your play work?"

"Now that's finally a good question! Dancing, resting in yourself, expressing yourself, trying out new things, laughing, rejoicing, smiling ... that's the game."

"That's the game?"

"That's the game."

"So not a game with rules?"

"No – expression of joy."

"Um ... you sound like some wise, laughing, Chinese Buddha ..."

"Have you ever talked to one?"

"Uh, no ... hey! You've got a sense of humor!"

"That's the game."

"Well, you're making me make statements and connections that I didn't expect at all. ... But I'm still looking for the overall message of your variety of forms ..."

"Joy."

"You create all these forms out of joy?"

"You create these forms – your collective subconsciousness."

"Um ... yes ... so that wants to rejoice?"

"It's always rejoicing – there's no 'wanting to rejoice'."

"Tell me – is that what I found on the second crop circle dream trip? That joy, that emotion, that 'grinning from ear to ear'?"

"Yes – that's what the essence of crop circles is."

"I think that's how I'm beginning to understand. Joy is the fruit on the tree of rightness ..."

"Yes."

"Isn't that what the ancient Egyptians said:

> *There is rightness: 'Ma'at.'*
>
> *One's portion of it is the soul: 'Ba'.*
>
> *This portion is related to a deity: 'Netjer em ib-i', – 'the deity in one's own heart'.*
>
> *If one is faithful to it, peace of mind arises: 'Hotep'.*
>
> *And from that comes joy: 'Reshut'."*

"Don't make it so complicated."

"Do you think it's too complicated?"

"Yes."

"And this Sumerian proverb 'Without one's Me (rightness, soul) one succeeds in nothing – with one's Me one succeeds in everything' – is that also too complicated?"

"Don't always tell everything you know."

"Um ... um ... all right – if you think so ... what do you think is essential?"

"Joy."

"Um ... yes well ... then I'll stick to that ..."

"It's good that you've started dancing again."

"You know everything too, don't you?"

"I am an expression of the collective subconsciousness, where everything is – and besides, I know everything you know, since I speak through you."

"Um, yes, well ... ... is it that for now?"

"If you have no more questions, I have no more answers."

"I've heard that before ... thank you, crop circle!"

"You're welcome."

"Ho!"

4th dream journey

47. butterfly man
(Niederlande, 2009)

This Butterfly Man crop circle invites you to talk to it …

"Hello, Butterfly Man – are you comfortable with me addressing you like this?"
"That's the picture you see."
"What do you mean? Do you see something different in yourself?"
"Are there butterfly people?"
"Well 'in reality' there aren't such people – only in myths."
"And are these myths well known in Holland – where I have been?"
"Probably not – more likely in Central America."
"What do you conclude from that?"
"Hmm ... that you are man's work?"

"I am anyway – either as the handiwork of a specific human being, or as the telekinetic work of your collective subconscious."
"Yes, well – I guess that's not a distinguishing criterion then ... What are you then?"
"The ideal of rightness – as you can see by my four 'da Vinci' arms and my four 'da Vinci' legs; and the ideal of lightness – as you can see by my wings."
"Do you have anything to do with the force fields depicted in some crop circles that resemble two wings?"
"I have four wings."
"So this is just an association?"
"Yes."
"Can you tell me anything else about yourself?"
"Joy is light. Joy is mobile. Joy dances."
"Um – letting go for advanced?"
"Presence for advanced."
"Um ... yes ... that seems very similar to me in the end."
"Letting go is the cure – presence is the healed state."
"So you crop circles have an impressively clear logic."
"We are, after all, symmetrical-logical-geometric forms."
"Yes ... there is actually a clear logic to be expected ... Tell me – is that the clarity you can also find as a human being, when you let your life force flow freely, when your kundalini is awakened, when you live out of your soul, when you are connected

275

to the gods?"
"Yes."
"I'm just realizing new things every time I go on a dream journey ..."
"Nice."
"Yes ... ... Thank you, butterfly person!"
"You're welcome."
"Ho!"

5th dream journey

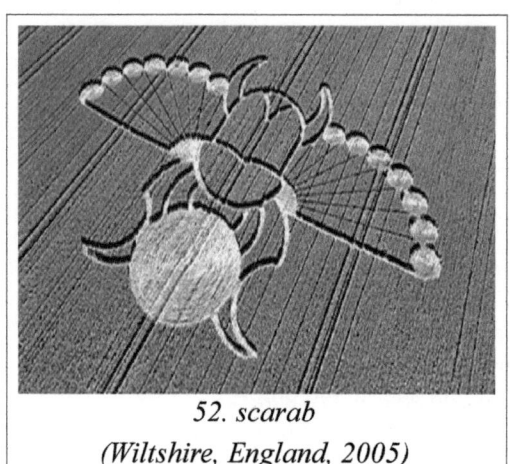

52. scarab
(Wiltshire, England, 2005)

This scarab also looks like a living being and hardly like a geometric structure. Therefore, a conversation seems most appropriate here as well.

"Hello crop circle – are you a scarab?"
"Yes – the image is me."
"You are the image of a scarab?"
"Isn't that obvious?"
"Well ... yes – but what lives in this picture?"
"Me."
"And what is that?"
"The parable between the sun rolling across the sky and the dung beetle rolling a dung ball before it."

"So it's the Egyptian image."
"Yes."
"And the wings of the winged sun ..."
"Yes – that's a closely related motif."
"Um – why did you appear as a crop circle?"
"Because Pluto in Leo longs for the glow of the soul."
"That glow is the sun? In the heart chakra, which also may be called the sun chakra?"
"Yes – the scarab was the heart chakra amulet."
"Is there anything you can tell me that I'm not clear about you yet?"
"Yes."
"What is it?"

276

"You don't dare to be a scarab yet, to be a winged sun."

"Now that is something said about me and not about you."

"If you don't dare to shine like me, you fear something in yourself – and in me."

"Ah – I see: That which I fear in you and in me is that which would be most precious to me if I could see it clearly."

"Yes."

"What is that?"

"Glow."

"Glow?"

"Glow."

"Um ... sounds like the problem of restricted social self-expression – throat chakra blockage ... I've seen that before ... And you can help me with that?"

"I am also the unrestrained self-expression: the rising sun."

"I should have rays like the rising sun?"

"Yes."

"Um – how do you do that?"

"Just start."

"Hm ... ... I guess what you mean ... just do it ... yes well ... It's like Zen and like Master Yoda – isn't it? ... ... Do you have any advice there?"

"That was the best advice there is on that."

"Yes ... it seems so to me ... yes then ... thank you very much, scarab!"

"You're welcome."

"Ho!"

6th dream journey

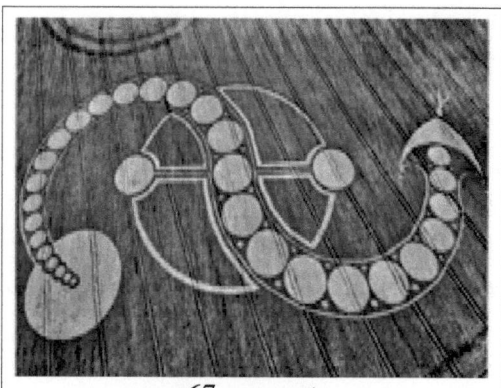

67. serpent
(Wiltshire, England, 2011)

This looks like a crop circle motif that I could go into.

I shift into the snake with my consciousness. I am powerful, limber, have a high body tension, I am very awake, very clear, I am one-pointed – I am doing exactly what I want.

I have an origin, I have a center, I have a goal – the white circle, the center circle, my head.

I am unwavering in my being, I am ruthless in my rightness, I am completely determined – I do what I want. I am straightforward, direct, present.

I am completely my body, I am completely my life force, I am me. The center radiates in warmth, the center transforms the tension of polarity into movement, I am in the center and the center is in me.

I am the fire of life.
I am the Kundalini.
I am the Caduceus.

I am Apophis.
I am Uraeus.
I am Quetzalcoatl.

I am the horned serpent of Marduk.
I am the horned serpent of Cernunnos.
I am the horned serpent of the Chinese Emperor.

I am the consciousness in Ida.
I am the consciousness in Pingala.
I am the consciousness in Sushumna.

I am the life.
I am the dance.
I am the breath.

I am the one you long for.
I am the one you fear.
I am the one you are.

Open yourself!
Live yourself!
Be yourself!

Ho!

I don't know if what I spontaneously wrote there as a crop circle snake can convey the feeling I had … this power and this body tension and this rightness, directness, life intensity, this action …
But I don't know any other words for it …

7th dream journey

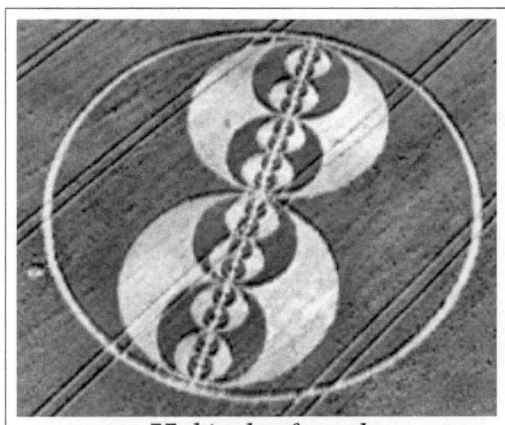

77. bipolar fractal
(Wiltshire, England, 2001)

What form of dream travel is most appropriate for this crop circle? I think walking around in this very regularly constructed crop circle is most appropriate.

I go inwardly to this crop circle and stand at first once on the small point on the left side of the circle. At this point I feel something firm, it has a binding quality – like an observer, guide, responsible person etc..
I go to the dark area in the big circle.
When I cross the outer ring, I feel a clear resistance – as if I were walking through a shell, through a vessel, through a protective area … a little bit this outer circle seems to me like the boiler of an old steam locomotive, in which the water is heated and which has to withstand a great pressure.
The dark area in the big circle is amazingly calm – no pressure, no movement, nothing …
I go into the light area of one of the two smaller circles. Here is more warmth, more

279

tension. It feels like I'm walking through several doors into a high security area – this was now the second room I've reached through these doors.

I walk into the dark area of the next smaller circle. Funny – there's hardly any heat or pressure here again – are they only in the light areas?

I go into the light area of the next smaller circle. Hardly any heat and pressure – only a little more than in the previous dark area and much less than in the previous bright area. Is this because this area is only half the size of the previous one?

I go into the dark area of the next smaller circle. Silence ...

I go into the light area of the next smaller circle – these are only the semicircle bulges at the light central axis. A slight tingling ...

And the central axis itself? There is a very strong pressure and movement – from top right to bottom left. It is as if this crop circle would produce a beam along its axis – which would fit well to the analogy of batteries, magnets or electric motors connected in series.

What is the quality of the beam? And what does it do? It is like a laser beam – one-directed, of uniform quality, the waves in it run synchronously. It clears the path in front of this beam. This reminds me of a Feng Shui rule: 'The Chi (life force) becomes a hard beam through long, straight lines, destroying whatever it hits.' If this ray is then additionally fed and strengthened by a series of polar circles, it is especially intense.

"Hello crop circle – what are you doing?"

"Showing what you're doing."

"Machines? Houses with straight edges? Right-angle thinking?"

"The first two points – there's nothing wrong with right angles in thinking – if you're looking at straight right angles."

"And this series of polar circles?"

"Gives intensity to the beam."

"Is there anything I haven't realized yet?"

"No – you have grasped this simple shape."

"Um, thanks. ... Ho!"

8th dream journey

85. three-polar Julia set
(Wiltshire, England, 1996)

What happens when you jump into a Julia set? Trying it out …

I jump inwardly through the picture as through a door-opening.

Wow! A violent vortex – I don't know if it pushes outwards or sucks towards the center … and I am in the middle of it …

Funny – first I saw blue, red and yellow, but that faded quickly and now I see only ochre and have the sensation of earth … the movement has stopped too … funny … what is this?

"Growth."

"Who is speaking?"

"Me."

"Who is 'I'?"

"The crop circle."

"What is your quality?"

"Earth."

"The earth is a vortex?"

"No – the earth is growth, flourishing and decay and new emergence."

"And what does that have to do with the Julia set?"

"She is a symbol of the earth – growth, unfolding. Look at leaves, ferns, the patterns of water in the sand …"

"I can see the resemblance to the plants, but not to the patterns in the sand."

"Tideways in the silt that go from thin threads to streams to small rivers."

"Um, yes well – if you mean simply the growing of the arms of the Julia set … ok. … Do you want to tell me something else?"

"I am something other than the vortex you can see in a polar circle – I am growth."

"Yes, I didn't distinguish that at first. Thank you, crop circle."

"There's something missing."

"What?"

"You need something of that quality yourself."

"How do I get it?"

"Stand consciously in me and open yourself."

"Okay, I will. … … … This dissolves the tensions in my body … this brings me back to my heart chakra … this reshapes everything from the heart chakra … This reminds me that in Tibetan Buddhism it is said that the innermost being of the created human being is a triple knot in the heart chakra – this is created at incarnation and dissolves again at death. Do you have anything to do with this knot, crop circle?"

"No – not directly. I am the growth. The knot is something else."

"What?"

"Ask the knot."

"Yes, well – some other time ... Then you are probably not related to the triskelis, that is, the three-legged sun, either?"

"No, I'm not. That's both similar to me in form, but I'm just the growth."

"Yes, thank you, crop circle."

"You are welcome."

"Ho!"

9th dream journey

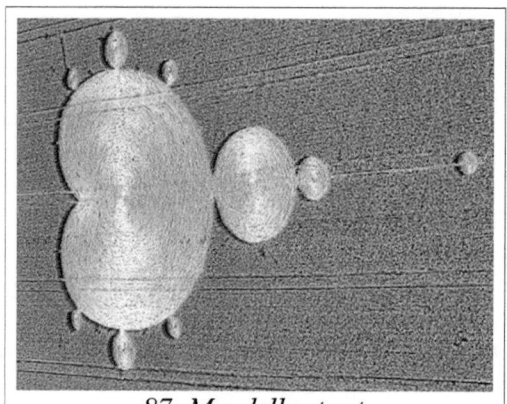

87. Mandelbrot set
(Oxfordshire, England, 1991)

This is one of the most famous crop circles ever. Which method? I think the conversation seems most appropriate to me.

"Hello crop circle – would you like to tell me something about yourself?"

"I'm not as important as you think – I'm just a conspicuous part of something much bigger."

"Um ... yes ... I once watched a film in which the fractal was depicted, of which you are a part. There a section of the picture was enlarged again and again and zoomed almost endlessly into the micros-copically small ... That you are only a striking part of something much bigger, I understand. But what does your striking form mean? Can you say something about it?"

"Concentration on the next step."

"Um – is that what makes you so fascinating to us?"

"Yes, most people can sense that, even if they couldn't put it into words."

"Yes, I couldn't have either. ... And why did you appear?"

"Because the next step is important."

282

"Um – isn't it always?"

"I am part of the answer to your longing for rightness."

"O.k. ... and why in a cornfield outside Oxford, of all places? Because that's where the mathematician Mandelbrot lives who discovered you?"

"The collective subconscious has a sense of humor – and it also likes to take associations as a crystallization point for its actions."

"I find that interesting about the crystallization point ... so the general pressure to create an Mandelbrot set as a crop circle became concrete near Oxford, because that was a tiny bit easier there by association to the mathematician Mandelbrot who lives in Oxford?"

"Yes – life force is also like water: it flows the easiest way."

"Um ... yes ... that is once again very simple and conclusive ... that seems to be typical for you geometric forms, after all."

"You know this also from dream journeys to deities."

"Yes ... yes, I guess it's true ... there's that quality too. ... ... Do you want to say anything else?"

"No."

"Thank you."

"You are welcome."

"Ho!"

10th dream journey

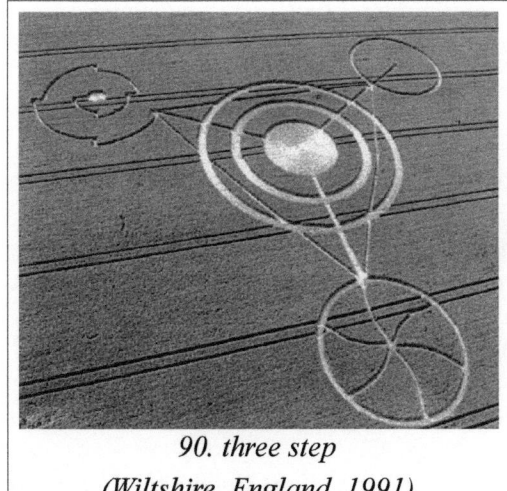

90. three step
(Wiltshire, England, 1991)

When this crop circle was made, I was very close by. I found out about it in the morning because a store in Glastonbury had hung the front page of a newspaper with this photo as a large copy in the window. On the newspaper, above the photo, was the headline, "Now explain this!" I was speechless at first, because I immediately recognized the three upper Sephiroth of the Kabbalistic Tree of Life.

So I am anything but neutral with this crop circle.

"Crop circle – did I recognize your character correctly?"

"Yes – and many others who have associated something have also recognized me correctly."

"Because the basic principle you express has already been formulated in many ways and in many systems?"

"That's the essence of archetypes, isn't it?"

"It depends on how you define 'archetype'."

"..."

"Yes, well ... Do you like to tell me something about yourself that I haven't seen yet? I suppose there is one or the other ..."

"No, I don't."

"Um – now that sounds like an emotional reaction ... I haven't experienced that with you crop circles before. You usually sound more like Mr. Spock from 'Enterprise'."

"Look closely."

"Where?"

"At you."

"Uh ... could you say a few words about that?"

"Why did you ask me? You think you understand this crop circle shape!"

"Ehm ... ... yes ... I think you are right ..."

"And why did you ask?"

"Um ... In the hope that there is still something coming? No, it wasn't that. ... I didn't mean to sound arrogant ... that's getting closer to it."

"You asked a question you didn't really ask. You thought you knew everything. You won't get an answer to a question like that."

"Hm ... yes ... I understand that. ... I was not completely attentive and sincere. ... Is there anything else, then, that would be good if it were here in this place in this book? Now this question is meant quite sincerely."

"I know. If you want to understand a crop circle, sit in it, walk around in it, feel into it. And then trust what you experience."

"Yes ... that also seems to me to be the most solid foundation. ... And do you want to say something else about yourself?"

"Stand at the centers of the three outer circles, one after the other, and then at the center of the middle circle."

"Yes, well ...

I'll start with the circle at the top left – with the 'form': ... relaxation, cave, lying down, Mother, the Sephirah Binah on the Tree of Life, home, community, effortlessness, form, letting go, being received, security, emergence of the laws of nature ... ...

The circle below – with the 'expansion': ... dance, light-storm, the Sephirah

Chokmah on the Tree of Life, widening, expansion, light, ecstasy, inhibition-lessness, freedom, unhindered self-expression, the inflationary universe right after the Big Bang, laughter, Shiva ...

The circle in the upper right – with the 'origin point': ... one, everything, undifferentiated, potential, the Sephirah Kether on the Tree of Life, the only one, unity, God ...

The circle in the center – I have never been there in my dream journeys to the Tree of Life: ... sage ... on my dream journey to sage I experienced these three areas at the top of the Tree of Life ... sage seems to be connected with it ... creation, serenity and complete security in doing ... a thriving garden ... the meadow with the apple trees far above the clouds, where I used to fly up to in my imagination as a child ... peace, everything is right the way it is ....

Hmm ... would you like to say something about that, crop circle?"

"That's all right ... and everyone has to fill this structure for himself with his own images, so that it comes alive for him."

"Archetypes come alive when you can link them to your own images?"

"No, archetypes are always alive – everyone understands a deity when he sees it. But geometric shapes have to be linked to one's own images for them to come alive – and crop circles are geometric shapes to begin with."

"Geometric shapes that express general relationships."

"Yes."

"I suppose that we have reached the end then?"

"If you have no more questions ..."

"No, not just now ... Thank you."

"You are welcome."

"Ho!"

11ᵗʰ dream journey

97. three rays
(Hampshire, England, 2016)

I'm really curious about this crop circle – these three tobacco leaves and these 20 characters … and then this background pattern of arch triangles …

"Hello crop circle, I'd like to ask you a few things."
"Then ask."
"Are those really tobacco leaves?"
"Yes."
"Why?"
"Because that used to be in Central America what incense is in Europe."
"Does this crop circle express something sacred?"
"If by 'sacredness' you mean 'rightness,' then yes."
"Why three leaves and three budding leaves between them, which then become indicated leaves further out?"
"The '3' is the number of creation. And creation is breath and tobacco smoke is the symbol of breath and life force."
"So this is a life force crop circle?"
"All crop circles are life force crop circles – they represent structures and dynamics of the life force."
"Then why the tobacco leaves in this crop circle."
"To remind you what tobacco actually is."
"An 'anti-smoking' crop circle???"
"No – you asked for rightness out of longing, and you get answers in many details that show rightness."
"Um, yes … this is ultimately the same statement, but it sounds very different. ... What about this scripture? Are these 20 characters a scripture?"
"Read it."
"Um … that's a little hard for me, because I don't even know if they're book letters … or word characters, or what language … or whatever …"
"How do you start reading something you don't know?"
"I look at it carefully."
"Then do that."
"Okay."

286

... ...

"What do you see?"

"Well – 20 different characters ... they're made up of arcs and dots, not straight lines ... two characters are the same after all, and they're also the only two symmetrical characters – they're pretty much right down to the left and right up opposite. So the inscription is divided in two: 2 separating characters and 9 characters between each."

"What else do you see?"

"There are more regularities ... hm, I think I must list these letters one by one and number them – then it is easier to talk about them. ... see you soon."

"See you in a minute."

I copy the characters into the following list – clockwise starting from the double character at the bottom left. The characters are rotated so that the side facing the center of the crop circle is at the bottom.

The sequence of characters

"Hello crop circle, I'm back."

"I know – I've been watching."

"I still haven't quite gotten used to the fact that you can be talked to ... The style of the letters reminds me a little of medieval writing.

Now with this list, I see a few more things I didn't notice before. Not only characters 1 and 11 are the same, but also characters 6 and 16, creating 4 groups of 4 characters between them – this doesn't look like a coincidence.

Some characters have 4 dots on their right edge. These are the characters 6, 10, 16 and 20. Again, they are arranged symmetrically.

The characters 8 and 18 qre the same. The characters 10 and 20 are also the same. The characters 5 and 15 could also be identical. The difference between characters 4 and 14 is very small.

Characters 3 and 13 look like mirror images of each other – or is it just the different shadow on the characters that is irritating here?

Characters 2 and 12 have the same structure, but their proportions are different.

So that leaves characters 7 and 17, which could also be the same – both have the basic shape of an 'H' with arcs attached.

So it looks like the same 'inscription' was written twice here.

Of course, it is not clear where the beginning of this inscription is. The character 1/11 is the only symmetrical character and could therefore be the beginning or the end of the 'sentence'.

The characters 6/16 and 10/20 have 4 dots on their right sides and are thus also highlighted. These 4 characters (6, 16, 10, 20) are also identical. They are the only characters that repeat within a line.

One could interpret these characters with the help of the Ba-Gua. This would give approximately the following qualities:

- 1/11: Going down from the center, incarnating, coming down to the ground, grounding something.

- 2/12: Power coming from the outside (top left), bringing down and coming to rest (opening to the bottom right).

- 3/13: A departure upward, restlessness, branching off from the "left-up"/"right-down" axis toward the upper right = striving towards a goal.

- 4/14: A movement to the upper left towards the "donor", which then, however, returns in an arc to the center; a root to the lower left towards one's own work; a swinging crash to the lower right towards rest; a small offshoot towards the goal at the upper right; is this altogether the attempt to become independent?

 *- 5/15: Anchored top left, middle left and bottom left – i.e. in all three past areas; circular movement towards the middle and down-right movement upwards or also towards the goal (top right); is this an attempt to become independent?*

 *- 6/16 and 10/20: Ascending through one's own work (lower left) and then receiving help (upper left); then recognizing what one wants to be in the world (upper) and from this creating one's own center (center), in which a line goes down to the right to relax; there then appear the four points which, seen from the circle, point down, down to the right and to the right, i.e. to the foundation, to rest and to the future; does someone want to improve his life here?*

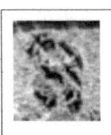 *- 7/17: Searching for one's own center (transverse stroke of the "H") between the past and the future (vertical strokes of the "H")?*

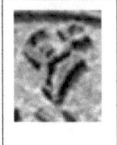 *- 8/18: Ascending from below and from below right – i.e. rise up and start something, pick yourself up; get help from above left and then concentrate on the goal (circle above right).*

 *- 9/19: Rising up from below – both past (left) and future (right); above one's center (lower cross line) something is being built up (upper cross line) – is this a striving for glory? Open to the top – seeking applause?*

One could see this as a whole as seeking help to find oneself. Possibly this is an invocation, that is, the invocation of a deity. This would also fit to the tobacco leaves, which were used in rituals – the tobacco smoke symbolized the breath, which connects the individual with the gods.

I noticed a few more things in the meantime:

> *- The 3 naturalistic leaves have six leaf transverse axes.*
> *- There are hexagonal shapes in the 3 leaves, which are only hinted at and shown in outline.*
> *- The arc triangles in the background are not so unrelated to the rest of the crop circle as I thought: They are arranged in such a way that they point from all six sides with one of their three points to the center.*

So in this crop circle the '3' and the '6' are emphasized: 'unfolding' and 'group'. Does this mean 'unfolding in a group and with the help of the group'? That would fit to the interpretation of the characters and also to the symbolism of the tobacco.

Are also the 33 sections of the outermost circular ring an emphasis of the '3'? So a '3·11=33'? But then what should the '11' mean?

So – now I have had a closer look at the crop circle mandala. What do you think of what I've come up with?"

"Not bad."

"So right?"

"No."

"Um ... can you tell me something about the meaning of this crop circle?"

"Invocation."

"So that part of my interpretation is correct?"

"That's already clear from the tobacco symbolism."

"With such a complex crop circle, you can probably say more, can't you?"

"Vision quest."

"So recognizing your own center? That would correspond to the symbolism of the '3' and the '6', after all."

"Yes."

"And the writing? Is that writing?"

"The signs encourage you to ask yourself how you can recognize your center and how you can then live out of it."

"Um ... yes ... that's one way to sum it up ... And also how I can get help with that."

"From your patron deity."

"From Osiris, yes."

"I have a suspicion that everyone will interpret these signs differently? But that nevertheless everyone who tries will ultimately come to the same conclusion?"

"Yes – that's the value of archetypes."

"Everyone tries to understand them in their own way, but ultimately comes to the same conclusion?"

"Yes – a goldsmith knows different things well than a farmer or a fabric merchant. But all three find the same basic structures when they look closely at life."

"And I just used my experiences to make this crop circle come alive for me?"

"Yes – so you understood what I was trying to say."

"Then you are something like a mirror, which on the one hand reflects the observer, but at the same time draws the observer's attention to certain contexts?"

"Yes."

"That's an interesting way of looking at crop circles – I like that way very much."

"It's also part of your view of the world, after all."

"So even that way of seeing crop circles – that it is a mirror for everyone – is part of my view? So part of how I experience the crop circles?"

"Yes."

"That gives it a fundamental-subjective interpretation, so to speak ..."

"Yes – you are the one who is experiencing your life."

"That's logical enough, but then what is the value of such a book as the one I'm writing here right now to others?"

"Inspiration. And the fact that everyone has his or her own view of the world doesn't mean that there are no similarities. Look at astrology: Everyone has the same 10 planets in their chart, but they're in a different relationship for everyone."

"Yes ... o.k. ... so there is a very subjective side to looking at crop circles, but these subjective views can match those of other people ..."

"Yes."

"O.k. ... I think that's enough for me for now ... Thank you, crop circle!"

"You're welcome."

"Ho!"

12th dream journey

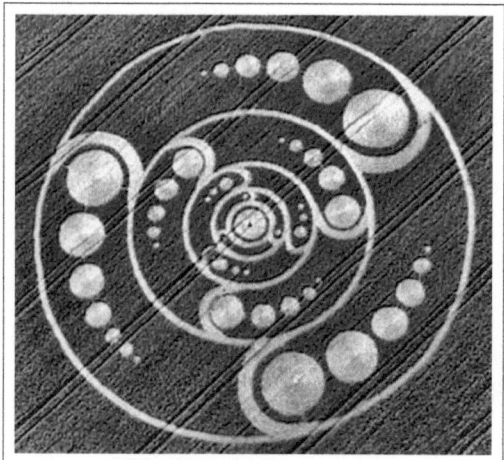

**100. four triple vortexes
(Wiltshire, England, 2001)**

I walk through this crop circle as through a door and see what comes next.

Clouds, fog, landscape, slightly sunny ... not what I expected ...

There is a triangular castle on a hill with black walls and a tower at each corner – that reminds me of the crop circle ...

I fly to the castle – I have until now seen the whole scenery from above. The walls and the towers are quite high. What is there inside? Just a castle courtyard and a fire in the middle. I fly down and now I stand in front of the fire.

The fire is blazing vigorously – a good 1.5m high. I can't quite make out what shape it has – is it round or triangular? Somehow its base is both ...

"Hello fire – who or what are you?"
"Life."
"Why are you here in a castle like this?"
"Protection."
"Um – protection?"
"Yes – it keeps me focused."
"I see – not 'protection from enemies', but 'protection from distraction'."
"Protection from distraction."
"Um ... and the castle? Does it have an outward effect?"
"It warms and invigorates the land."
"That sounds pretty much like a heart chakra mandala ..."
"Yes."
"And focusing on the essentials is also a characteristic of the heart chakra."
"Yes – and acting from the essentials."
"That's why these triple vortices?"
"There are four triple vortices – that's the 12 of unfoldment."
"Um ... yes ... Why are there '5, 4, 3, 1' points in the vortices and not '5, 4, 3, 2' points in the vortices? That would be a nice symmetry along with the center, wouldn't it?"
"Adding."

"Um – that's 3 times 13, or 39 points. I don't see any symbolism there."

"Wrong."

"??? ... Oh, I see - it's '6, 5, 3, 1' points and not '5, 4, 3, 1' points. I remembered that wrong ... O.k.: That would be a total of 15 or 3·15=45 points. Hm ... still doesn't make sense ..."

"1 – centering; 3 – expansion; 5 – straightening; 6 – shaping of an organic form."

"Straightening up is the symbolism of '5'?"

"Yes."

"O.k. ... The way you describe the meaning of the numbers, they make sense. But the '4' instead of the '5' would have made sense, too."

"Yes – but then it would have been a different crop circle."

"So there are always many possibilities?"

"You do choose different words, depending on what you want to say."

"Yes ... are there more?"

"If you have more questions."

"The 'questions-answers' principle seems to apply to all crop circles – is that so?"

"You'll see."

"Yes, well ... Then thank you very much, crop circle!"

"You're welcome."

"Ho!"

13th dream journey

102. triple vortex
(Wiltshire 2016)

I enter this crop circle by imagining its pivture and then using it as a door and walking through.

Forest, thorns, scrubs, through the trees I can also see open spaces – meadows or pastures, hills ...

"Where is the main thing here?"

Ah – behind me on the left.

Someone is standing there ... a man? A faun? Something like that ... a forest creature?

"Who are you?"

"Nice of you to come and visit me."

"Thank you. Who are you? What are you?"

"You are not yet fully living what you are."

"Um – you don't answer my questions at all..."

"Courage would do you good. More being in the forest, too. More sex, too. More people, too. More social stability, too. More fighting, too. Your Mars is not unfolded."

"Uh ... yeah, I can agree with you there ... and it's nice that you're telling me all this – but I actually wanted to get to know you."

"If you don't see what's there right now, you don't see anything."

"Um – yes, that's logical, but what do you mean by that? That you tell me and show me the essentials and I don't really listen to you?"

"Meaning instead of words."

I try to see him more clearly ... he is not wearing clothes, but has fur – or is he wearing something after all? There are also leaves or vines on him – is that clothing or is that part of his body? He seems brown-green, even if there are other colors ... A deer antler on his head? Sometimes yes, sometimes no ... He doesn't seem to have a very solid shape ...

"Who are you? What are you?"

"The urge of life to live."

"Hm ... the life force?"

"If you want to call it that – but you know little about it."

"Then tell me more."

"It cannot be told, but only lived and experienced."

"And in you I can see what that would be like?"

"Yes – you are beginning to ask better questions."

"Um ... that weird triple vortex in the center of the crop circle – what is that?"

"Wakan tanka."

"The Great Mystery? Life itself? Does it look like that because life remains permanently a mystery?"

"Yes."

"Um ..."

"If it weren't a mystery, you wouldn't want to experience it."

"I never thought of it that way ... but that makes sense ... And the order in the circular ring outside?"

"Isn't the world full of order and symmetries ... and full of crop circles?"

"Yes ... and at the same time a mystery?"

"Did you understand all the shapes then?"

"No."

"So the shapes are the expression of a Great Mystery."

"You have the convincing logic of all the crop circles ... Presumably, even if I understood all the shapes, I still can't understand the mystery, can I?"

"You are making progress."

"To understand the mystery, I have to go into the mystery and become the mystery, don't I?"

"Yes."

"May I cross over into you with my consciousness?"

"Yes."

I do ... ... relaxation and at the same time aliveness ... presence ... curiosity ... desire, joy ... and also happiness ... but above all desire ... desire to live, to experience, just to be there ... drinking the moment ....

"There is something as if you could become the whole forest and also all the creeks and animals and plants and the wind and the rain and the sunshine ... Is that so?"

"Yes – but stay inside me."

"O.k." ...

This feels like earth flowing through me ... an unfamiliar sensation ... doing what I feel like doing right now ....

"Any more?"

"That was the gist of it."

"Then thank you, crop circle, thank you so much!"

"M-m-m ..."

He goes whistling away deeper into the forest ...

"Ho!"

This being reminds me of Pan ...

14th dream journey

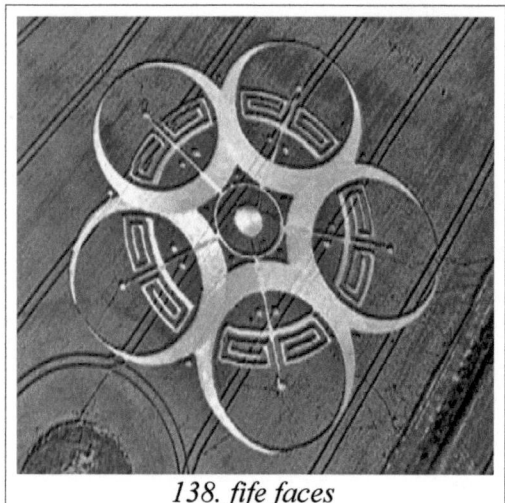

138. fife faces
(Wiltshire, England, 2010)

"Hello crop circle – I wonder if this is intentional, that the five crescents look like five faces."

"I see."

"Is that so?"

"Yes."

"Why?"

"Then you are more observant."

"Hm ... to what?"

"To the crop circle."

"Yeah – I get that. I mean, what are the viewers supposed to find when they're paying attention to the crop circle?"

"It's always the same: themselves."

"Could you also say 'their part in the rightness'?"

"Yes."

"By what means then can an observer of you, that is, of this crop circle, find himself?"

"By starting to think and feel into this pattern – just as you did."

"Hm ... it's not really clear to me yet ... so what is your message to the viewer?"

"Know thyself."

"Yes – that was written over the entrance to the temple of the Oracle of Delphi ... along with 'Nothing in excess.' ... but how does that work, that someone who looks at you recognizes himself?"

"He sees himself."

"I think I have to ask differently: What would be the question to You that would most help me understand you?"

"What do I want?"

"Um – do you mean that I ask you what you want?"

"No – that you ask yourself what you want."

"And that makes me understand you?"

"I am a mirror."

"Oh ... that's what another crop circle told me ... So: what do I want? ... Um ... I want to become completely healed and reach the rightness. ... Well – now I have asked myself and answered myself. And what do you have to do with it now?"

"I told you to ask yourself that."

"Tell me – is it perhaps an aspect of the symbolism of the '5' that everything

296

becomes a little bulky?"

"You could call it that."

"So the '5' isn't cooperative like the '6', nor is it spanning space like the '4', but rather a 'creative, developmental standing in the way'?"

"Nicely put."

"The provocateur among numbers?"

"Yes."

"Hmm ... well then ... ... I think that's enough for me for now ... Thank you."

"You're welcome."

"Ho!"

15th dream journey

148. hexagonal circle fractal
(Wiltshire, England, 2010)

"Hello crop circle ... According to your appearance you should be actually quite sociable and cooperative – because of the 6-symmetry. Is that right?"

"Yes."

"Would you like to tell me something about yourself?"

"Do what you just thought of: stand internally on the small dot above the top circle."

"O.k. ... I'll do it ... I'm immediately attracted to the crop circle and want to go inside it and become a part of the group."

"Then go inside."

"O.k. ... it feels solid, organical, moving, breathing, alive ... very pleasant ... I am drawn to the center ... it is not an essence nor a leader or the like, but an equal circle ... the circles in this crop circle form a cooperative, so to speak ... Would you like to give me a hint, crop circle?"

"Go to the right."

"Um ... yes, ok. ... I'm standing on one of the small circles ... that feels different than on the big circles ... they're more like fillers, insulators or something like that ... ... And the really small dots? ... They flow, are mobile, active, connect ... ... And the arc triangles? ... They build up a tension and maintain an order ...

Um ... and now?"

297

"That's it."

"That's what you are?"

"I am the group, yes."

"The crop circles have a very different character, don't they?"

"Yes."

"Even if, on the other hand, they are very similar – the expression of rightness and this mathematical-logical speaking ..."

"Yes."

"Thank you, crop circle."

"You're welcome."

"Ho!"

16th dream journey

161. blossom
(Italy, 2010)

I used the image of this crop circle as the door for a dream journey.

Light wind, warm air, flowers, a peaceful mood, lightness ...

Is there something important to see here? Where is the essence here? Um – the essence seems to be everywhere here, to be in everything ...

"Can the essence appear before me in a form I can understand?"

There is a woman ... her age is indeterminable – she seems young and old at the same time ... strange: she wears no clothes, but is not naked – this reminds me of an old Indogermanic riddle about the sun, which has been handed down by the Celts, the Teutons and the Indians and whose solution consists in the fact that the sun wears a net as clothes ... but what is this here?

She has long hair ... she seems delicate and very strong at the same time ... strange ... she also seems gentle and unpredictable at the same time ...

"Hello crop circle woman – who are you?"

"I am the crop circle."

"Hm – which characteristics do you have?"

298

"You have already described them."

"Can you add one or two more?"

"I am ... you are ... everything is ... and everything is movement, scent, color, change, sound ... and the wandering is a savoring, unfolding, dissolving, germinating ... that is what everything is ..."

"One could almost think that you are a butterfly ..."

"Butterflies understand me well."

"Is there something you can tell me – that is, something that is personally meaningful to me?"

"That which you have just noted: Think of encounters with people as something the wind brings you and something the wind takes away ..."

"Is that all?"

"No – think of the wind as the song that life sings."

"Hm ... it seems to me that it would be good to know the melody of this song."

"That's easy: dance as it comes to your mind – play on your harp as it flows from your heart right now – sing as your soul wants it right now ... then you will see the wind of life blowing ..."

"Yes ... I know this side of me ... Is there anything you would like to say to those who will read these pages?"

"Come to me and see for yourself."

"Hm, yes ... I could almost have guessed that ... ... Thank you, wind crop circle!"

"You're welcome."

"Ho!"

17th dream journey

162. four, six and twelve
(Oxfordshire, England, 2013)

"Hello crop circle, would you like to tell me something about your being?"

"I am who I am."

"Hm – is it possible to be a little more differentiated?"

"That will do."

"Hm ... wouldn't it possibly be helpful for me to understand your structure, if I haven't arrived at the 'I am who I am' yet?"

"Yes, it is. Organic concentration in solid form, which is the expression of essence."

"Aha ... organic – diamonds; concentration – center; solid form – square; expression – circle and rays; essence – center. ... O.k., I understand ... but can't it be a little more descriptive? That would please me."

"Love yourself, then the world will love you."

"Um ... yes ... so ... o.k. – that is however a well tangible and plausible statement. And that is what you represent?"

"Yes."

"Um ..."

"Shine and it will become bright all around you."

"You sound like a prophet."

"Open your heart to become what you are – and the world will reflect you and become a perfect place."

"Um – is there more of this?"

"That's enough – if you don't understand these three sentences, you won't understand the other possible sentences."

"Sounds to be a rather economic thinking."

"Crop circles are an economic representation of the essential."

"O.k. ... yes, you represent the essential in the simplest possible way ... ... Thank you, crop circle – I like your three sentences!"

"And you don't like me?"

"Hey – you have humor and know irony!"

"Of course – when you are yourself, you can dance ... and play with things and

words."
"That's freedom, isn't it?"
"Yes."
"Thank you!"
"You're welcome."
"Ho!"

18th dream trip

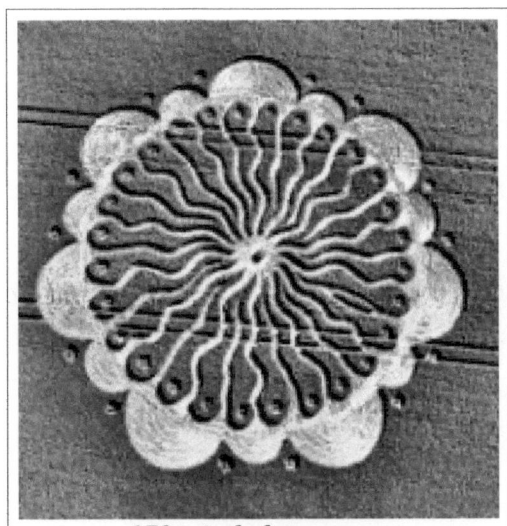

172. circle heptagram
(Wiltshire, England, 2009)

"Hello crop circle – what are these 28 worms?"

"The force that creates one leaf each as a pair."

"The 14 outer circles?"

"Yes."

"I hadn't noticed that they travel in pairs. ... What is the goal of this power?"

"Creation."

"And what do they want to create?"

"Love."

"Um – are they sperm?"

"If you want, yes ... but that's very narrowly put."

"What are they, then, if you take that more broadly?"

"Creation, ascension, emergence, expansion, kundalini, return from the underworld, soul serpents ... whatever you want ..."

"And why a 7-corner?"

"Because it fits well."

"I have not been able to find any structural symbolism of the '7' – that is, a symbolism that is not based on a rather arbitrary tradition like, for example, the assignment of the '7' to Venus. What, then, is the symbolism of '7'?"

"Unfolding."

"That which comes after the '6' of the Sun?"

"That which arises from the organic form of the '6'."

"I don't find that quite conclusive yet ... that sounds more like the traditional

301

number symbolisms like the view that '13' destroys the harmony of '12' and is therefore an unlucky number."

"Look at it any way you want."

"Um – am I asking the wrong questions right now?"

"There are no wrong questions. But there are questions whose answers don't lead very far."

"Is the question about the symbolism of '7' such a question?"

"That depends on how you answer it."

"And what would be a creative and fruitful way of answering?"

"Use the crop circle as a door."

"O.K., I will." ... ...

Earth, cave, snake in the cave, a big snake ... dark ...

"Who are you, snake?"

"The soul of the crop circle."

"Um ... and what do you want?"

"To be what I am."

"You crop circles really all have a very characteristic way of speaking and having conversations ..."

"We are crop circles. That's our nature."

"Yes, well ... what happens when you are there, when you are active, when you express yourself?"

"I move."

"Do you mean that you are crawling around?"

"Yes."

"And this 'area' could also be my body?"

"Then I would be your Kundalini."

"Are you the flow of the life force?"

"Yes – I am the flow of life and the flow of the life force – which is ultimately the same thing."

"Why are there so many snakes in the crop circle? And why are they all crawling outward?"

"Because the life force is multifaceted. Because the life force sings a total song, dances a total dance."

"And out of this commonality, then, do the beautiful geometric patterns emerge?"

"No – they are expressions of one aspect of the flow of the life force. The common is there because multiplicity is the expression of unity – the essence of unity is seen in multiplicity. And the shapes of the crop circles are words in the song that unity sings, steps in the dance that unity dances."

"It sounds like the crop circles are very closely related to the Kabbalistic Tree of Life."

"They are – except that the Tree of Life is one form for everything and the crop circles are many forms for the One."

"I like this 'geometric poetry' ... I have liked it for a very long time ... Thank you, crop circle, thank you very much!"

"You're welcome."

"Ho!"

19th dream journey

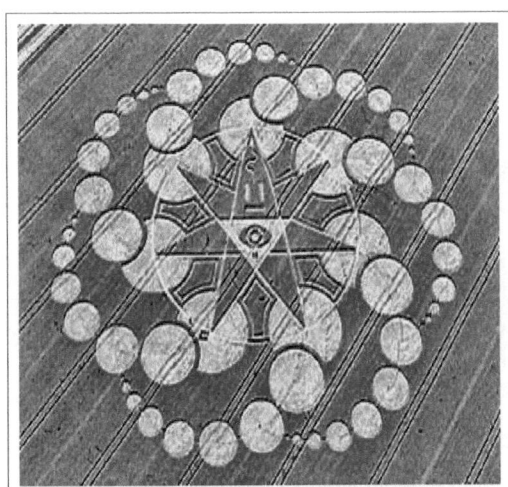

175. complex heptagram
(Wiltshire, England, 2008)

"Hello crop circle – I am not sure if I have grasped your meaning correctly. Can you tell me something about it?"

"Yes, gladly. I am heaven."

"Um ... I can't say that I understand ..."

"I am that which is above, that which has ascended, that which has awakened, that which has become conscious."

"Sounds good and sounds like Kundalini – but I still don't really understand it. Is the snake at the top of the heptagram the Kundalini?"

"Yes."

"What do you mean by 'heaven'?"

"Well, what you also mean by it – the desired state."

"Oh, I see ... you are showing us the rightness, the state we long for. That is the 'heaven'. Can you describe heaven a little bit? Or tell me in what way this crop circle, that is you, describes a certain aspect of the sky?"

"Look."

"Hm ... a seven-rayed vortex ... an eye and a snake ... and the eye is unusually in an inverted triangle ... and between the eye and the snake is a 'U'. ... But what does it all mean?"

"Striving."

"Hmm ... the snake is striving upward – that's what I see. But the eye is looking down – why?"

"Attachment to the detail. Lack of looking at the whole."

"Above is unity and below is multiplicity?"

303

"Yes – and above is the crown chakra and below is the kundalini in the root chakra."

"So to attain rightness, you advise awakening the Kundalini?"

"In rightness, the life force flows unimpeded. When the Kundalini rises, it dissolves all blocks in the life force."

"O.k., that's logical. ... Is that all there is to it? And why the '7'? In the previous crop circle, the snake has also been linked to the '7' – the '7' is supposed to mean 'unfoldment'."

"Yes."

"Yes good ... ... Thank you."

"You're welcome."

"Ho!"

21st dream journey

182. talons
(Wiltshrie, England, 2008)

I use the picture as a gate for a dream jurney and walk through it.

Angular rocks ... a sense of fire somewhere nearby ... danger ... there is something I don't see ....

"Who or what is there?"

"Me."

"Who are you?"

"The perfect warrior."

"Will you show yourself to me?"

"If you can stand it."

"Try."

Something comes around some trees and rocks that feels like a tiger, but isn't a tiger. What is it? ... male ... well, that's not certain – more likely male and female at the same time ...

"Why can't I see you clearly?"

"Because you are afraid. I'm not hiding – you're not looking."

"Um ... are you Mars?"

"Something similar to it."

"How can I see you?"

"By looking."

"O.K. ... I'll try again ... ... I feel fire, but I don't see anything clear ..."

"You have to look with your heart."

"That's what the 'little prince' said too ... but well, you're both right ... I'll try ... ... centering, power, being my own thread, being the experiencer, being independent of others ... Is that the letting go I finally want to learn?"

"This fire is the foundation – if you have it, you let go where it is beneficial for you."

"Hm ... I'll go on again ... ... the quality is getting deeper, but I don't feel anything new ... Did I actually correctly identify the eight strange shapes in the crop circle as 'claws'?"

"Claws, knives, weapons – it doesn't matter ..."

"This is what I defend myself with?"

"That's the shape of fire."

"Flames?"

"For example."

"The circle inside rotates counterclockwise – the flames outside clockwise. Why?"

"Fire is in motion. A warrior is in motion. It's a constant change of motion."

"Um, yes well ... thank you, crop circle."

"You're welcome."

"Ho!"

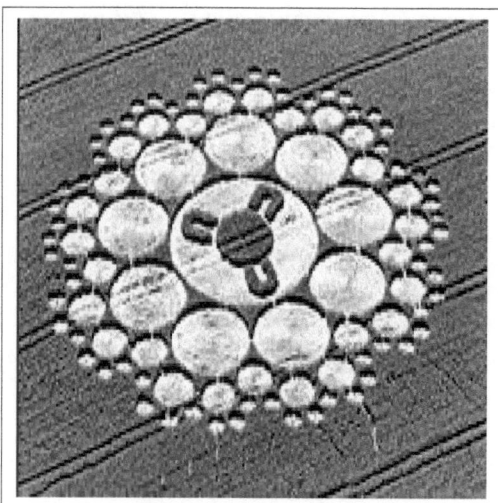

186. circle nonagram
(Wiltshire, England, 1998)

"Hello crop circle – can you tell me something about yourself?"

"If you ask something, yes."

"Why are actually the three 'U's in your central circle not symmetrical? The bottom one points exactly to the center of the circle in front of it; the top two don't – the one on the right is turned 10° too far counterclockwise, the one on the left 10° too far clockwise. And they don't have the angle of three times 120°. Why?"

"I'm glad you noticed that after all."

"That doesn't really make any sense, does it?"

"No, it doesn't."

"Then why is there this inaccuracy?"

"Untrained beginners."

"You mean the circle was made by humans?"

"Yes."

"That's why it's the only crop circle with such 'U's in it?"

"Yes."

"But the arrangement of the circles was plausibly and precisely made, wasn't it?"

"Yes."

"A crop circle is not 'wrong' just because people made it, is it?"

"If by 'right' you mean that the crop circle expresses rightness, then a man-made crop circle is not necessarily wrong, no."

"Then this crop circle is merely inaccurate, but otherwise an expression of rightness?"

"In principle, yes, but inaccuracy destroys rightness – it therefore expresses only the pursuit of rightness."

"I'd like to see how that plays out when I use the crop circle as a dorr for a dream journey. I'm going to go inside you now, okay?"

"O.k."

... ...

"Um ... a shallow scree slope ... lots of rocks from 20cm to 50cm in diameter ... they could break loose and form an avalanche ... um – what would happen if the avalanche actually rolled off? Let's see ... um – something else comes to light ... the

306

top of a building made of rocks? ... a spaceship made of stone? ... What is that? ... I imagine that the remaining stones are rolling away, too. ... It looks more like the Hagia Sophia ... a temple with a dome-roof, which is pointed in the middle ... strange architectural style – I have not seen this style before ... it seems powerful, somehow mighty and also a bit dominant ... it feels like dominance ... is it also a palace?

I'll go inside ... hm, it has no doors or windows ... is it hollow? ... There's a spherical cavity in the middle ... what's in there? ... I wish myself in there ... empty, bright, a kind of quiet fire-light, warm ... that is potential, but not active ...

I wish myself back outside. I wish to see this temple as it would look if the three 'U's were in place. The building starts to glow, continues to form, many more details emerge – towers, roofs, ornaments, windows, gates. Colors ... now it really looks like a temple ... is it 3-symmetrical? ... it has several symmetries – 3, 4 and 6 – I can't see a 9-symmetry right now, but maybe the picture is not quite finished yet ...

What is inside now? ... a large room with a flat floor, on the floor is a mandala – a 9-polar mandala, a central circle ... this resembles the crop circle ... the mandala shines and lights up the room ...

I start to sweat, but I don't know if it's because of the crop circle, because I've been hot all day today – from the inside. Although fire would fit well to a 3-polar crop circle mandala.

I stand in the middle of the mandala. ... heat, glow, great intensity, expansion, self-expression, radiance, living from within ... that seems to be a solar plexus and throat chakra quality that originates in the heart chakra ... I could do with a bit more of that than I have ... I let this radiance into me ... ... hm – there's not much happening ... I think the heat just now and my sweating was already this energy that flowed through me ....

Thank you, Temple!"

I go back out of this 'dream journey within a dream journey' into the primordial dream journey in which I spoke to the crop circle.

"What do you think about what I saw, crop circle?"

"Good."

"What do you mean?"

"It's good the way you did it. It's good for you. And it's good to see what I would be like if I were whole."

"By 'whole' you mean if the three 'U's were in their proper places?"

"Yes."

"Thank you, crop circle."

"Your are welcome, Harry."

"Oh – you call me by my name? That's not what the other crop circles did ..."

"You did something for me."

"Ah ... yes, well ... thank you."

307

"You're welcome."
"Ho!"

23rd dream journey

189. nonagram castle
(Wiltshire, England, 2007)

(the right way up)

"Hello crop circle. Can you tell me something about yourself? I would be especially interested in the meaning of the crescent. Otherwise, the symbolism of the '3' and the '9' is quite clear."

"The crescent is serenity and protection and resting in oneself."

"I take it that the middle of the crescent in the upper right is the baseline of this crop circle?"

"Yes – turn the crop circle the right way around and then look at it again."

"O.k., I'll do that – I'll be back soon."

I make a rotated version of this crop circle and paste it on this page.

"It was a bit of a pain to make, but I see now what you mean. You can't miss the serenity. Without the crescent it would look quite different. I'll make another version without the crescent, okay?"

"Go ahead - that's probably the easiest way to see the significance of the crescent."

So I make my first crop circle fake … not perfect, but it serves its purpose.

"This crop circle without the crescent looks empty, boring, straightforward and without tension. The crescent clearly does more than add serenity. The crescent also

makes the crop circle come alive, it adds a second element that is different from the others, which all have the 3-polarity or the 9-polarity. This second element gives the crop circle a tension and makes it alive. Without the crescent, the crop circle does not shine. This is impressive – I would not have expected such a big effect ...

(without crescant)

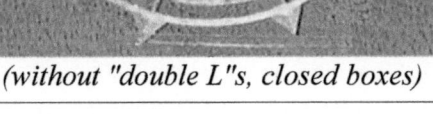

(without "double L"s, closed boxes)

With the crescant it has also something of 'sun-birth' or 'Isis and Horus' or 'Mary and Jesus' ... I didn't notice that before ...

What do those 9 'boxes' in the outer ring actually do?"

"Stability."

"Um – actually there are always two 'L's' ... Why?"

"Imagine them closed."

"Shall I make another 'fake'?"

"If you want – it's the most effective way to tell."

"All right."

This time, however, the 'faking' was a bit easier.

"Um ... you can feel the difference, but you can't see directly what the difference actually is ... now the grain circle seems limp – or like soup without salt ... What are those gaps in the boxes actually doing?"

"Turning."

"Um ... that's right – they give the impression that the crop circle is rotating counter-clockwise. That really paid off, making that rotation of the crop circle and the two fakes. It made it much easier for me to see which elements of the crop circle have which effect.

Thank you, crop circle!"

"You're welcome."

"Ho!"

309

24th dream journey

205. sixteen (detail)

"Crop circle – what are these pairs of triangles doing in the ring segments?"

"Go from the whole to the detail – it's easier."

"O.k. ... The whole thing is a kind of 'sun-flower with inscription'. The '16' indicates perfection – possibly it is also a reference to the throat chakra, which is traditionally depicted with sixteen petals. There are three rings to be seen, of which the two middle ones are 'inscribed'. The outer ring directs the 'scripture boxes' to the rays on the outside, which are also 'labeled' by the dots in them. Untill now I don't understand these 'code'. Is it worth another try?"

"Check it out."

The "crop circle code"																
rays	•	•	o	•	o	•	•	o	o	o	•	o	o	o	o	o
	•	o	•	•	•	o	•	•	o	•	o	•	•	•	o	•
	o	o	o	o	o	o	o	o	•	o	o	•	o	o	o	o
	•	o	o	•	•	o	o	•	•	o	o	•	o	o	•	o
	o	•	•	o	•	•	•	•	o	o	o	•	•	•	•	•
	•	o	o	o	o	o	o	o	o	o	o	o	o	o	o	•
	o	o	o	o	o	o	o	o	o	•	o	o	o	o	o	o
	•	•	•	•	•	•	•	•	•	•	•	•	•	•	•	•
middle circle	oo	oo	oo	oo	--	--	--	•o	o•	o•	••	•o	••	oo	oo	•o
inner circle	oo	•-	--	--	••	••	oo	•o	oo	oo	•o	oo	••	oo	oo	•o

"What could this mean? On the inner ring the triangles point with their tip inwards, on the middle ring outwards. Together with light/dark this results in 4 different triangles – the 4 elements? Hm ... they would then be irregularly distributed: 10 inside/dark, 17 inside/light, 9 outside/dark and 17 outside/light. And what should the gaps mean? You can't fill up the missing triangles evenly with them, because half of 32 triangles per ring are 16, but of two kinds there are already 17 triangles each. So this is probably no element symbolism.

310

There are a total of 12 signs in each ray, but whether this has anything to do with the zodiac is also very questionable.

In total there are 76 dark signs, 105 light signs and 11 gaps – there is no systematic distribution discernable.

The only recognizable regularity is that all rays begin with a dark circle.

Help me out here, crop circle."

"You've now realized that there is no pattern."

"Yes."

"What do you conclude from that?"

"Hm – these are actually too few characters for a script – at least too few to be able to decipher anything. The columns in the table would also have to be read as a whole, since there are only 4 different characters in total in the two rings, which is too few for a script. In the 16 columns, there is not a single one that matches another, which would also be atypical for letters. Does this mean that the distribution of dots is purely decorative?"

"What else could it be?"

"Um – I didn't expect anything purely decorative here ..."

"So what effect does this distribution have?"

"It loosens up the impression and arouses curiosity."

"And what element does that correspond to?"

"Air."

"Rightness does not have to be strict."

"Um ... that's an interesting aspect ... So rightness can be ruleless at times? Just colorful?"

"Why not?"

"I never thought of it that way ... I always thought that rightness was always competely pre-determined – like when I tune my harp: There is always only one correct pitch for each string. ... So there is also freedom in rightness? Is this freedom arbitrariness?"

"Rightness is not fixed in all individual parts. It can be shaped in many ways – and that includes joyful colorfulness."

"Hm – you bring me to a whole new way of looking at things ... I have savor that slowly ... So the distribution of the light and dark characters and the gaps in the crop circle is simply playful colorfulness?"

"Yes."

"Indeed! ... yes well ... Thank you very much, crop circle! ... Once again, I'm learning a great deal on these dream journeys – as I do on all dream journeys, actually ... Thank you."

"You're welcome."

"Ho!"

311

25th dream journey

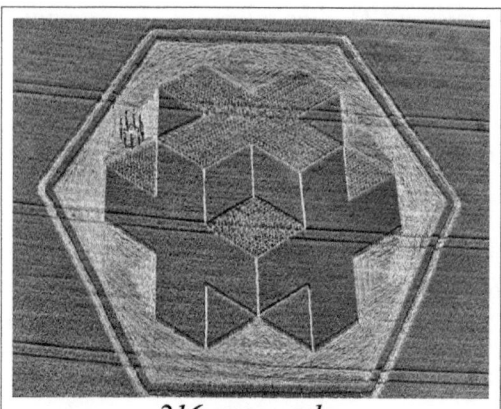

216. cross cube
(Wiltshire, England, 2010)

"Well, crop circle ... the way you look, I would guess that a geometry-enthusiastic person made you. Is that right?"
"Yes."
"After all, the production of gray tones in crop circles is something decidedly creative ...
And also the outline, which is exactly hexagonal, has already been skillfully made. ... Um, I'll make a version with guide lines. See you soon!"
... ...

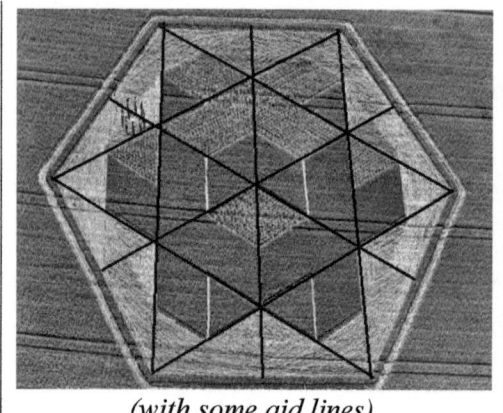

(with some aid lines)

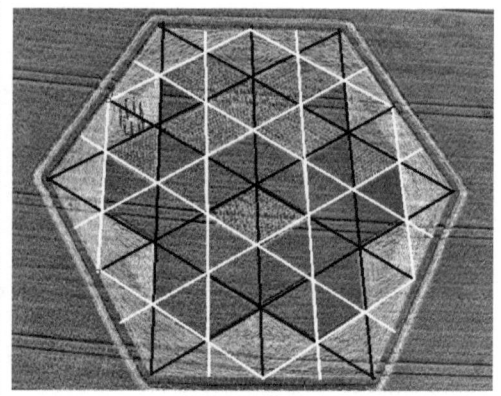

(with some more aid lines)

"Have a look: You can make the 'cross cube' entirely out of diamonds – I didn't expect that ... Can you tell me anything about yourself, crop circle?"
"You already said it: a geometrical gimmick."
"So without deeper meaning?"
"Yes – but with a lot of fun."
"Hm – that actually also sounds like a decidedly good motivation ..."
"It is – what else could be such a good motivation?"
"Er ... by talking to you crop circles, I'm beginning to get a significantly broader idea of what you are, and what your value can be to us. It's significantly more diverse

and joyful than I first thought."

"Dancing the rightness can be great fun."

"Um, yes ... that's probably the best reason for seeking and living rightness, too ..."

"Yes."

"Thank you, crop circle!"

"You're welcome. And have fun!"

"Thank you. ... Ho!"

26th dream journey

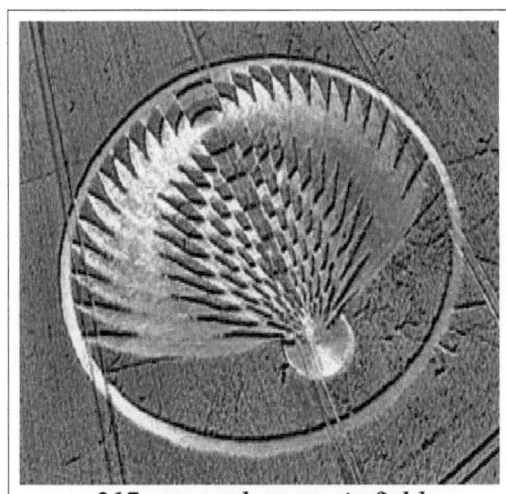

217. sun and magnetic field
(Oxfordshire, England 2006)

"What are you, crop circle? A sunrise or an explosion?"

"The light at sunrise."

"I'm going to look at it from the inside, o.k.?"

"Sure."

"Well ... ... I'm standing on a high hill, in front of me is a plain, in the distance is a mountain range, above it the sun rises and colors the sky and the clouds in different colors – mainly red and pink, but also blue and turquoise ... a pleasant sight ... and very powerful ... ... now the sun comes up over the horizon and shines intensely golden yellow ... it is clearly larger than in reality, more than 1° in diameter ... I am waiting for an echo to this sunrise in me, a radiation of my heart chakra or similar, but there is not much happening right now ... but the sight is very beautiful ...

I return from the 'dream journey within the dream journey' to the original dream journey.

"Is there anything else you could tell me, crop circle?"

"No – you have seen the essence."

"Yes, well ... thank you."

"You're welcome."

"Ho!"

313

27th dream journey

218. decentralized sun
(Ravenna, Italy, 2015)

"Crop circle – what is this 'lid' on the rays of the sun?"

"A lid."

"Um – that doesn't make me any smarter now than I was before."

"It is a lid."

"But what's it doing there? And why does it have a hole?"

"It covers the sun – but never completely."

"Is the lid a bad thing? And is the hole for the lid to never completely cover the sun?"

"The lid can be sleep. But also trauma. And the hole is the possibility of finding the inner sun again."

"So simple is the message of this crop circle?"

"Yes."

"Good ... Thank you!"

"You're welcome."

"Ho!"

28th dream journey

224. sun god
(Wiltshire, England, 2009)

"Hello crop circle – your picture has been on the shelf above my desk for many years ... Would you like to tell me something about yourself?"

"Ho mitakuye oyassin!"

"Er – that's the Dakota greeting used at sweat lodges: 'I greet all my relatives!' ... That's what you're saying?"

"Ho."

"Um ... are you just joking with me or is that what you mean?"

"That's what it is."

"Um ... then I'll ask it another way: is that supposed to be a face?"

"Yes."

"Is that the sun?"

"Yes – Grandfather Sun ... Tunkashila."

"Why don't the feathers have a symmetrical pattern?"

"Because feathers are never exactly the same."

"Um - could you call that 'playful realism'?"

"Yes."

"Why do the spirals all spin in the same direction, but start alternately at the top and bottom?"

"That's the course of the sun. And if the spirals were all the same, it would look lax and boring."

"Hm ... I still have to get used to this reasoning ... and why double spirals? And wahy are always two of them connected to each other?"

"Otherwise they would fall apart."

"Yes – I can imagine the impression that would make. ... Is that the face of a human or a bird?"

"Tunkashila and Wambli."

"So Grandfather Sun and the Eagle of the East. Then is that the sun eagle, the winged sun?"

"Yes."

"Hm – this crop circle is at the same time very complex and full of details, but also very simple and clear. Some good Indian or Tibetan deity images also have this quality, reminiscent of some kinds of dream travel images and visions that also have

315

this quality."

"This is what distinguishes a good 'sacred image'."

"And the depiction of rightness is a 'holy image'?"

"What is right other than holy? And what is holy other than right?"

"Yes ... o.k. ... I'm convinced ... is there anything else you want to say?"

"Come into me."

"Shall I use your image as a dream journey door or shall I cross over into your graphic/shape with my consciousness?"

"Cross over with your consciousness."

"O.k. ... ... oh, that's good! ... I feel far above, big, stable, safe – so I feel completely sure of myself, radiant ... that's really good! ... that is free ... the spiral-rays are something quite natural ... there is also play and laughter ... light-heartedness ... being filled with oneself and with life ... being in the moment ... that is effortless ... just flowing ... yes, that is how I want to live! ... that is good! ... Thank you, Tunkashila-Wambli, for giving me this advice! Thank you, cop circle!"

"You are welcome! ... And come here often – it will do you good."

"Yes, certainly! Thank you! ... Ho!"

29ᵗʰ dream journey

225. abstract sun god
(Oxfordshire, England, 2005)

"Are you essentially the same crop circle as before?"

"First turn me around properly and then look at me again."

"O.k. - so again a little tinkering ..."

... ...

"Now the head and the beak are recognizable again – so again Tunkashila and Wambli in one, sun-god and eagle ... Also the spirals are there as in the previous picture and also the playful-systemless distribution of the light and dark stripes on the 'feathers', from which here a ring has become. Do you want to tell me anything else about this, crop circle?"

226. abstract sun god – the right way up
(Oxfordshire, England, 2005)

"Cross over into me with your consciousness."

"O.k. ... this is calmer, warmer, simpler, brighter than the previous crop circle ... it is fundamentally the same, but, so to speak, the sun on a different day ...

I still notice that this sun-man-eagle-face is pointed downwards and that this looks a bit like the faces of the aliens in the man-made crop circles. Is this where the 'alien' face shape originated?"

"Yes."

"Thank you, crop circle."

"You're welcome."

"Ho!"

30ᵗʰ dream journey

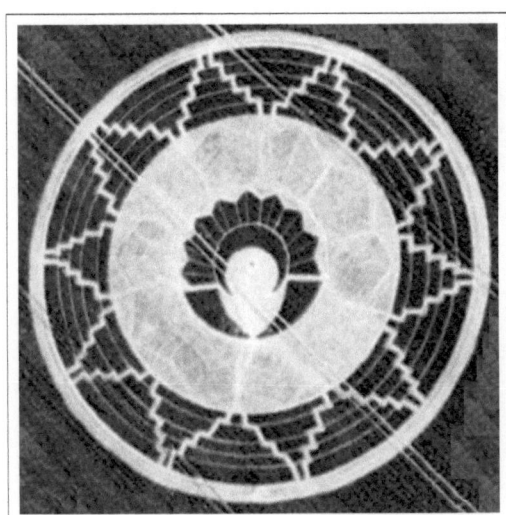

227. pyramid of the sun
(Wiltshire, England, 2011)

"Hello crop circle – how do you differ from the previous two crop circles? You have the beaked face with the feather crown again but no irregular pattern and instead of spirals here are mountains – or step pyrmids."

"Look at it."

"Cross over into you with my consciousness?"

"Yes."

"O.k. ... it's a feeling rather than a picture, what I perceive ... bright, airy, aloft, vastness, calm certainty, clarity ... and I keep seeing your face cross over to the downward pointed face of the 'aliens' and then back again ... All three crop circles are the sun, but they feel different each time.

317

Is there more to see, crop circle?"

"Go down the 10 mountains."

"O.k. ... They are the times of day – each mountain corresponds to 2.4 hours, so 144 minutes ... um – nice number ... 12·12=12² ... but that's only because of our time system ...

Um ... crop circle – why is your face not quite regular? There are eight and a half feathers – and the two half-sickles under your face are of different lengths ... Was this crop circle made by humans?"

"Yes."

"By people inspired by the collective subconscious?"

"Yes – inspired, but mainly by the two older crop circles and only partly directly from the collective subconscious."

"The direct inspiration is the ten step pyramids?"

"Yes."

"Thank you, crop circle."

"You're welcome."

"Ho!"

31ˢᵗ dream journey

229. winged sun
(Wiltshire, England, 2004)

This crop circle is older than the previous three. I present the four „sun face" crop circles below side by side in their correct chronological order.

318

The Four Bird/Wing Sun Faces

   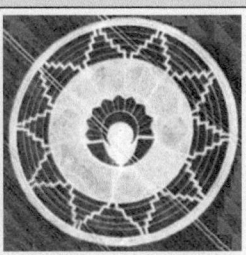

| *Wiltshire, 2004* | *Wiltshire, 2005* | *Wiltshire, 2009* | *Wiltshire, 2011* |

"Crop circle, do I see correctly that you represent a winged sun? With curved wings instead of the usual straight ones?"

"Yes."

"What do the double spirals, squares and dashes mean?"

"Movements in the water, currents, rays in the sky."

"That means it's actually about the double spirals – the squares and the dashes just indicate the water and the sky?"

"Yes."

"Um – is there anything more to say or see about this? This crop circle is, after all, quite plain in the end."

"Look at it from the inside."

"Cross over into you with my consciousness?"

"Yes."

"O.k. ... It's fire, great intensity, glowing and flaming from the center, that's really very intense, that's in the middle of the sun ... that's sublime, that's high up, that's flying, that's really the winged sun, the sun-eagle ... ...

Thank you, crop circle!"

"You're welcome."

"Ho!"

The comparison of the direct experience of these four quite similar crop circles was extremely interesting – the similarities and the differences were both very clear.

236. molekule
(Wiltshire, England, 2020)

"Hello crop circle ... actually you can't be called a 'circle' anymore, because you have a completely different shape. You are to my knowledge also the only crop circle of this kind. Can you tell me something about yourself?"

"What do I remind you of?"

"The new logo of the Merck corporation in Darmstadt in Germany, that is producing pharmaceutics and the like – it has a font of letters that is very similar to your shape."

"You thought of that every time you saw me."

"Yes – the Merck logo is presumably meant to represent biotechnology, i.e. the production of new, complex chemical and biologic compounds, including with the help of genetic engineering. I see this logo often when I visit my son in Darmstadt. Is this crop circle meant to evoke such associations?"

"No."

"What is it supposed to awaken in the viewers?"

"What does it awaken in you, if you leave aside the logo of the pharmaceutical company Merck?"

"Hm ... seed and plant ... but also biochemistry ... the circle of eight dots at the bottom looks like a seed. Is that supposed to be that way?"

"Yes."

"This crop circle is not made of symmetrical or at least simple geometric shapes, but of curved shapes that emerge as a neighborhood of dots. What is it supposed to be?"

"Growth. Core and envelope. Impulse and unfolding."

"Is this model from 2020, that is, from this summer, the prototype of a new kind of crop circles with biochemical shapes?"

"It could be."

"Um ... can't you tell me something else about it?"

"I told you what to say about it."

"O.k. ... thank you."

"You're welcome."

"Ho!"

33rd dream journey

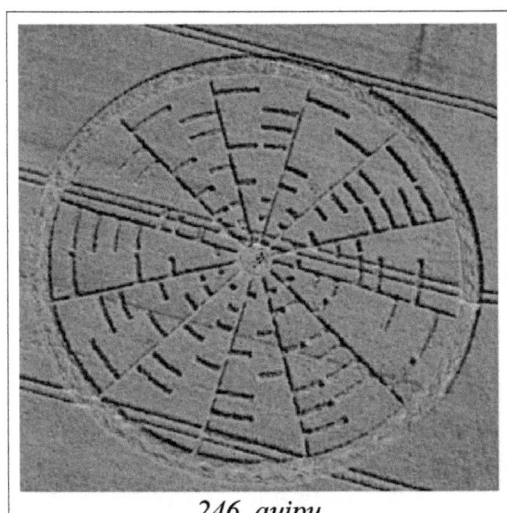

246. quipu
(Wiltshire, England, 2010)

"Hello crop circle – does this crop circle have a meaning? I mean, are the horizontal lines on the 12 rays something like letters or numbers or are they just ornaments?"

"Ornaments."

"Hm ... a lot of effort for an ornament ... and besides, this crop circle consists almost only of ornaments, a central circle, 12 rays and an outer ring."

"Yes."

"Hm – I could check if there are any regularities. There are 12 rays, each with cross strokes on the left and right. There are always 8 strokes – always left or right, but never two or none. This results in 12 sequences of 'o' for 'right' or 'l' for 'left'. Altogether 96 characters – that is still clear. At the bottom of the table are the strokes at the center of the crop circle.

The strokes at the rays											
1.	2.	3.	4.	5.	6.	7.	8.	9.	10.	11.	12.
l	o	o	l	o	o	o	o	l	l	l	l
l	l	l	l	l	l	l	l	l	o	o	l
l	l	l	l	l	l	l	o	l	l	o	l
o	o	o	l	o	o	l	o	l	o	o	o
l	l	l	o	l	l	o	o	o	o	o	l
o	o	o	o	o	o	o	o	o	l	l	o
o	o	l	o	o	l	l	l	l	l	o	l
l	l	l	l	o	l	l	l	l	o	l	l
Total											
5 l	4 l	5 l	5 l	3 l	5 l	5 l	3 l	6 l	4 l	3 l	6 l
3 o	4 o	3 o	3 o	5 o	3 o	3 o	5 o	2 o	4 o	5 o	2 o

In total, 54 'l' and 42 'o' are found – so not an even distribution.

Column 3 and 6 are equal. Otherwise, neither vertically nor crosswise equal strings can be found. That's not much in results ... So it really seems to be a random distribution.

*   Crop circle – are you really such a 'random representation'?"*
*   "Yes."*
*   "So an uninspired crop circle made by humans?"*
*   "Yes – a pretty free design."*
*   "Hmm ... all right ... thanks."*
*   "You're welcome."*
*   "Ho!"*

34th dream journey

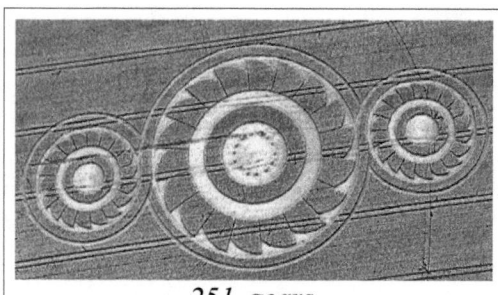

251. gears
(Oxfordshire, England, 2008)

*   "What is that which has been represented by you, crop circle? Three equally built circles with 18 gear-wheels each – the middle circle has only additional 14 points in the circle in the middle ..."*
*   "Polarity, movement – and there is still the common outer ring as a continuous 'S'."*
*   "Hm, yes ... so this is a simple polarity circle?"*
*   "Yes – the paddle wheels indicate the direction of rotation."*
*   "Oh! Right ... they are paddle wheels not gear wheels ... ... Why 18 paddles? And why 14 points?"*
*   "That has no deeper meaning ... they could have been other numbers. But the '18' has an unusual aesthetic – it's very rare to see something like that."*
*   "Um – the crop circles want to stand out, too?"*
*   "Why not create something special?"*
*   "Um – I have not seen this aspect before either. Doesn't that contradict the principle of rightness?"*
*   "Rightness can have different depths," he said.*
*   "The '12' would have given the crop circle more depth?"*
*   "Yes."*
*   "And so only the polarity principle has been represented, but not the zodiac or the superstring?"*
*   "Yes."*
*   "Um ... so crop circles have different depth and are 'right' on many different levels,*

322

so to speak?"
"Yes."
"I like the crop circles with 'deep rightness' better."
"Yes."
"Thank you, crop circle."
"You're welcome."
"Ho!"

35ᵗʰ dream journey

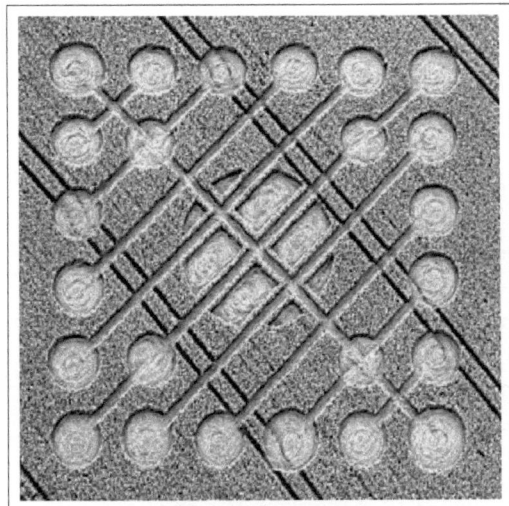

252. circle square
(Oxfordshire, England, 2012)

I use this crop circle as a door for a dream journey.

... ...

Gold in rocks ... sun in a cave ... circle in a square ... ... that feels stable and warm and solid ... and valuable ... a bit like a treasure ... also like a seed in the earth ... ...

I come back from the crop circle.

"Crop circle, is there anything else to see?"

"No – it's what you just said."

"O.k. ... thank you."

"You're welcome."

"Ho!"

36th dream journey

254. jet
(Wiltshire, England, 2012)

"Crop circle – what are you? Or: Who are you?"

"I."

"What is your quality, what are your qualities?"

"Love, striving, centering."

"Now this is unexpected ... The centering can be seen, yes, and the striving could be the alignment to the left ... is that so?"

"The centering yes, the striving no. I am striving towards the small right circle – I have already arrived there ... at the child."

"The small right circle with the dark crescent is a crop circle child?"

"Yes."

"Um ... is the big crescent then the mother – or the womb?"

"It is the mother's womb."

"Yes ... that's conclusive ... And the pointed cross is the mother?"

"Yes."

"And I thought that was the bow and arrow at first ... but it's much more plausible that way. ... That's probably what you can say about it, isn't it?"

"Go on in."

"Yes, well ... I cross over to you with my consciousness ... ... security, semi-darkness ... the mother is strong, she rests in herself, the child thrives, they are connected and at the same time both independent – and that already at this age of the child ... there is above all strength ... and space for the child ... the cross gives strength and power and space and protection ...

Thank you, crop circle!

"You are welcome!"

"Ho!"

37th dream journey

262. Triskelis
(Wiltshire, England, 2008)

I enter the crop circle, that is, I use it as a door for a dream journey.

... ...

I am looking down at the earth from the perspective of the sun ... well, actually I am looking down at the earth from the clouds, but I am in the sun ... this is the childlike image of the 'sun in the sky' ... this is light and carefree ...

"Do you want to say anything more about that, crop circle?"

"No."

"This is a triskelis, isn't it? A sun-face with three legs?"

"Yes – the sun wanderer."

"Thank you, crop circle."

"You're welcome."

"Ho!"

38th dream journey

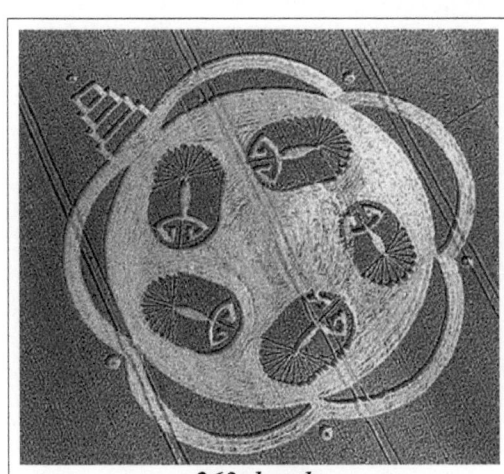

263. beetle
(Wiltshire, England, 2011)

"Hello, crop circle beetles – am I correct in thinking that you are beetles?"

"Something like that."

"What are you guys? Trilobites?"

"Something like that."

"And what are you exactly?"

"Living, individualized movement."

"So not concrete beings, but rather living-being archetypes?"

"Yes."

"Why five?"

"Because it is a pentagon."

"And why is it a pentagon?"

"Just because ..."

"Is this the 'artistic license' again,

which sometimes creates shapes without deeper symbolism?"
"Yes."
"Tending to be created by people without deeper inspiration?"
"Yes."
"Does that also apply to the somewhat leaning four-story tower or this slightly crooked stepped pyramid?"
"Yes."
"All right ... thank you, crop circle!"
"You're welcome."
"Ho!"

39th dream journey

I use this crop circle as a door for a dream journey.

195. ornamental circle
(Oxfordshire, England, 2009)

Earth, thriving, fields, avenues with fruit trees, pastures, gardens, small forests, streams and rivers, sunshine ... just idyllic ...
"What is the essence here?"
There is a shining stone in the earth ... it is quite big ... at least 1.5m in diameter ... it is almost transparent, the light in it is bluish, bright, partly also whitish – it is a quiet glow but no radiance ... strangely enough, despite these colors, it does not seem cold at all ...
"Who are you, light-stone?"
"The thriving, the blessing, the sun in the earth."

"The sun in the earth?"

> *"The sun that makes the plants flourish;*
> *the sun in the nocturnal under-world;*
> *the sun-god in his winter barrow;*
> *the warmth in the earth;*
> *the seeds in the earth;*

326

the flourishing of the earth;
the primeval giant Ymir;
the earth-god Atum, Yama, Yima, Pan Gu ..."

... ...

"*Yes ... I can feel that ... I have already met these deities on my dream journeys ... yes, the crop circle feels like that ... that's right ... ... Should I do anything in particular?*"

"*No – just enjoy that quality.*"

"*Yes, I am. ... Thank you very, very much! Now that was really unexpected! Thank you!*"

"*You're welcome.*"

"*Ho!*"

40th dream journey

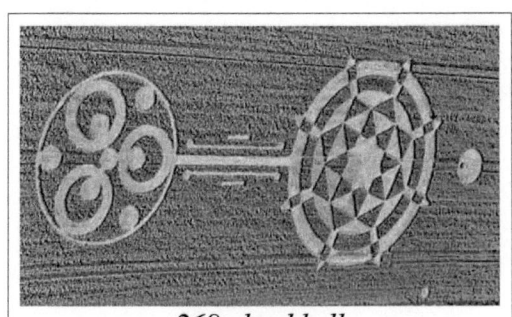

268. dumbbell
(Wiltshire, England, 2007)

"*Who or what are you, crop circle?*"

"*Polarity – only here represented a little more differenzied: round and angular, '3' and '8', directed inward and directed outward, development and differentiated form ... and in the center on the straight line the tension is held.*"

"*And the circle with the dot on the far right?*"

"*That's the viewer: the psyche with the memory of the soul and its directionality for its incarnation.*"

"*Is the small dot in this circle the memory of rightness?*"

"*Yes.*"

"*Is this the same 'circle with a hole' as in crop circle 218?*"

"*Yes.*"

"*Thank you.*"

"*You are welcome.*"

"*Ho!*"

41st dream journey

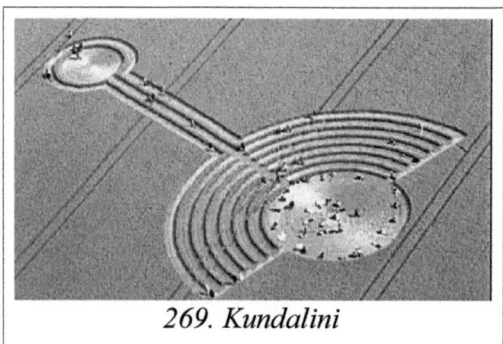

269. Kundalini
(Wiltshire, England, 2010)

"What are you, crop circle? Are the two circles a polarity? But then what are the seven semicircles?"

"It is the polarity, yes. The semicircles are the chakras – they are created by polarity and by unfoldment."

"Why are the seven semicircles only on one of the two circles?"

"On the left is the root chakra, on the right is the crown chakra, the straight line is the sushumna, the semicircles are the sevenfold ascended kundalini."

"Is that what is meant in some Buddha depictions – the upper ends of seven serpents above the head of Buddha? Not seven kundalinis, but the seven chakras healed by kundalini?"

"Yes – and the Kundalini experienced in the seven chakras. It is also represented sevenfold because it is experienced differently in each chakra."

"Yes, I can confirm this diversity. ... Is there something else? ... Is the triple straight line also the sushumna along with Ida and Pingala?"

"It's not primarily meant that way, but you can see it that way – that's an accurate analogy."

"Thank you, crop circle."

"You're welcome."

"Ho!"

42nd dream journey

270. „parachute“
(Dorset, England, 2014)

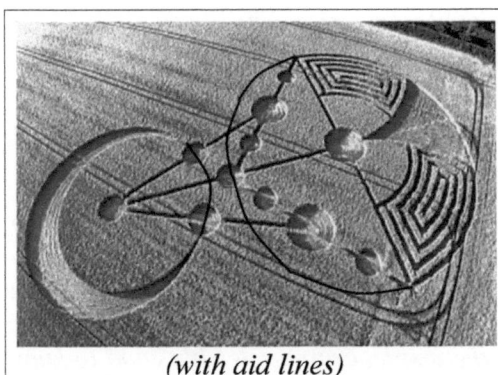

(with aid lines)

"What are you crop circle? Or: Who are you? Is that a polarity again?"

"Yes – but not a creating polarity, but a structural polarity."

"Can you explain that to me in more detail?"

"The crescent on the left collects and concentrates – the semicircle on the right transmits – the line in between directs the collected power from the crescent into the transmitter."

"The shape of the two spirals in the semicircle shows that this semicircle is also a receiver."

"Yes."

"When does it receive and when does it transmit?"

"Conception and birth."

"Er ... I think I'll draw in the two circles of which the crescent and the semicircle are a part – I want to know how those go."

"That's a good idea."

"Thank you. ... ...

So: the outer circle of the crescent goes through the centers of the two circles at their vertices. The outer circle of the semicircle goes right through the center of the circle where the three straight lines meet. So none of the spheres is between the two systems.

If you describe this as 'procreation and birth,' the system on the right would have to be a mother's vagina and the system on the left would have to be a mother's womb."

"Yes."

"Hm ... rather abstract ..."

"But precise and understandable."

"Yes ... well ... now on the second try."

"That doesn't matter."

"Yes, well ... thank you."

"You're welcome."

"Ho!"

43rd dream journey

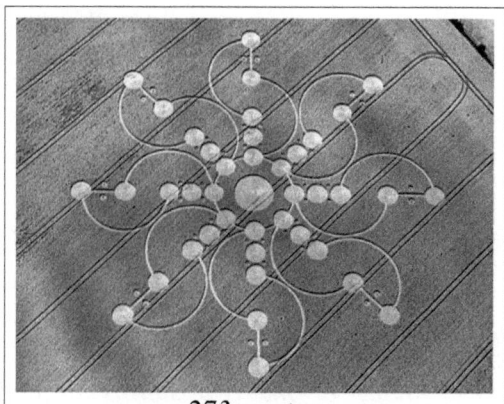

273. vortex
(Wiltshire, England, 2009)

"With this crop circle, I'm curious – what does the arrangement of the three circles and the polar system mean? Can you tell me, crop circle?"

"From the inside unfolding, outward protection."

"That's pretty simple when you put it that way."

"And overall? What does the overall crop circle mean?"

"Relaxed self-realization."

"Um, yes ... so purely from the impression I can agree with that ... the rather airy 'flames of power' ... the centre in the middle of the perfection of the eight circles ... the stabilization points ... yes, o.k., I can see that 'relaxed self-realization' describes this crop circle well."

"Go inside."

"O.k. ... ... there's a sense of life there above all: radiance and independence, but still in contact with everything ... but above all this radiance and independence ... there's a very clear distinction between inside and outside – that's because of the eight polar systems ...

Thanks for the advice to look at this from the inside, crop circle! It's good to know this attitude and this feeling of life. ... Thank you!"

"You're welcome."

"Ho!"

44th dream journey

274. gathering
(Wiltshire, England, 2009)

"Hello, crop circle, what do you represent? A gathering?"

"The community of the different ones."

"Um – sounds interesting. Do you mean the 12 signs of the zodiac?"

"They are a good image for it."

"Why do I always have to ask you crop circles every question specifically in order to get an answer? Why can't you just tell about yourselves? It's quite different with dream journeys to deities, power animals or plants."

"We are what we are: geometric shapes with an inner logic. That's where we speak out of, too."

"O.k. ... so geometric-mathematical conversations ... all right ... Are the 12 rays supposed to be people?"

"Double-humans."

"What's a double-human?"

"They have two faces."

"Yes, I can see that – is that supposed to represent polarity? Root chakra and crown chakra?"

"Yes – the inner face looks inward, the outer face looks outward."

"So the root chakra on the inside and the crown chakra on the outside?"

"The three inner and outer chakras respectively."

"Yes, logically ... the straight line is then the sushumna?"

"You can see it that way – with Ida and Pingala next to it."

"Why are the triangles not 3·4 shapes, but 6+3+3 shapes? That doesn't really fit the zodiac at all, does it?"

"That's right."

"Does that mean it could have been done better?"

"Yes."

"Um ... can I conclude that this crop circle was made by humans? It seems a little strange to me to think that everything I don't understand and that you crop circles can't explain to me is 'man's work' – isn't that a little presumptuous of me?"

"You can recognize what you can recognize – and that has its limits."

"Yes, I see it that way, too. But what does that mean now? That it's OK for me to

assume that this crop circle was made by people, and that they didn't do an aspect of this crop circle as well as they could have?"

"Yes."

"But I may yet find at some point that I was wrong and that the '6+3+3' division makes sense."

"Then see your findings as provisional."

"Yes, I already do it that way – I am happy about what I see, but at the same time I know that I do not see a lot of things (yet?). ... What do the two arcs on the double people mean?"

"The protection when looking outward and the support from within when looking outward."

"That would be an aspect of the rising Kundalini, then, wouldn't it?"

"Yes, it is – it establishes the self-knowledge, the self-assurance, and the inner-pressure that one needs to stand securely in the world."

"Then these two arcs are the same symbols as the seven arcs on crop circle 266?"

"Yes."

"Er ... is that all you can tell me about this crop circle for now?"

"No."

"What else is there?"

"Go inside."

"O.k., I'm using the crop circle as a door for a dream journey ... ... a castle or fortress on a flat hill, a moat, inside a big hall, a light in the middle, a mandala on the floor ... around it are many people – in twelve groups? ... apparently sorted according to their zodiac sign ... in the middle is the source, the life, the area of the souls – from there everything radiates, there all people are aligned ... I go once into this middle ... yes, there is my soul as a golden light, this middle is like the sun ... also all others can go here ... and then you can go with this light in you again outside into the world ... this castle or this castle is actually a temple ...

Yes, to let the light of one's center radiate outward through one's psyche unhindered – that is what makes sense ..."

I come back from the 'dream journey within the dream journey'.

"Thank you, crop circle!"

"You're welcome."

"Ho!"

45th dream journey

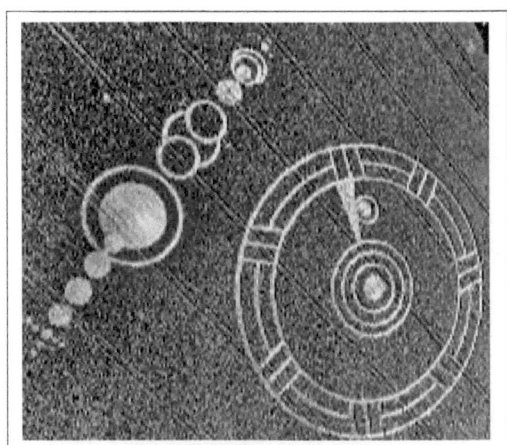

280. double crop circle
(Essex, England, 2014)

"Well ... I interpreted this crop circle as 'man and woman'. Is that accurate this way, crop circle?"

"Yes, it can be taken that way."

"And how else?"

"More generally as the interaction of two principles."

"Does that mean that this crop circle is a variant of the Yin/Yang symbol and the polar systems?"

"Yes."

"And the two different structures merely represent the shifting of the two poles?"

"Yes."

"Um ... yes well ... can you tell me something more about this?"

"You will experience something about it in your life."

"Um ... soon?"

"You'll see."

"All right ... thank you, crop circle."

"You're welcome."

"Ho!"

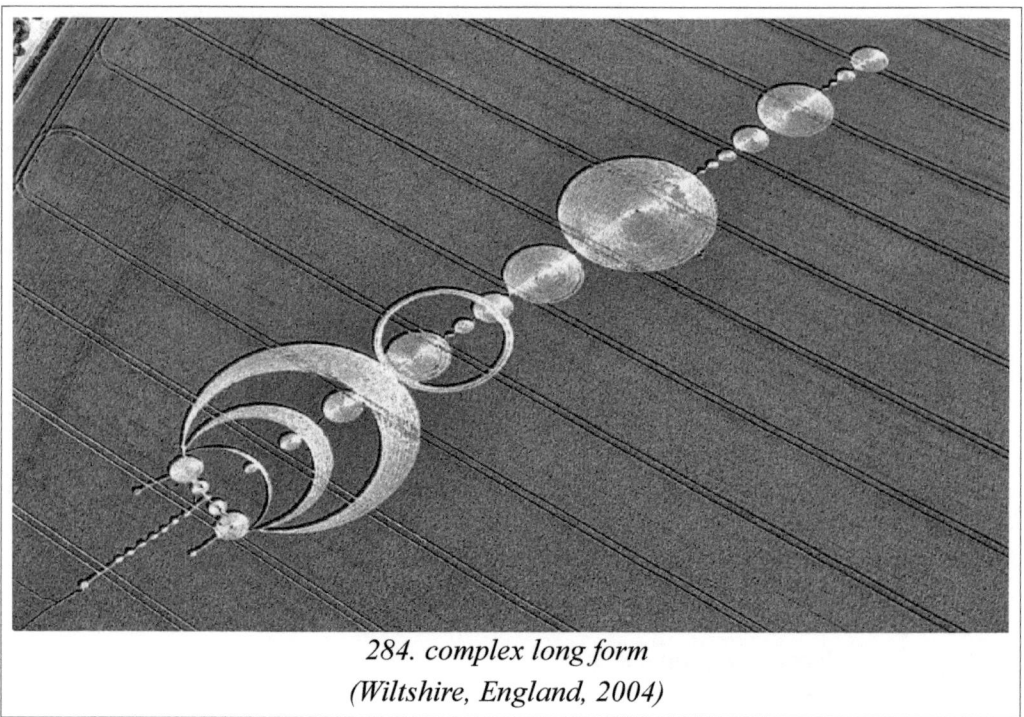

284. complex long form
(Wiltshire, England, 2004)

"Hello crop circle ..."
"Hello Harry."
   "You look a bit like a magic wand and from your charisma you remind me of the Caduceus wand of the Greek god Hermes."
"That's true."
"I take it that I have not yet fully understood this staff?"
"That is also true."
"Can you tell me what I haven't understood there yet?"
"What it means to you."
"Um – what does it mean to me?"
"Independence."
"Can you say a few more words about that?"
   "You are your own thread. Your life is about expressing who you are, not about accomplishing anything. The sun shines – and it doesn't ask what happens to the light it emits."

"Er – that's a nice image ... the image with the sun. I understand that, yes. ... ...
Is there anything else to understand about the details of this crop circle, then?"
"That's not so important – stay with the image of the sun and its rays."
"Yes, I will do that. Thank you crop circle!"
"You're welcome."
"Ho!"

47th dream journey

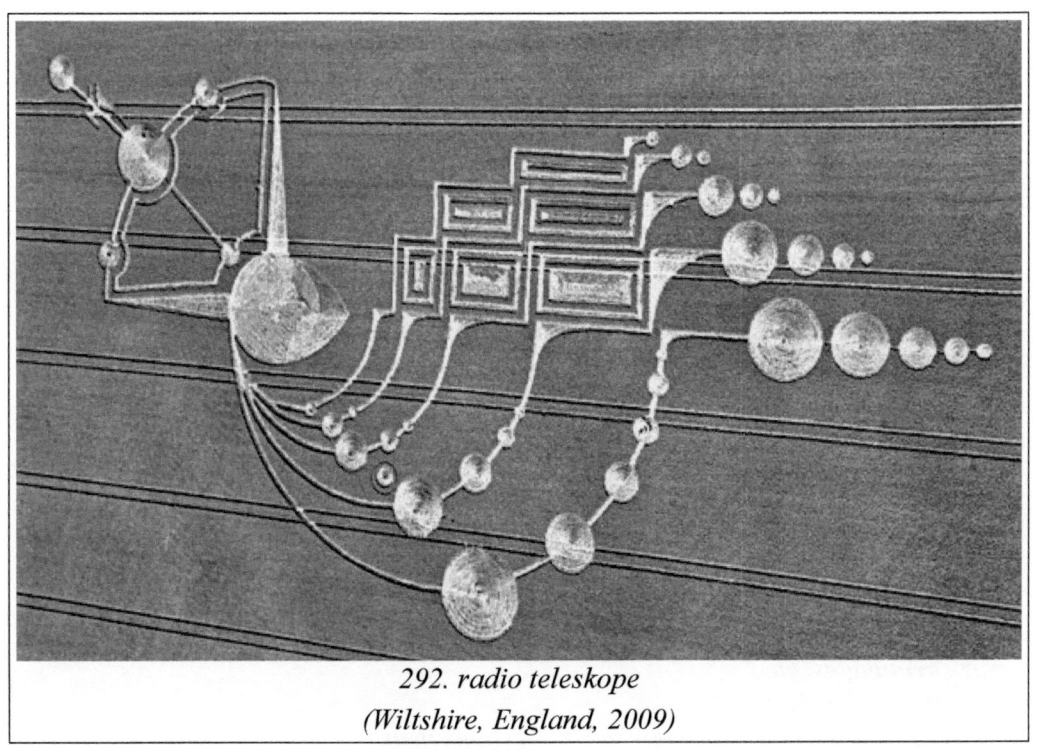

292. radio teleskope
(Wiltshire, England, 2009)

"Hello crop circle – are you a technician, a machinist, an engineer?"
"From your point of view, certainly."
"And from your point of view?"
"Not."
"Then what would you describe this crop circle as?"
"As a heart."

335

"I have to admit that this doesn't make sense to me off the top of my head. Can you tell me a little bit about it?"

"The heart is connected to everything and it radiates."

"I assume you are talking about the heart chakra?"

"Yes. The drop is the heart, the telescope is the radiance, and the five lines are the roots."

"Is the radiance the self-expression?"

"Yes."

"But what are the five roots? Is there a reason that there are five? Or is this once again 'artistic license'?"

"It could be other numbers."

"And what are these roots?"

... ...

"Why don't you say something, crop circle?"

"You have mixed your own thoughts with your dream journey perceptions. That's where you got lost."

"Then help me please again on the correct way back."

"Use the crop circle as a door for a dream journey."

"O.k. ... I see the system of acupuncture meridians and in the center the heart chakra ... ... the picture stays like that, nothing happens there ..."

I come back from the 'dream journey within the dream journey'.

"O.k. ... this is how I understand the image of the crop circle ... What are the rectangles?"

"Your body."

"And what are those arcs in the angles that lead to the rows of circles on the right side?"

"The transitions of the meridians to the other chakras."

"Um ... and the circles on the arcs?"

"The acupuncture points."

"I guess the numbers aren't literal here, are they? – The numbers of rays, arcs, circles, rectangles, etc."

"No, they're just 'many'."

"Um ... I guess I don't have any more questions then."

"Then I don't have any more answers either."

"Thank you."

"You're welcome."

"Ho!"

336

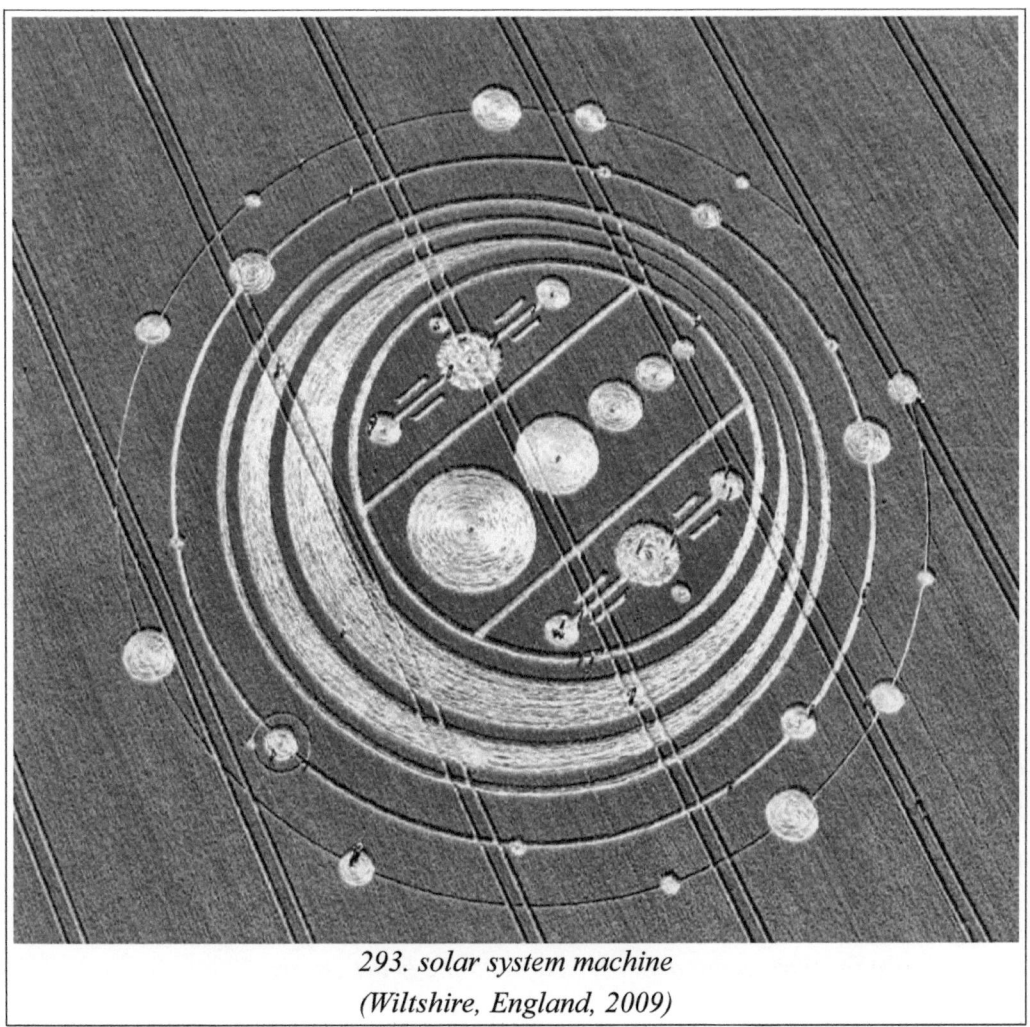

293. solar system machine
(Wiltshire, England, 2009)

"Hello crop circle ... what are you? Or, who are you?"
"Me."
"And what qualities do you have?"
"Movement."
"What movement?
"Expansion, expression, migration."

"Um ... are the two polar systems to the left and right of your center your 'driving machines', so to speak?"

"Yes."

"What is the actual meaning of the '5', that is, the five circles in your center?"

"Movement."

"The '5' is movement?"

"More generally, it is action and attitude."

"12 points on the outer ring and 9 points plus 1 moon on the inner ring – are these supposed to be the 12 signs of the zodiac and the 10 planets?"

"Yes."

"This looks a lot like a 'flying saucer' in space ..."

"That's humor ..."

"Er ... are you saying that the collective subconscious knows that there are no flying saucers, but that it has the fun of nevertheless depicting this image, which people collectively carry within themselves and which has been inspired by the images of the galaxies, in a cornfield?"

"You're getting closer to the point. The circle is also a galaxy: it moves through space – the five circles; it pulls everything together and pushes outward – gravity as the centripetal force and momentum as the centrifugal force."

"O.k. – from these two forces the shape of the galaxy is formed: the sphere in the center and the disk in the plane of rotation ... But why two polar systems?"

"That is only a symmetrical representation, no differentiation of content."

"Well, I still haven't got used to this 'artistic freedom' with the crop circles – I still see them mainly as geometrical correlations, mathematical formulas or as construction plans ..."

"That's essentially what they are."

"Tell me – are the two crescents and the circular ring around them the solar wind, the shock front, and the bow wave in the space around the sun?"

"You can look at them that way – the triple shroud is a principle found in many places."

"Yes ... like the three pairs of chakras around the heart chakra."

"Yes."

"Um ... is that it then?"

"If you have no more questions ..."

"No, I don't ... Thank you, crop circle!"

"You're welcome."

"Ho!"

V Usage

At the latest after all these contemplations, analyses and dream journeys, the question also arises, what these crop circles are good for.

1. first of all, one can simply enjoy their appearance, provided that one is attracted by this kind of aesthetics – which seems to be the case with many people.

2. You can also take a closer look at what effect looking at crop circle images has on you. This can be comparable to looking at a sunset, a seashore or any other natural scenery.

One sees, so to speak, also in the crop circles the forces of nature at work, which form the surface of the earth. In nature scenes as well as in crop circles one can feel, suspect and to some extent recognize the character of the forces shaping them.

3. It is a little more tedious to go to a crop circle and to stand inside it and to feel how its different parts feel. The consequences of such an experience can be very different, because on the one hand different things can be experienced and on the other hand people build these experiences into their world view in different ways according to their character.

4. By looking more closely at the crop circles, one can get to know their symmetries, structures and inner dynamics in more detail. This can lead one to discover more general principles such as the eternal change caused by the Yin/Yang opposition.

These contemplations of the crop circles can also lead one to connect the forms in the crop circles with various systems such as astrology, the Kabbalistic Tree of Life, or the symbolism of some numbers – as has been done in the present book.

Through these comparisons, the basic principles according to which this world unfolds can be more precisely recognized: the integration of the '1', the polarity of the '2', the cohesion and unfolding of the '3', the space of the '4', the group of the '6', the ambient space of the '12', the conservation laws, the unfolding in the form of the Chakras, etc.

Through all these comparisons one finally gets a feeling for the inner dynamics of the world. Finally, this sense makes it possible to use the rules of this dynamic for one's own actions – one gets a sense for the right, i.e. the effective way to a goal.

5. One of the most valuable methods are the dream journeys, because through them one can get to know the quality of a crop circle in a direct way. One can feel it, see it, have it explained to one …

This kind of contact can be extended and one can connect with the quality of a crop circle. You can take it in through visual imagination or by imagining drinking it – there are many possibilities. This is basically the same as taking a homeopathic globule or invoking a deity.

One should see in which way one can connect most intensively with the quality of a crop circle:

- by frequent dream journeys to it;
- by giving the crop circle a name and then using the name as a mantra;
- by drawing it on one's arm like a small tattoo;
- by drawing the crop circle itself or one of the visions on the dream journey to it as a picture and hanging it up in one's own room;
- by drawing it on a piece of paper, putting this paper in a glass of water and then drinking the water;
etc.

Again, there are many possibilities …

6. Furthermore, the crop circles can be used as symbols in magic. However, it is advisable to thoroughly research the crop circle in question before using it as a symbol, as a talisman, as a sigil, in evocations, etc., so that one knows what one is emphatically calling into one's life.

7. It would be conceivable to derive from the crop circles and from related fields like astrology, Feng-Shui, Kabbalah etc. as well as from physics the basic structure of the world and to represent it graphically. Presumably, this would result in various kinds of benefits that are not yet foreseeable.

8. It might also be possible to have conversations with the collective subconsciousness by means of the crop circle symbolism. Possibly, however, dream journeys would be simpler and more effective for this purpose. However, this would have to be researched first.

English Books by Harry Eilenstein

- Living Magic (261 p.)
- The Synthesis of Physics and Magic (192 p.)
- Astral Projection for Beginners (60 p.)
- Invocations for Beginners (52 p.)
- Evocations for Beginners (62 p.)
- Auto-Movement for Beginners (60 p.)
- Elves for Beginners (56 p.)
- Hypnosis for Beginners (56 p.)
- Shamanism for Beginners (52 p.)
- Crop Circles for Beginners (344 p.)
  These books will be puplished soon:
- Telepathy for Beginners
- Telepathy for Advanced Learners
- Telekinesis for Beginners
- Life Force for Beginners
- Meditation for Beginners
- Kundalini for Beginners
- Chakra-Magic for Beginners

- Astrology for Beginners
- Ritual Magic for Beginners
- Mandalas for Beginners
- Money Magic for Beginners
- Love Magic for Beginners
- Magic Research for Beginners
- Self-awareness for Beginners
- Symbolism of Numbers for Beginners
- Language of the Moon – for Beginners
- Magic Chant for Beginners
- Prophecy for Beginners
- Magic Objects for Beginners
- Da'ath-Magic for Beginners
- Feng Shui for Beginners
- Magic for Beginners – Anthology I
- Magic for Beginners – Anthology II
- Magic for Beginners – Anthology III
- Magic for Beginners – Anthology IV

Bücher von Harry Eilenstein

Religion allgemein
- Die sieben Schritte des Lebens (428 S.)
- Muttergöttin und Schamanen (168 S.)
- Göbekli Tepe (472 S.)
- Die Göttin von Göbekli Tepe (144 S.)
- Totempfähle (440 S.)
- Christus (60 S.)
- Dakini (80 S.)
- Vajra (76 S.)

Ägypten
- Hathor und Re 1: Götter und Mythen im Alten Ägypten (432 S.)
- Hathor und Re 2: Die altägyptische Religion – Ursprünge, Kult und Magie (396 S.)
- Isis (508 S.)

Indogermanen
- Die Entwicklung der indogermanischen Religionen (700 S.)
- Wurzeln und Zweige der indogermanischen Religion (224 S.)

Germanen
- Die Götter der Germanen (87 Bände – siehe nächste Seite)
- Odin (300 S.)

Kelten
- Cernunnos (690 S.)
- Taliesin (228 S.)
- Der Kessel von Gundestrup (220 S.)
- Der Chiemsee-Kessel (76)

Psychologie
- Über die Freude (100 S.)
- Das Geheimnis des inneren Friedens (252 S.)
- Das Beziehungsmandala (52 S.)
- Gefühle und ihre Verwandlungen (404 S.)
- einsgerichtet (140 S.)
- Liebe und Eigenständigkeit (216 S.)
- Von innerer Fülle zu äußerem Gedeihen (52 S.)

Heilung
- Die Symbolik der Krankheiten (76 S.)

Kunst
- Herz des Tanzes – Tanz des Herzens (160 S.)

Drama
- König Athelstan (104 S.)

Bücher von Harry Eilenstein

„Magie für Anfänger"

- Telepathie für Anfänger (60 S.)
- Telepathie für Fortgeschrittene (52 S.)
- Telekinese für Anfänger (52 S.)
- Lebenskraft für Anfänger (60 S.)
- Meditation für Anfänger (56 S.)
- Kundalini für Anfänger (100 S.)
- Hypnose für Anfänger (56 S.)
- Auto-Movement für Anfänger (56 S.)
- Chakra-Magie für Anfänger (148 S.)
- Astralreisen für Anfänger (56 S.)
- Astrologie für Anfänger (120 S.)
- Ritual-Magie für Anfänger (56 S.)
- Mandalas für Anfänger (68 S.)
- Geldzauber für Anfänger (56 S.)
- Liebeszauber für Anfänger (52 S.)
- Invokationen für Anfänger (52 S.)
- Evokationen für Anfänger (60 S.)
- Elfen für Anfänger (56 S.)
- Magie-Forschung für Anfänger (140 S.)
- Selbsterkenntnis für Anfänger (52 S.)
- Zahlensymbolik für Anfänger (60 S.)
- Die Sprache des Mondes – für Anfänger (116 S.)
- Zaubergesänge für Anfänger (100 S.)
- Zukunftschau für Anfänger (60 S.)
- Schamanismus für Anfänger (52 S.)
- Magische Gegenstände für Anfänger (68 S.)
- Da'ath-Magie für Anfänger (64 S.)
- Kornkreise für Anfänger (348 S.)
- Feng Shui für Anfänger (96 S.)
- Magie für Anfänger – Sammelband I (696 S.)
- Magie für Anfänger – Sammelband II (664 S.)
- Magie für Anfänger – Sammelband III (580 S.)

„Traumreisen"

- Traumreisen zu Heilpflanzen (700 S.)

Magie

- Handbuch für Zauberlehrlinge (408 S.)
- Tarot (104 S.)
- Physik und Magie (184 S.)
- Die Synthese von Physik und Magie (200S.)
- Die Magie-Formel (156 S.)
- Krafttiere – Tiergöttinnen – Tiertänze (112 S.)
- Schwitzhütten (524 S.)
- Mythen und Magie der Harfe (116 S.)
- Magie heute – Berichte aus der Praxis (288 S.)

Meditation

- Der Lebenskraftkörper (230 S.)
- Die Chakren (100 S.)
- Das Chakren-System mit den Nebenchakren (296 S.)
- Organe und Chakren (64 S.)
- Die platonischen Körper in den Chakren (156 S.)
- Meditation (140 S.)
- Drachenfeuer (124 S.)
- Kundalini I (676 S.)
- Reinkarnation (156 S.)
- einsgerichtet (140 S.)

Astrologie

- Astrologie (496 S.)
- Photo-Astrologie (428 S.)
- Die astrologischen Aspekte (88 S.)
- Horoskop und Seele (120 S.)

Kabbala

- Kursus der praktischen Kabbala (150 S.)
- Eltern der Erde (450 S.)
- Blüten des Lebensbaumes:
  - Die Struktur des kabbalistischen Lebensbaumes (370 S.)
  - Der kabbalistische Lebensbaum als Forschungshilfsmittel (580 S.)
  - Der kabbalistische Lebensbaum als spirituelle Landkarte (520 S.)

Die Themen der 87 Bände der Reihe „Die Götter der Germanen"

1. Die Entwicklung der germanischen Religion
2. Lexikon der germanischen Religion
3. Der ursprüngliche Göttervater Tyr
4. Tyr in der Unterwelt: der Schmied Wieland
5. Tyr in der Unterwelt: der Riesenkönig   Teil 1
6. Tyr in der Unterwelt: der Riesenkönig   Teil 2
7. Tyr in der Unterwelt: der Zwergenkönig
8. Der Himmelswächter Heimdall
9. Der Sommergott Baldur
10. Der Meeresgott: Ägir, Hler und Njörd
11. Der Eibengott Ullr
12. Die Zwillingsgötter Alcis
13. Der neue Göttervater Odin   Teil 1
14. Der neue Göttervater Odin   Teil 2
15. Der Fruchtbarkeitsgott Freyr
16. Der Chaos-Gott Loki
17. Der Donnergott Thor
18. Der Priestergott Hönir
19. Die Göttersöhne
20. Die unbekannteren Götter
21. Die Göttermutter Frigg
22. Die Liebesgöttin: Freya und Menglöd
23. Die Erdgöttinnen
24. Die Korngöttin Sif
25. Die Apfel-Göttin Idun
26. Die Hügelgrab-Jenseitsgöttin Hel
27. Die Meeres-Jenseitsgöttin Ran
28. Die unbekannteren Jenseitsgöttinnen
29. Die unbekannteren Göttinnen
30. Die Nornen
31. Die Walküren
32. Die Zwerge
33. Der Urriese Ymir
34. Die Riesen
35. Die Riesinnen
36. Mythologische Wesen
37. Mythologische Priester und Priesterinnen
38. Sigurd/Siegfried
39. Helden und Göttersöhne
40. Die Symbolik der Vögel und Insekten
41. Die Symbolik der Schlangen, Drachen und Ungeheuer
42.a Die Symbolik der Herdentiere I
42.b Die Symbolik der Herdentiere II
43. Die Symbolik der Raubtiere
44. Die Symbolik der Wassertiere und sonstigen Tiere
45. Die Symbolik der Pflanzen
46. Die Symbolik der Farben
47. Die Symbolik der Zahlen
48. Die Symbolik von Sonne, Mond und Sternen
49.a Das Jenseits I – Das Hügelgrab
49.b Das Jenseits II – Der Jenseitsweg
50. Seelenvogel, Utiseta und Einweihung
51. Wiederzeugung und Wiedergeburt
52. Elemente der Kosmologie
53. Der Weltenbaum
54. Die Symbolik der Himmelsrichtungen und der Jahreszeiten
55.a Mythologische Motive I
55.b Mythologische Motive II
56. Der Tempel
57. Die Einrichtung des Tempels
58. Priesterin – Seherin – Zauberin – Hexe
59. Priester – Seher – Zauberer
60. Rituelle Kleidung und Schmuck
61. Skalden und Skaldinnen
62 Kriegerinnen und Ekstase-Krieger
63. Die Symbolik der Körperteile
64.a Magie und Ritual I
64.b Magie und Ritual II
64.c Magie und Ritual III
65. Gestaltwandlungen
66.a Magische Angriffs-Waffen
66.b Magische Verteidigungs-Waffen
67. Magische Werkzeuge und Gegenstände
68. Zaubersprüche
69. Göttermet
70. Zaubertränke
71. Träume, Omen und Orakel
72. Runen
73. Sozial-religiöse Rituale
74. Weisheiten und Sprichworte
75. Kenningar
76. Rätsel
77. Die vollständige Edda des Snorri Sturluson
78. Frühe Skaldenlieder
79.a Mythologische Sagas I
79.b Mythologische Sagas II
80. Hymnen an die germanischen Götter